Battle Colors / Volume IV

BATTLE COLORS

Insignia And Aircraft Markings Of The U.S. Army Air Force In World War II

Volume IV

European-African-Middle Eastern Theater Of Operations

Robert A. Watkins

THIS VOLUME IS RESPECTFULLY
DEDICATED TO ALL USAAF PERSONNEL WHO SERVED IN THE
MEDITERRANEAN THEATER OF OPERATIONS
DURING WORLD WAR TWO

Book Design & Illustrations: Robert A. Watkins

Library of Congress Control Number: 2009930151

Printed in China.
ISBN: 978-0-7643-3401-6

We are interested in hearing from authors with book ideas on related topics.

Published by Schiffer Publishing Ltd.
4880 Lower Valley Road
Atglen, PA 19310
Phone: (610) 593-1777
FAX: (610) 593-2002
E-mail: Info@schifferbooks.com.
Visit our web site at: www.schifferbooks.com
Please write for a free catalog.
This book may be purchased from the publisher.
Please include $5.00 postage.
Try your bookstore first.

In Europe, Schiffer books are distributed by:
Bushwood Books
6 Marksbury Avenue
Kew Gardens
Surrey TW9 4JF, England
Phone: 44 (0) 20 8392-8585
FAX: 44 (0) 20 8392-9876
E-mail: Info@bushwoodbooks.co.uk.
Visit our website at: www.bushwoodbooks.co.uk
Try your bookstore first.

Preface

Those readers familiar with the first three books of this series are aware of my acknowledgement that these efforts represent a *work-in-progress*, and the same is true in the case of this, the fourth in the 'Battle Colors' series.

My primary concern is with the unofficial images that were so common during this period. Even with the advent of the Army's Heraldic Section, many units continued to display insignia that had not gone through the official approval process, in addition to tactical aircraft markings that, for one reason or another, did not become part of a units official history. This was especially true once hostilities broke out and many of the AAF combat units were dispersed throughout the globe. Before this historical imagery is hopelessly buried, my goal is to collect and catalogue as much as possible concerning unit insignia and tactical markings of all combat & support units of the United States Army Air Forces.

My interest in the subject of unit insignia and tactical aircraft markings began at an early age, and has remained with me throughout a professional career as a Graphic Designer. I have amassed a considerable library on this period of our nations history, including numerous volumes which deal with the topics in question to one extent or another. As an individual who has spent his entire professional life dealing with visuals , it has been both a source of amazement and frustration that so many words were used in an attempt to deal with this visual subject.

This, coupled with a desire to 'fill-in-the-blanks', has been and continues to be the motivation behind the 'Battle Colors' series. Are words important? Of course they are! When dealing with a visual subject however, visuals should be the dominate vehicle used to present that subject, with words as a support mechanism rather the primary medium. Ergo 'Battle Colors'!

As much as I might hope to fill in every blank in this aspect of the history of the Army Air Forces during the course of World War II, I know that this is not realistically going to happen. It is my hope however, that other individuals will continue to look for these missing images and eventually we will have successfully 'filled-in-*all*-the-blanks'.

Why is the subject of group / squadron insignia important? Simply because it was important to so many of the young men who fought this conflict. If one questions the veracity of this statement, I would suggest that individual spend a little time perusing wartime photographs. This is the only way to get an idea of just what part these images played in the daily lives of the USAAF airmen who fought in WWII.

For this reason, I am committed to an ongoing effort, to chronicle subject matter relating to unit insignia and tactical aircraft markings of the USAAF during this conflict. I encourage those readers who may have in their possession data pertinent relating to these subjects to contact me at the address below.

Robert A. Watkins
8462 Road 41, Mancos, Colorado 81328-8945 USA

Introduction

Very few pre-war military strategists on either the Axis or Allied side gave much thought to Africa's northern deserts as a potential battleground for the coming conflict. The strategic importance of the Suez Canal was of course obvious to everyone but still the primary focus of Allied planners in particular was Europe proper, the Pacific and the Far East. The Northern Deserts contained no target rich environments such as the industrial complexes of the Ruhr Valley in Germany, or oil production and refinement centers the likes of Ploesti, in Romania. Targets were few and for the most part, mobile.

The air war in the North Africa was, for the most part, tactical in nature, and thus caught most military thinkers off guard and ill prepared for what was to unfold. Prior to this, precious little attention had been given to the monumental problem of logistical support inherent with maintaining multiple combat air units as a viable force under constantly mobile conditions. Part of the problem can be attributed to an antiquated 'Maginot Line Mentality', which presumed that ones opponent would have the common decency to fight when and where you expected him to fight. This 'toe-to-toe' philosophy to war conculded that any conflict over control of the Suez Canal would obviously be in or immediately around the Canal proper. The Axis forces, ultimately under Field Marshal Erwin Rommel, had other plans than a frontal assault of course, and the Allied forces soon began what would prove to be a long and painful learning curve in the Sahara Desert.

When the United States found itself thrust into World War II following the Japanese attack on Pearl Harbor, British Commonwealth forces had been combating a combined German/Italian Axis coalition for slightly more than one year in what has sometimes been referred to as the 'see-saw war' of the Western Desert.

The American air commanders were able to draw upon their British counterparts for many valuable and early hard learned lessons. Air Vice Marshal Arthur Coningham's prime doctrine concerning the effective utilization of tactical air operations, readily adopted by Gen. Dwight Eisenhower, provided the basis upon which the U.S. air forces built. The previous, ineffective 'penny packet' method of piecemeal assigning specific air units to provide support for specific ground units was totally thrown out. In its place was instilled a policy of concentrated effort under a unified Theater Command structure. This theory was expressed in Air Power In The Land Battle, published by the British Air Ministry which led to British Army Training Instruction No. 6, which in turn was adopted, modified and culminated in the development of U.S. Army Field Manual FM-31-35, Air / Ground Operations. The lessons contained within this publication were even further expounded upon on U.S. FM-100-20, Command And Employment Of Air Power, which reiterated Air Vice Marshal Coninghams theories concerning centralized control and flexibility of air assets.

So it was that the Allied air offensive slowly found cohesion and a mutual sense of purpose, but this didn't last much beyond the confines of North Africa.

Winston Churchell once quipped that the only thing worse than fighting without allies was fighting with them.

By the time the Sicilian Campaign was under way both the U.S. and British commanders were attempting to exert control over the other for one reason or another. In the final analysis, even though Allied forces continued to work together towards the mutual goal of defeat of the Axis Powers, at no time would they ever again reach the level of integrated air power as that attained over the sands of the Sahara Desert.

Evolution Of U.S. Army Aircraft Markings

1st Pattern

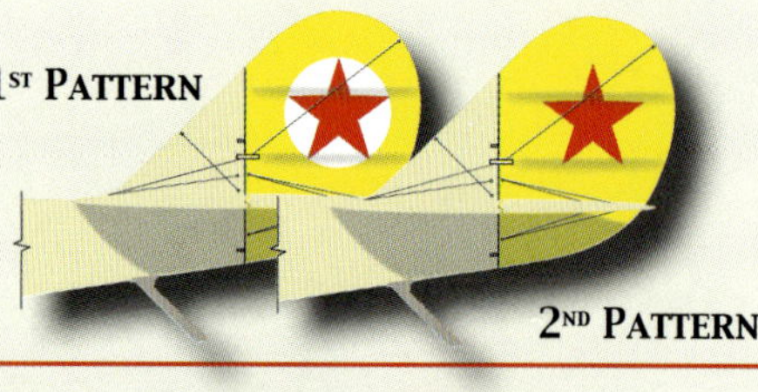

2nd Pattern

• Circa 1916 •

Original U.S. Army Signal Corps aircraft markings. Developed at the North Island Aviation School in California, there was originally no fuselage or wing identification symbols. Although in use prior to WWI, these were never officially adopted.

• 17-May-1917 •

This combination of both fuselage, wing and tail markings were in use briefly during the United States initial involvement during World War I.

1st Pattern

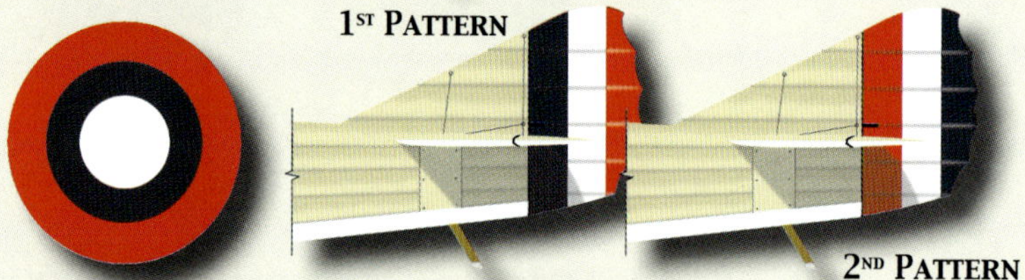

2nd Pattern

• 11-January-1918 •

For reasons not quite clear today, this combination of national symbols was adopted for use on all Allied Expeditionary Forces aircraft for the remainder of the war. The previous markings were re-adopted following WWI in May of 1919.

• Circa 1920's •

The 'U.S. Army' Identification label was adopted for use on under wing surfaces of Army Air Service aircraft in 1924 and the rudder and tail fin markings configuration was modified later in 1927.

Insignia Specification No.24102-K
Amend.#3

• 28-May-1942 •

In the Pacific Theater, there were numerous problems with 'friendly fire ' incidences due to gunners mistaking the U.S. national insignia for the Japanese Hinomaru, or 'meatball'. As a result the red center of the U.S. insignia was ordered deleted.

Insignia Specification No.24102-K
Amend. #3/Memo #9

• 9-October-1942 •

A two-inch Identification Yellow outline was directed to be applied to all AAF aircraft serving in Great Britain and later (Nov-'42) similarly applied in North Africa. Use of this device was officially discontinued in both theaters c.April / May, 1943.

USAAF / AN-1-9a

• 29-June-1943 •

In an ongoing effort to better differentiate U.S. national markings from other nationalities, the 'Star and Bars' insignia was first introduced with an Insignia Red outline. The application of yellow to the center bars was a short lived modification.

USAAF / AN-1-9b

• 29-June-1943 •

The final USAAF national insignia of World War II. This pattern would remain in service until 1947 when the United States Air Force was formed. A modified version of this design continues to be used by all USAF military aircraft to this day.

Markings And Other Matters

There are numerous excellent reference books available today that provide the researcher with precise sizing and positioning of everything from USAAF national insignia to unit tactical markings. As valuable a tool as these sources are it must be emphasized that these were *factory* specifications, and all too often have little correlation with actual combat aircraft.

One of the most typical errors one will find in many models or paintings of combat aircraft, especially when dealing with WWII, is that all to often look like they just rolled off the assembly line. Now if a factory fresh representation is what the artist or craftsman is looking for, fine. But anyone who has seen what actual combat conditions have on the cosmetic appearance of any war bird knows that there is little correlation between a factory fresh airframe and one that has been subjected to the rigors of intense field use. One does not need to have spent time 'in country' to appreciate what metal fatigue and weather can do to an airframe, careful study of high resolution photographs should provide anyone with a general idea. Aluminium skins show signs of stress to the airframe, while paint and metal become mottled and stained with any number of elements ranging from mud to fuel and oil, and this does not even factor in surface skin patch repairs. So research and study become critical elements in accurately recreating an authentic representation of a war bird of any period, and this applies particularly to WWII combat aircraft.

RAF Fin Flashes

There are a several points regarding tactical markings as they relate to the Mediterranean Theater that need to be addressed. The first item has to do with the RAF fin flashes. These Allied Friendly Forces Recognition Markings were adopted by the USAAF shortly after beginning combat operations. Original *Pattern-1* specifications called for three 8" X 27" vertical bars: red, white and blue respectively. The red element was always supposed to face forward but there were instances where this pattern was reversed on some field applications, as did size and placement frequently vary, even within the same squadron.

Pattern-1

The white center bar on *Pattern-2* applications was reduced in size to a width of 2". when questions of camouflage were brought up, due to the frequency of enemy attacks on Allied airfields and Advanced Landing Grounds.

Pattern-2

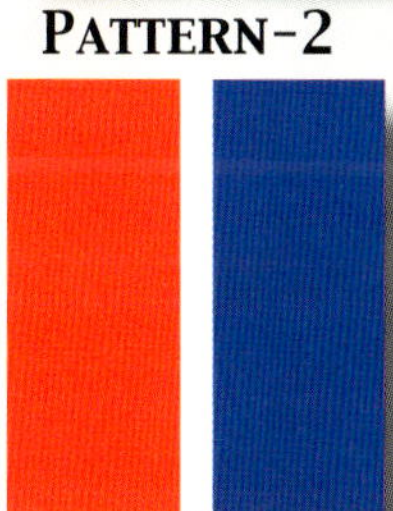

The final formal modification to this device, *Pattern-3*, called for a revision in size to 24" square, but most field applications measured approximately 18"X 24" in the final analysis. On B-24's these markers were often applied to both outward and inward facing sides of both vertical stabilizers. Use of these tactical markers diminished as the war progressed and had disappeared from virtually all USAAF combat aircraft by mid-to-late 1944.

Pattern-3

The Issue Of Spinners

A question frequently posed concerns the red propeller spinners on many USAAF fighter aircraft in the Mediterranean Theater. The use of this particular color is present on some U.S. fighters while clearly absent on others.

Research to date has failed to disclose any specific regulation concerning the application of Insignia Red to the fighter spinners, this much however is certain, RAF serving units of the Desert Air Force (most notably RAF No.112, 'The Shark Squadron') had, for some time before the arrival of AAF units, been using Signal Red (or similar shade) on the spinners of their Lend-Lease Curtiss P-40 Models I-IIB 'Tomahawks' and Models IA-IV 'Kittyhawks'. Painting their spinners red was one more attempt to reduce friendly fire incidences.

Upon arrival in the Middle East for combat operations in mid-summer 1942, the AAF 57thFG readily adopted the now 'friendly forces' red spinners as well. Other U.S. fighter units tended to follow suit, some in a more or less random fashion, but most viewed it prudent to benefit from the experience hard learned earlier by the RAF.

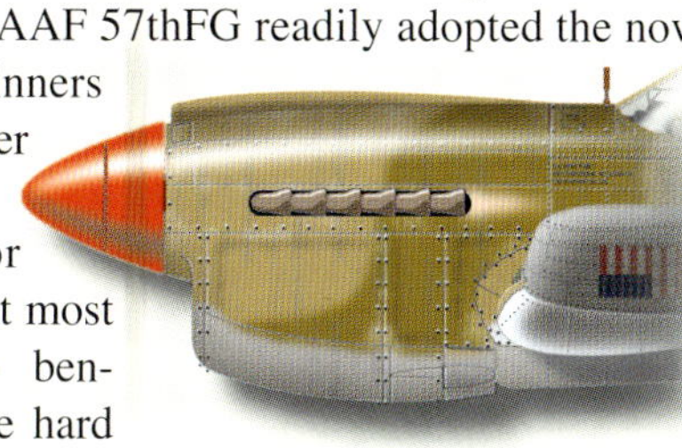

Later, as the Allies began to gain dominance over the skies of the Mediterranean, some AAF units elected to adopt Spinner and cowling colors other than red. With a few exceptions however, Insignia Red remained the dominant color of choice on the majority of MTO serving AAF fighter aircraft until wars end. This, in spite of the fact that apparently no official directive regarding this topic was ever issued by either the Ninth, Twelfth or Fifteenth Air Forces during the course of World War II.

Allied Recognition Stripes

First used by the RAF in North Africa in 1942 as a 'friendly forces' recognition marking, these devices were later adopted by fighter units of the AAF upon arrival in the MTO and applied as 12" yellow bands around the rear fuselage and on both upper and lower wing surfaces. Later in the war, several AAF fighter units displayed similar bands of varying colors in very much the same manner, however these were squadron identification markings and should not be confused with the original tactical use.

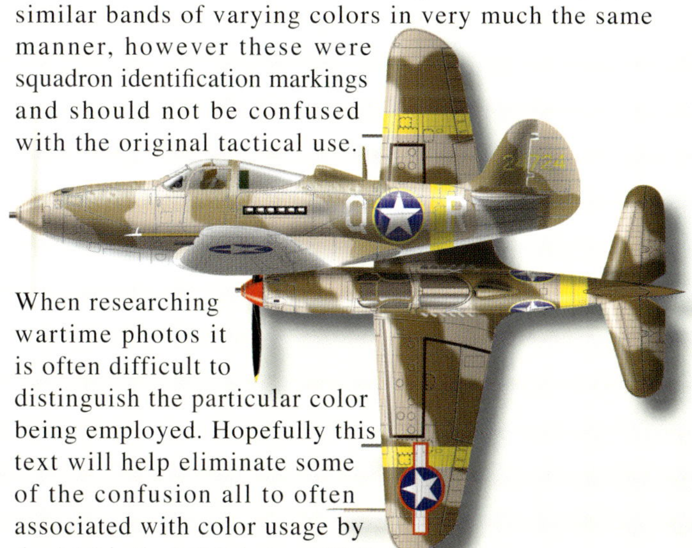

When researching wartime photos it is often difficult to distinguish the particular color being employed. Hopefully this text will help eliminate some of the confusion all to often associated with color usage by the AAF in the MTO during WWII.

Non-Tactical Markings

The images below represent *mission markings* and have no tactical significance whatsoever. However due to the presence of such markings on so many war time photographs, they are presented here for the benefit of those readers who may not have a working understanding as to their purpose or meaning. There were other symbols utilized but these represent the most commonly used. Additionally, there were no precise configurations adhered to when painting these markings to the fuselage of any given aircraft, therefore variations were common.

Yellow or white was the dominant choice of color for these symbols when applied to an olive drab surface. Red was sometimes also selected for use on both camouflaged and metal surfaces, however black paint was the dominant selection for most applications to a natural metal airframe.

The method of application varied greatly and ran the gambit of markings crudely slapped on freehand with a brush by a ground crew member lacking artistic skill, time or both, to still other examples painstakingly applied, sometimes using multiple colors.

Bombardment Units

Bombing Mission | Decoy Mission | Railroad Facility | Aerial Kill | Supply Drop | Turn-Around

Fighter Units

Aerial Kill | Escort Mission | Top Cover Bomb Mission | Railroad Locomotive Rail Supply Train | Fighter Sweep

Transport Units

Cargo Drop | Supply Drop | Medical Evacuation | Paratroop Drop | Glider Tow | Red Cross Flight

Antisubmarine & Reconnaissance Units

U-Boat Sinking | Visual Recon | Photo Recon | Visual Recon | Photo Recon

Variant Mission Markers

Ship Sinking | Maritime Attack | Bombing Mission | Fighter Kills Or Airfield Attack

Basic Aircraft Nomenclature

The following diagrams have been included to assist those readers perhaps unfamiliar with certain aircraft terminology used frequently within this text.

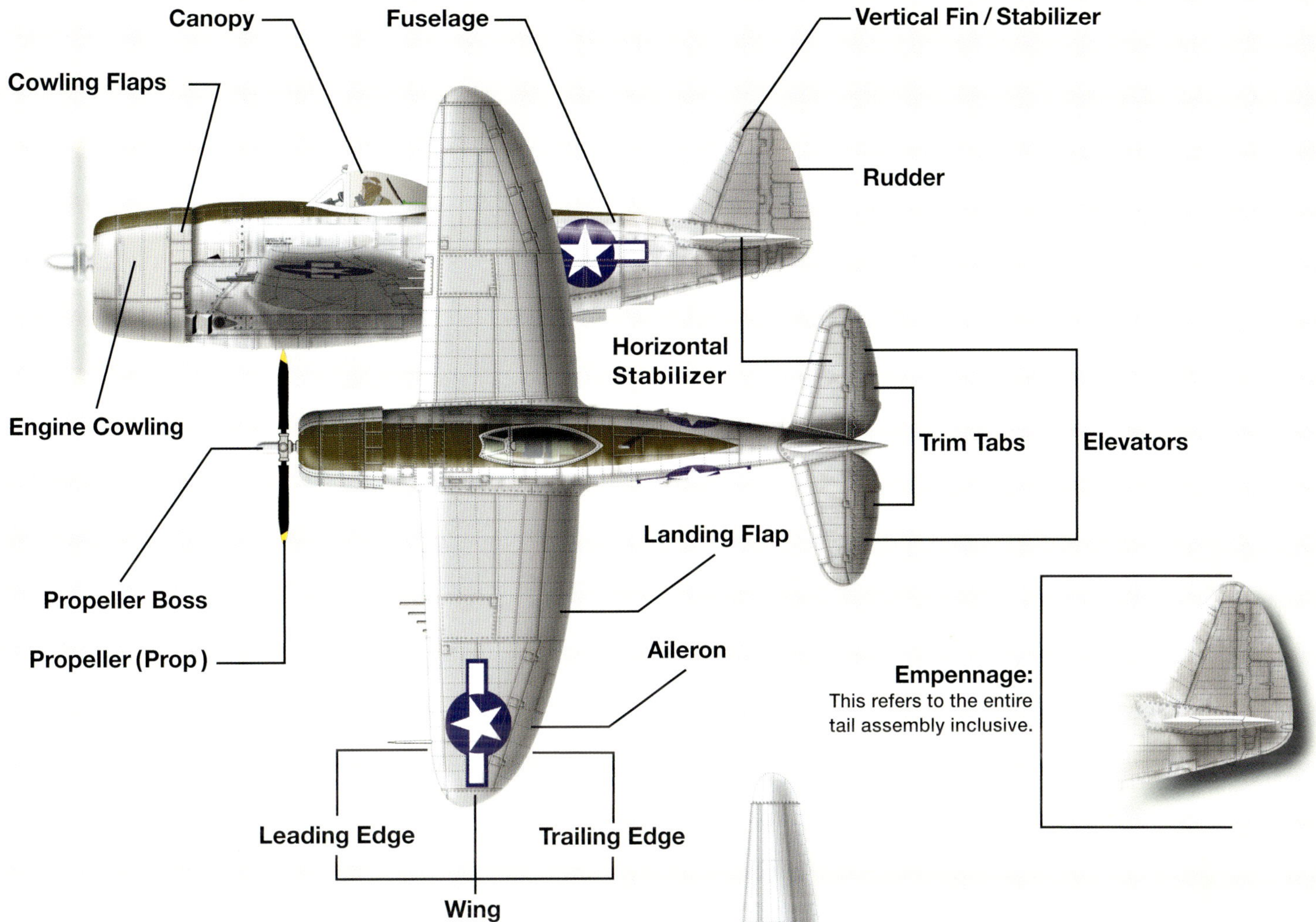

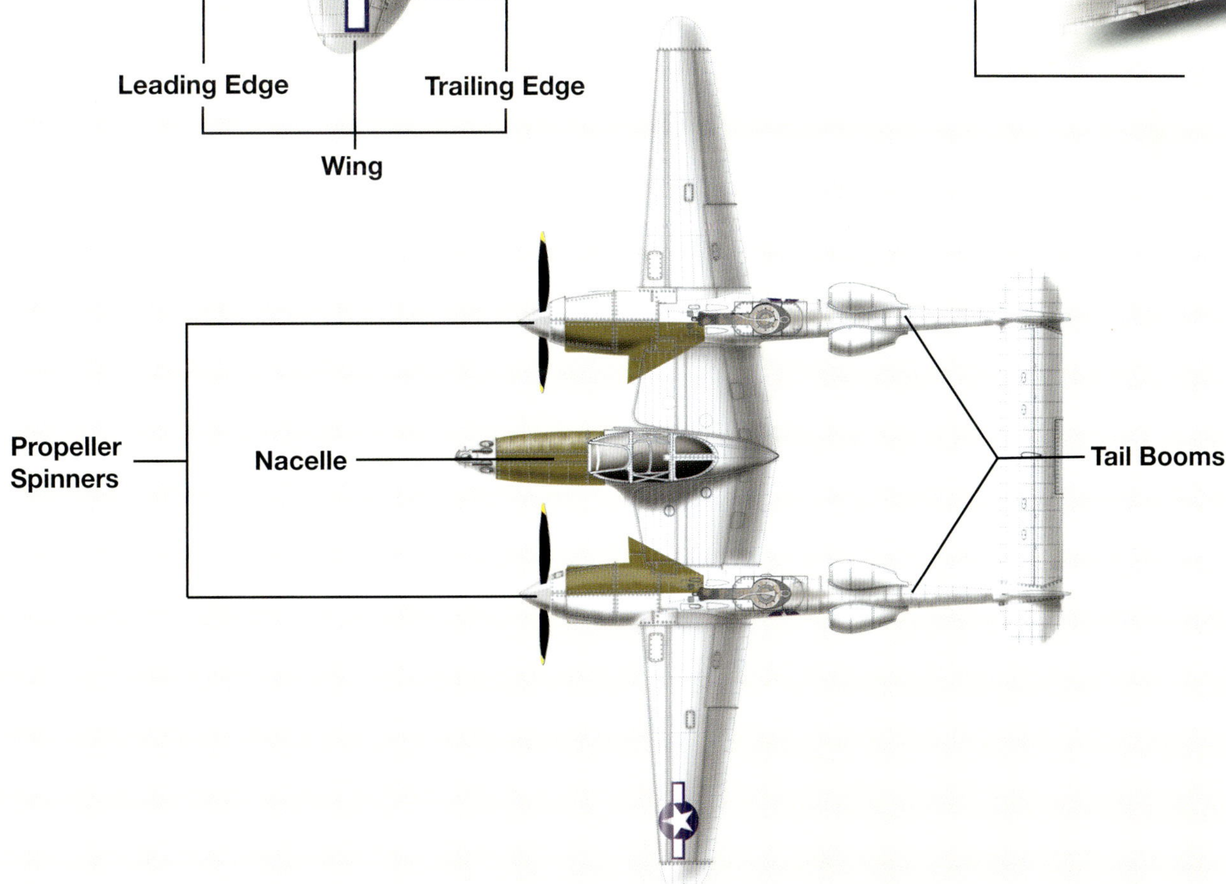

U.S.A.A.F. FIGHTER GROUPS

MEDITERRANEAN THEATER OF OPERATIONS

Perhaps the single noticeable difference between the fighter units of the Twelfth and Fifteenth AAF's and an organization such as the Eighth AAF was in the use of unit insignia on their respective aircraft. It has been stated that the Eighth AAF discouraged the practice of adorning their fighters with group/squadron insignia for security reasons. This line of thinking might have had a bit more merit had it not been for the fact that the Germans maintained a constantly updated list of both RAF and USAAF fuselage codes, not only for our fighters but for virtually every Allied aircraft operating out of Great Britain during the war.

Whatever the logic, it did not appear to have had much influence on the fighter units serving in the MTO. Squadron as well as group insignia were to be found in abundance throughout this theater during the course of the war. It was recognized by many commanders that these symbols helped build a sense of esprit de corps within their units. It is often overlooked that both the men flying and maintaining these war birds were only recently out of high school or college where the mascots and sports rivalries went hand in hand, and had played an important part of their lives. Combat insignia was only a natural extension of this tradition. In short, it was good for morale.

Why more AAF officers in a position of leadership couldn't see this is difficult to understand. All one had to do was look across the waters to the Allies greatest aerial adversaries, the Luftwaffe. One would be hard pressed, until the final stages of the war, to find a German fighter sans unit insignia, and there is no doubting the esprit de corps within their ranks, even when facing defeat.

As to the tactical aircraft markings, the units serving in the European-African-Middle Eastern Theater quickly adopted several of the methods already developed by the RAF through that organizations previous combat experience. The RAF recognition flash on Allied aircraft vertical stabilizers and yellow wing markings among them.

With the exception of the 33d Fighter Group, all USAAF fighter groups that served in the MTO adopted aircraft identification marking systems. Whereas the RAF utilized a two-letter fuselage code system, most AAF units opted to eventually utilize a system based upon Arabic numerals, sometimes however incorporating a letter as part of the code like the 324th and 350th FG's. A few groups stuck to the RAF two-letter system they had adopted earlier during their time in England, I.E. the 31st and 52d FG's while a few like the 27th and 82d FG's made it through the whole war on a single letter method of aircraft recognition.

During the early stages of the war, two and three color camouflaged airframes were the order of the day. This was due directly to the threat of aerial attacks on Allied airfields by both the German Luftwaffe and Italian Regia Aeronautica. The use of camouflaged airframes by the AAF decreased in direct proportion to Allied dominance in the skies over the Mediterranean. With the diminished threat of attacks to their air bases, the U.S. fighter groups quickly opted to discard the camouflaged paint schemes in favor of the increased benefits of increased range and speed inherent with a natural metal finished airframe, and by wars end little remained of camouflaged AAF fighters.

• Assigned Eighth AAF, Jun-42 ; Twelfth AAF, Nov-42 ; Fifteenth AAF, Nov-43 thru V-E Day •

5TH BOMBARDMENT WING

XII TACTICAL AIR SUPPORT COMMAND

306TH FIGHTER WING

1ST FIGHTER GROUP

INSIGNIA/APPROVED: 10-FEB-24
MOTTO: 'CONQUER OR DIE'
CONSTITUTED: 1ST PUR GRP/5-MAY-18
REDESIGNATED: 1ST PUR GRP (INTEP)/DEC-39
REDESIGNATED: 1ST FTR GRP (FTR)/MAR-41
REDESIGNATED: 1ST FTR GRP/MAY-42

EARLIER INSIGNIA

©
71ST PURSQDN

94TH PURSQDN

27TH FTR SQDN

INSIGNIA/APPROVED: 4-MAR-24

CONSTITUTED: 21ST AERO SQDN/15-JUN-17
REDESIGNATED: 27TH AERO SQDN/23-JUN-17
REDESIGNATED: 27TH SQDN/14-MAR-21
REDESIGNATED: 27TH PUR SQDN/25-JAN-23
REDESIGNATED: 27TH PUR SQDN (INTEP)/6-DEC-39
REDESIGNATED: 27TH PUR SQDN (FTR)/12-MAR-41
REDESIGNATED: 27TH FTR SQDN/15-MAY-42

71ST FTR SQDN

INSIGNIA/REPLACED: 10-OCT-47

CONSTITUTED: 71ST PUR SQDN (INTEP)/14-DEC-40
ACTIVATED: 1-JAN-41
REDESIGNATED: 71ST PUR SQDN (FTR)/12-MAR-41
REDESIGNATED: 71ST FTR SQDN/15-MAY-42

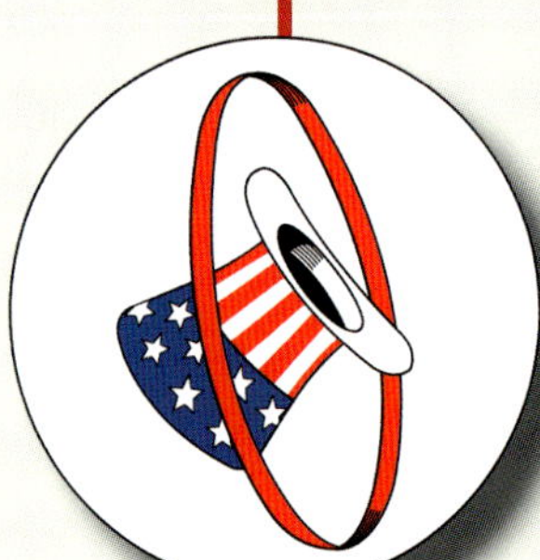

94TH FTR SQDN

INSIGNIA/REINSTATED: 9-JUL-42

CONSTITUTED: 94TH AERO SQDN/20-AUG-17
REDESIGNATED: 94TH SQDN/14-MAR-21
REDESIGNATED: 94TH PUR SQDN/25-JAN-23
REDESIGNATED: 94TH PUR SQDN (INTEP)/6-DEC-39
REDESIGNATED: 94TH PUR SQDN (FTR)/12-MAR-41
REDESIGNATED: 94TH FTR SQDN/15-MAY-42

• Twelfth USAAF •

Wings:
With the assignment of individual squadron colors, wing tips, and in some cases the entire leading edges of both wings, were soon displaying these new tactical markings.

Lockheed P-38 'Lightning'
circa: Aug-44 thru V-E Day

Squadron Codes:
With the transfer from the Eighth to the Twelfth AAF, the 1stFG continued to use the same two-letter squadron codes originally assigned while stationed in England. These codes were nearly always located directly on the outward facing radiator housings, and were accompanied by an individual aircraft call letter, usually separated from the squadron code by use of a hyphen. This entire configuration was applied with either white or light gray paint.

Squadron Colors:
Upon initial deployment, the propeller spinners of all a/c within the group received an application of the appropriate squadron color.

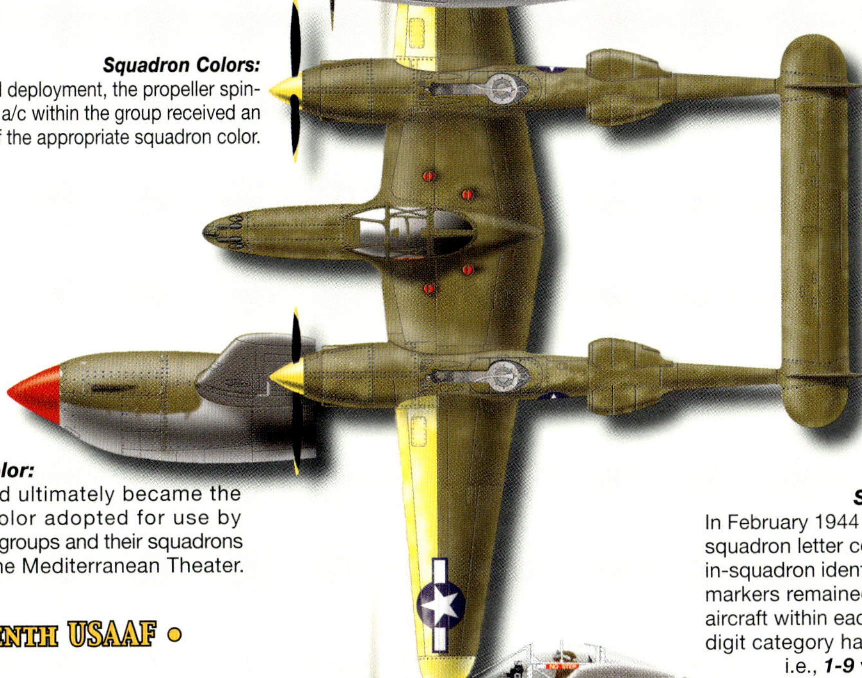

Spinner Color:
Insignia Red ultimately became the standard color adopted for use by most fighter groups and their squadrons serving in the Mediterranean Theater.

• Fifteenth USAAF •

Squadron Codes:
In February 1944 the 1stFG dispensed with the use of squadron letter codes and replaced them with a 'number-in-squadron identification system. Location for the new markers remained on the radiator housings. Those aircraft within each squadron falling within a single digit category had a 'zero' precede the number; i.e., ***1-9*** was represented as ***01-09***

Squadron Colors:
As a new tactical marking both boom surfaces, immediately aft the radiator, received a vertical band of appropriate squadron color. This graphic device was quickly expanded to encompass the entire rear boom tail, with the color terminating at the empennage seam. **Note:** The 71stFS adopted the use of Black as a tactical marking color on all metal finished replacement aircraft.

Squadron Colors:
At the same time that squadron colors began appearing on the aft boom areas, the nose sections of the groups aircraft also received an application of the identical tactical color.

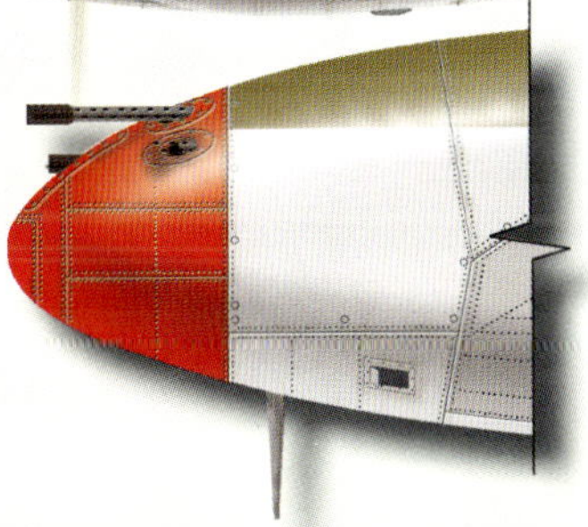

• Assigned Eighth AAF, Jul-42 ; Twelfth AAF, Nov-42 ; Fifteenth AAF, Nov-43 thru V-E Day •

5th Bombardment Wing

XII Air Support Command

306th Fighter Wing

305th Fighter Wing (Prov)

14th Fighter Group

Insignia/Approved: 17-Jun-42
Motto: 'To Fight To Death'
Constituted: 14th Pur Gr (Ftr)/20-Nov-40
Activared: 15-Jan-41
Redesignated: 14th Ftr Grp/May-40

Earlier Insignia

48th SchSqdn

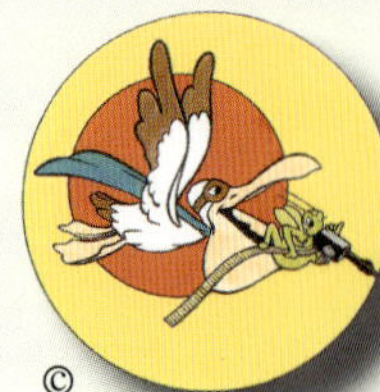

©

37th PurSqdn

37th Ftr Sqdn

Insignia/Revised: 9-Sep-58

Constituted: 37th Pur Sqdn (Intep)/20-Nov-40
Activated: 15-Jan-41
Redesignated: 37th Ftr Sqdn/15-May-42

©

48th Ftr Sqdn

Insignia/Replaced: 5-Jun-53

Constituted: 48th Aero Sqdn/04-Aug-17
Redesignated: 435th Aero Sqdn/1-Feb-18
Redesignated: 462d Aero Sqdn/3-Mar-18
Redesignated: 48th Sch Sqdn/6-Feb-23
Redesignated: 48th Pur Sqdn/1-Mar-35
Redesignated: 48th Pur Sqdn (Ftr)/20-Nov-40
Redesignated: 48th Ftr Sqdn/15-May-42

49th Ftr Sqdn

Insignia/Replaced: 23-Jul-54

Constituted: 49th Pur Sqdn (Ftr)/20-Nov-40
Activated: 15-Jan-41
Redesignated: 49th Ftr Sqdn/15-May-42

• TWELFTH USAAF •

LOCKHEED P-38 'LIGHTNING'
CIRCA: OCT-42 THRU V-E DAY

Squadron Codes:
When the 14thFG arrived in North Africa the 48th & 49th FS's continued to operate with the same two-letter tactical marking codes assigned to them while with the Eighth AAF. These were applied as shown above with Insignia White or R.A.F. Sky.

• FIFTEENTH USAAF •

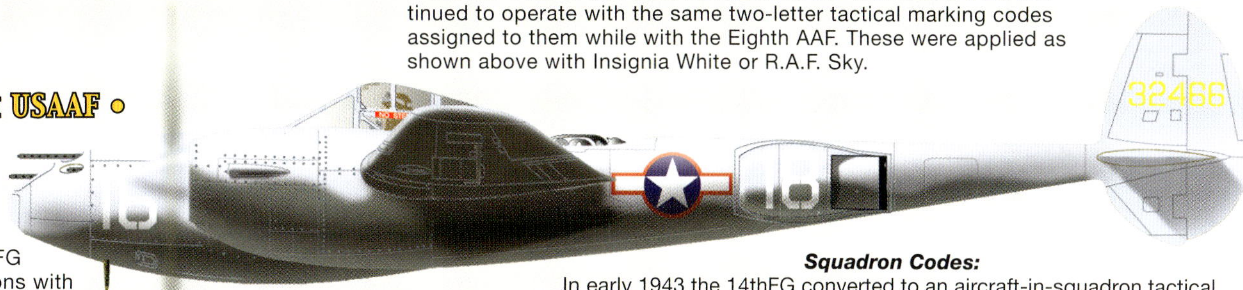

Airframes:
After a period of refitting the 14thFG resumed operations with many of the groups P-38's painted in a two-color 'dull, blue gray' over Olive Drab in preparation for the extensive reconnaissance missions the group's squadrons would be called upon to perform.

Squadron Codes:
In early 1943 the 14thFG converted to an aircraft-in-squadron tactical marking system These numbers were applied to both outboard radiator surfaces and nacelle surfaces with White paint.

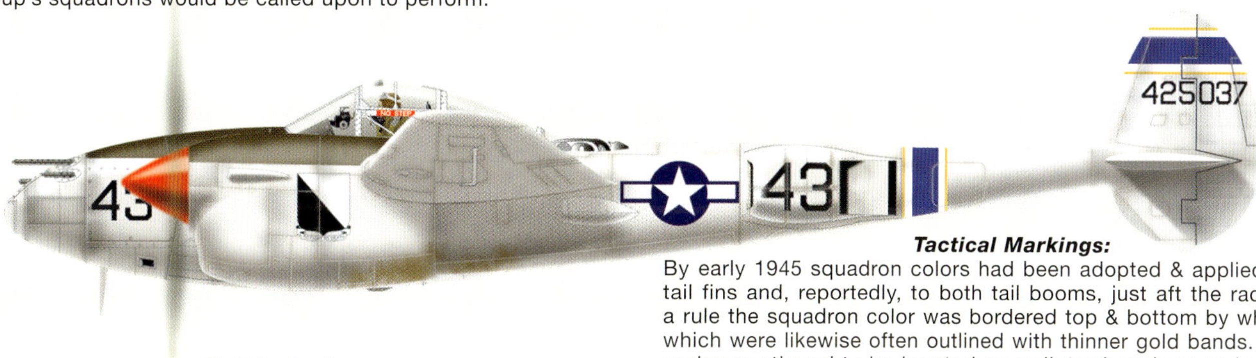

Tactical Markings:
By early 1945 squadron colors had been adopted & applied to upper tail fins and, reportedly, to both tail booms, just aft the radiators. As a rule the squadron color was bordered top & bottom by white bands which were likewise often outlined with thinner gold bands. Squadron codes continued to be located on radiator housings and were often duplicated on the forward nacelle area.

Unit Insignia:
Both the group and individual squadron insignia were known to have been applied on some 14thFG outer engine housings. In such cases squadron insignia appeared on the right side, group insignia the left.

50TH FTRSQDN:
The 50thFS, an original component of the 14thFG, was temporarily reassigned 14-Nov-42. It would however eventually be replaced by the 37thFS on 1-Mar-43.

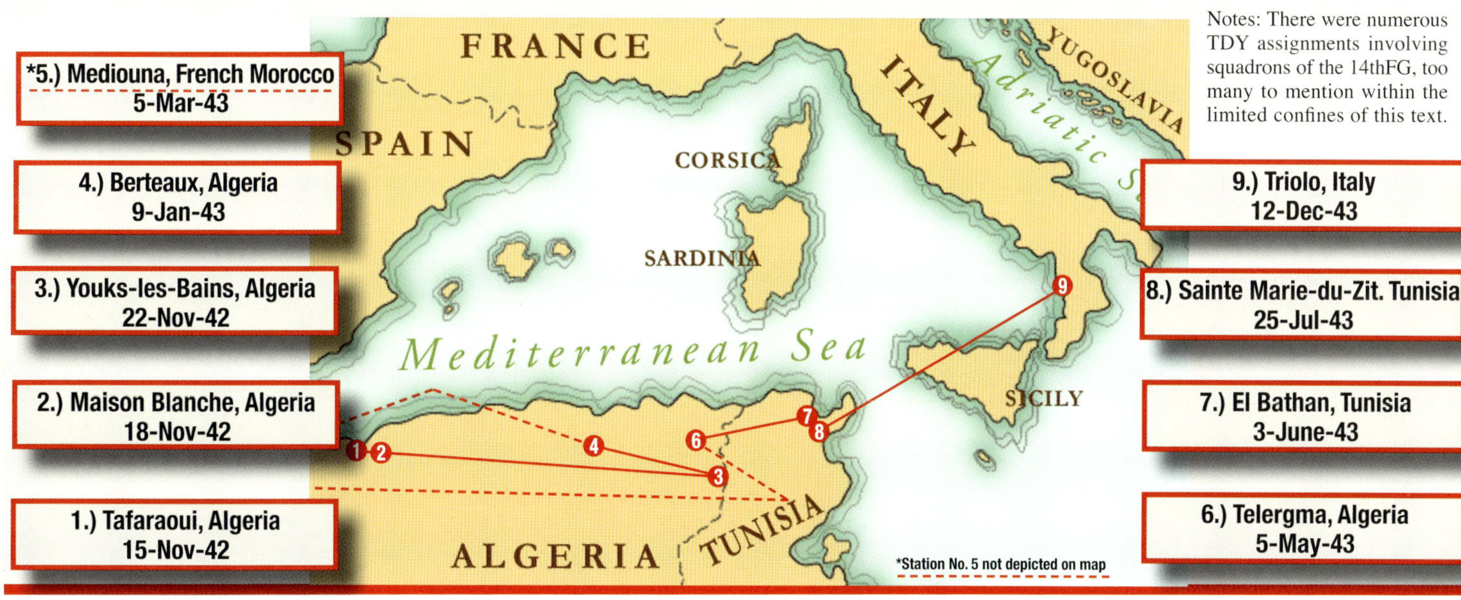

Notes: There were numerous TDY assignments involving squadrons of the 14thFG, too many to mention within the limited confines of this text.

• Assigned Twelfth USAAF: Jun-1943 / V-E Day •

64th Fighter Wing

XII Tactical Air Support Command

27th Fighter (Bmr) Group

Insignia/Approved: 12-Sep-40
Motto: 'Intelligent Strength'
Constituted: 27th Bomb Grp (Lt)/22-Dec-39
Activated: 1-Feb-40
Redesignated: 27th Ftr-Bmr Grp/Aug-43
Redesignated: 27th Ftr Grp/May-44

522d Ftr (Bmr) Sqdn

Insignia/Replaced: 25-Jun-51

Constituted: 16th Bomb Sqdn (Lt)/22-Dec-39
Activated: 1-Feb-40
Redesignated: 522d Ftr-Bmr Sqdn/23-Aug-43
Redesignated: 522d Ftr Sqdn/30-May-44

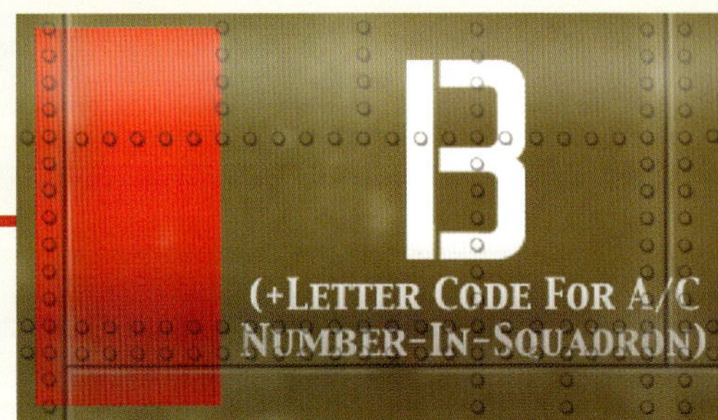

523d Ftr (Bmr) Sqdn

Insignia/Replaced: 5-Jan-51

Constituted: 17th Bomb Sqdn (Lt)/22-Dec-39
Activated: 1-Feb-40
Redesignated: 523d Ftr-Bmr Sqdn/23-Aug-43
Redesignated: 523d Ftr Sqdn/30-May-44

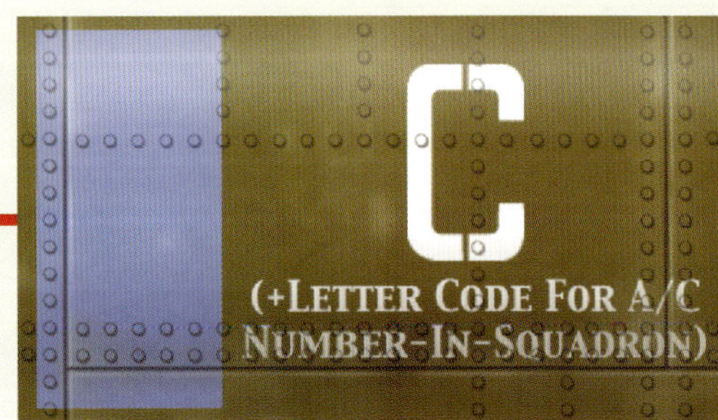

524th Ftr (Bmr) Sqdn

Insignia/Replaced: 21-Jan-55

Constituted: 11th Rcn Sqdn (Lt)/20-Nov-40
Activated: 15-Jan-41
Redesignated: 91st Bomb Sqdn (Lt)/14-Aug-41
Redesignated: 524th Ftr-Bmr Sqdn/23-Aug-43
Redesignated: 524th Ftr Sqdn/30-May-44

• Twelfth USAAF •

North American A-36 'Apache'

circa: Jun-43 thru Feb-44

Squadron Colors:
Beginning in June 1943, propeller spinners were painted with recently adopted squadron colors.

Squadron Codes: All three squadrons utilized a stacked two-letter code on the vertical stabilizer applied with Insignia White paint. The A/C serial numbers were relocated to the fuselage in an enlarged form, just aft the national insignia.

Curtiss P-40 'Warhawk'

circa: Feb-44 thru Jun-44

Tactical Markings:
The P-40's acquired by the 27th were all hand-me-downs from other groups and flown only briefly while awaiting permanent replacement P-47 aircraft. The only tactical marking utilized during this period was the appearance of a an Insignia Red tail section reportedly displayed by various 27thFBG aircraft. By this time most Allied fighters were displaying the standard MTO Insignia Red 'Friendly Forces' propeller spinner.

Squadron Colors:
The P-47 newly redesignated 27thFG carried over the same squadron colors as had been displayed on the earlier A-36's, the only exception being the 524thFS which supplemented Orange/Yellow for Insignia White on natural metal airframes.
Empennage: In all three cases these colors were applied to the upper vertical stabilizer as horizontal bands, often bordered top and bottom by thin Black bands.
Engine Cowlings: Squadron colors were applied to alternating cowling flaps.

Republic P-47 'Thunderbolt'

circa: Jun-44 thru V-E Day

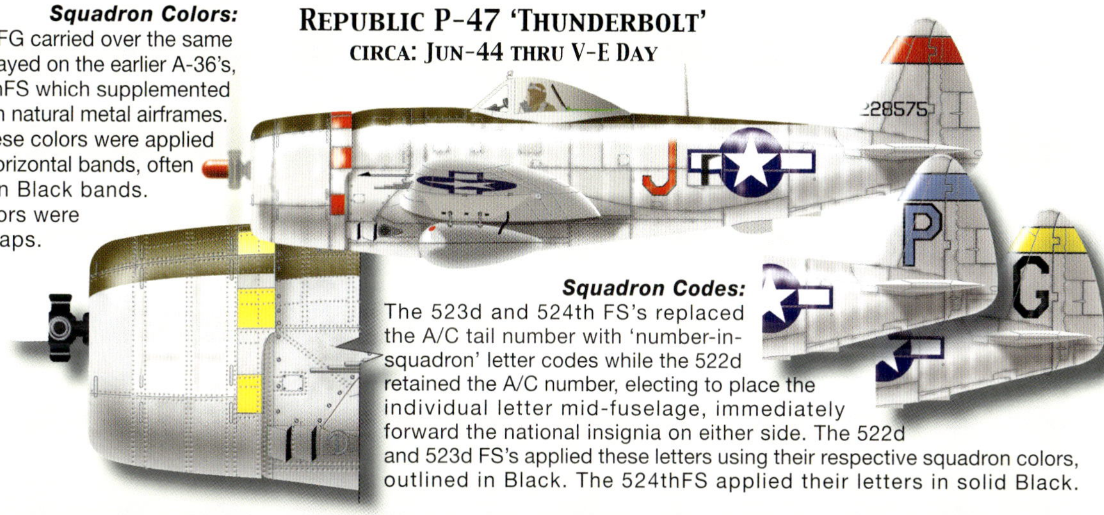

Squadron Codes:
The 523d and 524th FS's replaced the A/C tail number with 'number-in-squadron' letter codes while the 522d retained the A/C number, electing to place the individual letter mid-fuselage, immediately forward the national insignia on either side. The 522d and 523d FS's applied these letters using their respective squadron colors, outlined in Black. The 524thFS applied their letters in solid Black.

8.) Pomigliano, Italy Jan-44	9.) Castel Volturno, Italy Apr-44	11.) Ciampino, Italy Jun-44	13.) Serragia, Corsica Jul-44
7.) Paestum, Italy Nov-43	10.) Santa Maria, Italy May-44	12.) Voltone, Italy Jul-44	14.) Le Luc L/G, France/Aug-44 15.) Y-16 Salon, France/Aug-44

- 6.) Capaccio, Italy — Sep-43
- 5.) Gela, Sicily — 26-Dec-42
- 4.) Korba, Tunisia — Jun-43
- *3.) Ras el Ma, French Morocco — Apr-43
- 2.) Nouvion, Algeria — Jan-43
- 1.) Sainte-Barbe-du-Tlelat, Algeria — 26-Dec-42

*Station No's. 3, 16, 19, 20 & 21 not depicted on map

- *16.) Y-25 Loyettes A/F, France — Sep-44
- 17.) Tarquina, Italy — Oct-44
- 18.) Pontedera, Italy — Dec-44
- *19.) A-64 St.Dizier A/F, France — Feb-45
- *20.) A-96 Toul/Ochey A/F, France — Mar-45
- *21.) Y-78 Biblis A/F, Germany — Apr-45

• Assigned Eighth AAF, May-42 ; Twelfth AAF, Oct-42 ; Fifteenth AAF, Apr-44 thru V-E Day •

64th Fighter Wing

XII Air Support Command

306th Fighter Wing

31st Fighter Group

Insignia/Approved: 28-Jun-41
Motto: 'Return With Honor'
Sobriquet: 'The Peppermint Group'
Constituted: 31st Pur Grp (Intep)/22-Dec-39
Activated: 1-Feb-40
Redesignated: 31st Ftr Grp/May-42

Earlier Insignia

©

308th FtrSqdn

©

309th FtrSqdn

©

307th Ftr Sqdn

Insignia/Approved: 16-Oct-44

Constituted: 307th Pur Sqdn (Intcp)/21-Jan-42
Activated: 30-Jan-42
Redesignated: 307th Ftr Sqdn/15-May-42

308th Ftr Sqdn

Insignia/Replaced: 10-Jan-62

Constituted: 308th Pur Sqdn (Intcp)/21-Jan-42
Activated: 30-Jan-42
Redesignated: 308th Ftr Sqdn/25-May-42

©

309th Ftr Sqdn

Insignia/Revised: 3-Nov-55

Constituted: 309th Pur Sqdn (Intcp)/21-Jan-42
Activated: 30-Jan-42
Redesignated: 309th Ftr Sqdn/15-May-42

○ Twelfth USAAF ○

The 31st brought their inventory of Spitfires with them when the unit transferred from the U.K. to the Mediterranean. Original paint schemes consisted of an R.A.F. tri-color camouflage pattern consisting of Dark Green and Ocean Grey over Medium Sea Grey. Replacement aircraft were painted in a standard Allied Tropical Land Scheme/MTO pattern comprised of Dark and Mid Stone over Azure Blue. For a brief period, propeller spinners retained their original R.A.F. Sky blue paint. Also retained were the 24in. tall, two-letter codes that had been assigned to the squadrons while stationed in England. The placement of these codes would remain unchanged throughout the war. (These same codes incidentally, were later duplicated and assigned to the 78thFG when that unit was assigned to the 8thAAF in November 1943, following the departure of the 31stFG from the UK.) The use of individual a/c call letters were similarly retained until wars end.

Supermarine 'Spitfire'

circa: Jun-42 thru Apr-44

Fuselage: Sqdn Codes applied Insignia White or R.A.F. Sky Blue with Black drop-shadows

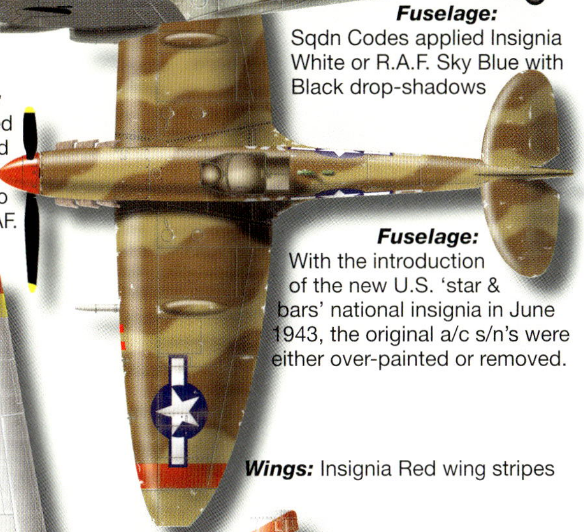

Spinners: Insignia Red was adopted soon after transfer to the 12thAAF.

Fuselage: With the introduction of the new U.S. 'star & bars' national insignia in June 1943, the original a/c s/n's were either over-painted or removed.

Wings: Insignia Red wing stripes

○ Fifteenth USAAF ○

North American P-51 'Mustang'

circa: Apr-44 thru V-E Day

Empennage: A single diagonal band of Insignia Red was applied over both sides of the vertical fin and rudder. The a/c serial numbers were generaly over-painted with this marker application.

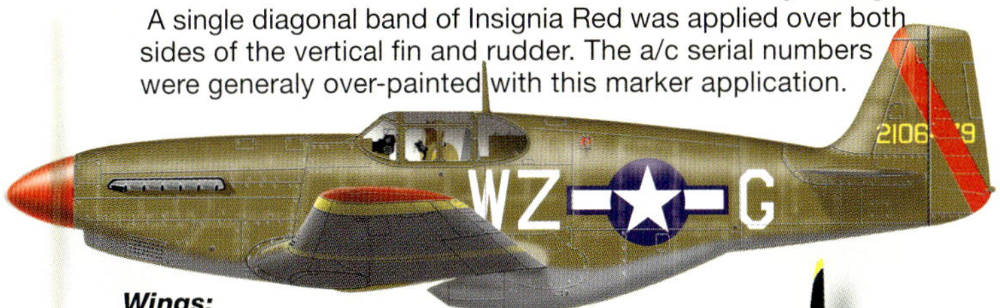

Wings: All group a/c painted wraparound color bands of Insignia Red & Orange Yellow color to both outermost wing edges.

Horizontal Stabilizers: Diagonal Insignia Red 'Candy Stripes' were applied to some of 31stFG's aircraft.

• *Empennage:* The 31stFG's signature 'Candy Stripes' began replacing the single stripe by the summer of 1944. Originally the lower stripe did not drop below the horizontal stabilizers.

Fuselage/Cowling: Vertical Insignia Red color band applied aft the a/c call letter, later relocated to the engine cowling area. Squadron codes and call letters were applied with Insignia White on camouflage and Black on natural metal finished aircraft.

Empennage: Serial numbers re-applied over existing 'Candy Stripes' in addition to the lower diagonal stripes now being extended below the horizontal stabilizers.

1.) Tafaraoui, Algeria 8-Nov-42

2.) La Senia, Algeria 12-Nov-42

*3.) Cazes, Casablanca (308thFS) Jan-43

4 & 8.) Thelepte, Algeria 7-Feb-43 / 11-Mar-43

5.) Tebessa, Algeria 17-Feb-43

6.) Youks-les-Bains, Algeria 21-Feb-43

7.) Kalaa Djerda, Tunisia 25-Feb-43

9.) Djilma, Tunisia 7-Apr-43

10.) Le Sers, Tunisia 12-Apr-43

11.) Korba, Tunisia 15-May-43

12.) Gozo Island, (Malta) 30-Jun-43

13.) Ponte Olivo, Sicily 13-Jul-43

14.) Agrigento, Sicily 21-Jul-43

15.) Termini, Sicily 2-Aug-43

16.) Milazzo, Sicily 2-Sep-43

17.) Monte Corvino, Italy 20-Sep-43

18.) Pomigliano, Italy 14-Oct-43

19.) Castel Volturno, Italy 19-Jan-44

20.) San Severo, Italy 2-Apr-44

21.) Mondolfo, Italy 3-Mar-45

• Assigned Twelfth AAF, Nov-1942 • Tenth AAF, Feb-1944 thru V-J Day •

64th Fighter Wing

XII Air Support Command

33d Fighter Group

Insignia/Approved: 21-Feb-42
Motto: 'Fire From The Clouds'
Constituted: 33d Pur Grp (Intep) / 20-Nov-40
Activated: 15-Jan-41
Redesignated: 33d Ftr Grp / May-42

99th Fighter Squadron

This outfit was attached originally to the 33dFG and stationed at Fardjouna Airfield, Tunisia until serving briefly with the 79thFG. With the arrival of the 332dFG to the Meditterean Theater, the 99th was permently assigned to that unit as its fourth squadron in May '44.

58th Ftr Sqdn

Sobriquet: 'The Gorillas'
Insignia/Replaced: 30-Mar-51

Constituted: 58th Pur Sqdn (Intcp)/20-Nov-40
Activated: 15-Jan-41
Redesignated: 58th Ftr Sqdn/15-May-42

59th Ftr Sqdn

Sobriquet: 'The Golden Pride'
Insignia/Approved: 24-Jul-44

Constituted: 59th Pur Sqdn (Intcp)/20-Nov-40
Activated: 15-Jan-41
Redesignated: 59th Ftr Sqdn/15-May-42

60th Ftr Sqdn

Sobriquet: 'The Fighting Crows'
Insignia/Approved: 15-May-42

Constituted: 60th Pur Sqdn(Intcp)/20-Nov-40
Activated: 15-Jan-41
Redesignated: 60th Ftr Sqdn/15-May-42

• Twelfth USAAF •

Curtiss P-40 'Warhawk'

circa: Nov-42 thru Oct-44

Spinners: Original P-40's assigned to the 33dFG bore no distinctive tactical nose markings. By 1943 all squadron aircraft spinners displayed a coat of Insignia Red, the typical Allied fighter aircraft marking within the MTO.

Empennage: The use of squadron colors on the Groups aircraft appears to have been a somewhat sporadic application. When utilized, the respective colors were applied as a single thin diagonal stripe.

Stars & Stripes: The U.S. flag was displayed on both sides of the fuselage, in front of the national insignia, blue field facing forward. A similar image was located on the left wing undersurface during the early months of deployment. This application was done in the hope of reducing losses due to 'friendly fire' from Allied gun crews unfamiliar with the silhouette characteristics of the P-40.

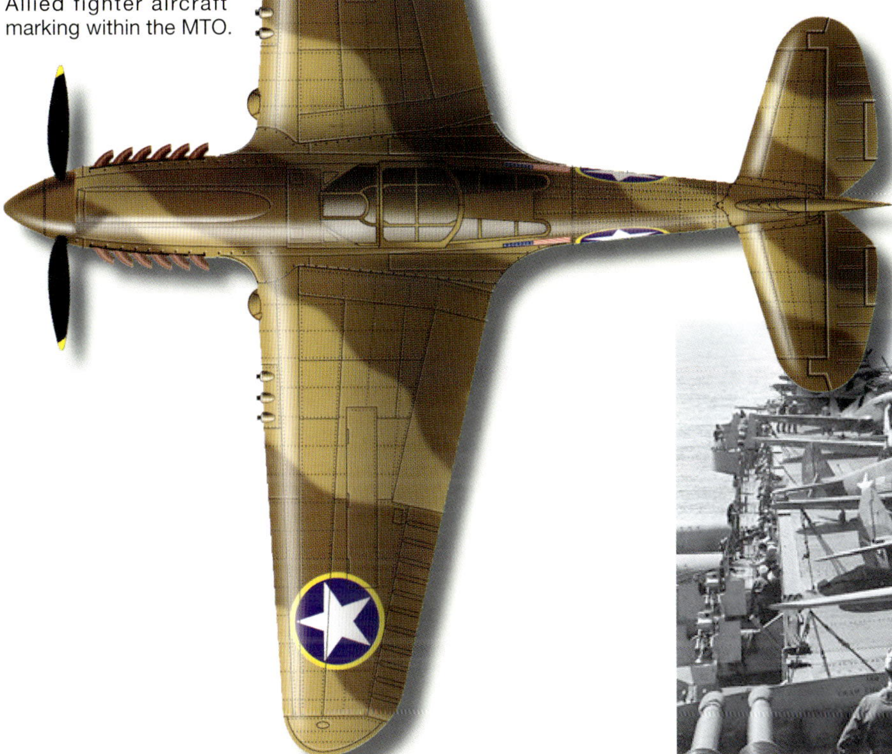

Special Delivery: Factory fresh Warhawks aboard the USS Ranger en route to the AAF fighter units awaiting their arrival in North Africa.

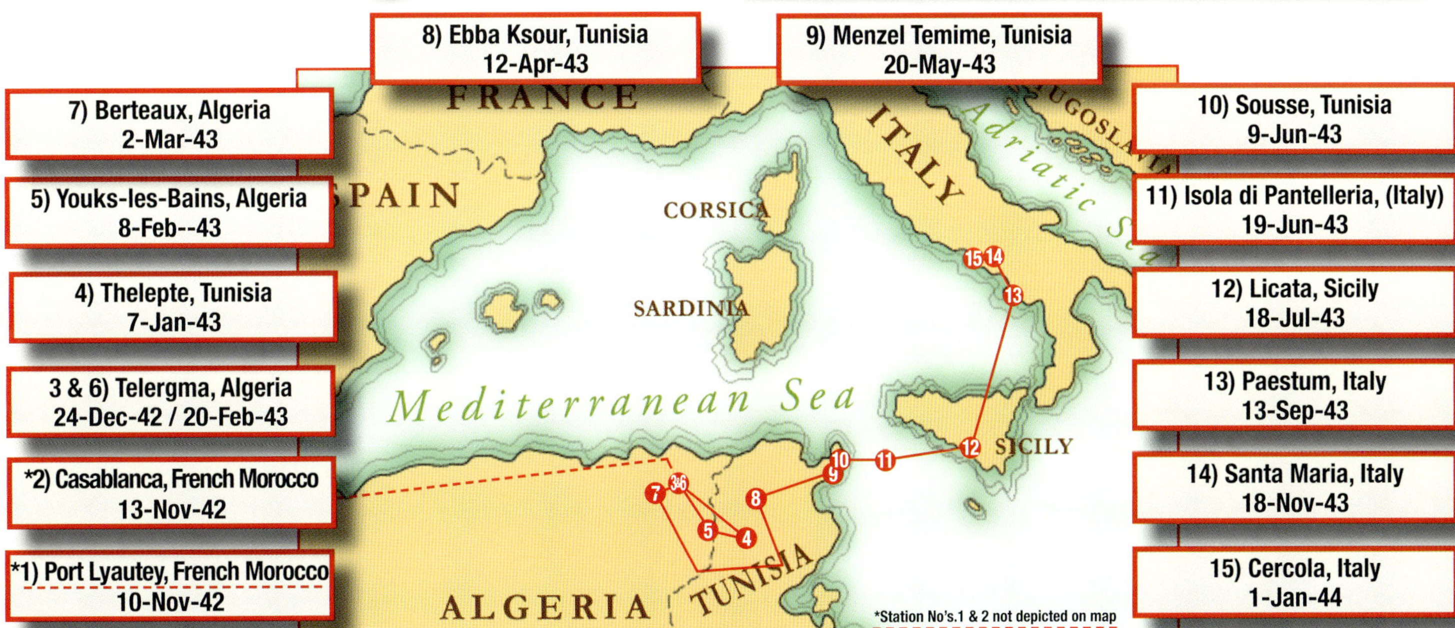

• Assigned Eighth AAF, Jul-42 ; Twelfth AAF, Nov-42 ; Fifteenth AAF, Jul-44 thru V-E Day •

63D Fighter Wing 1943-1944

62D Fighter Wing 1943

XII Air Support Command

306TH Fighter Wing

52D Fighter Group

Insignia/Approved:28-Jun-41
Motto: 'Seek-Attack-Destroy'
Sobriquet: 'Yellow Tails'
Constituted: 52D Pur Grp (Intep)/20-Nov-40
Activated: 15-Jan-41
Redesignated: 52D FtrGrp/May-42

2D Ftr Sqdn

Sobriquet: 'American Beagle Sqdn'
Insignia/Replaced: 5-Mar-59

Constituted: 2D Pur Sqdn (intcp)/20-Nov-40
Activated: 15-Jan-41
Redesignated: 2D Ftr Sqdn/15-May-42

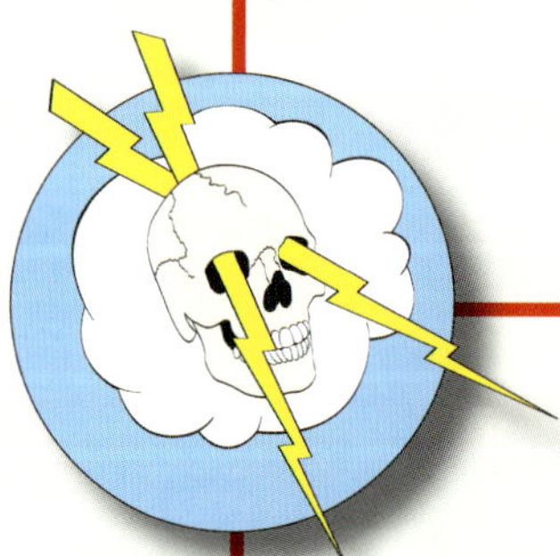

4TH Ftr Sqdn

Sobriquet: (unknown)
Insignia/Replaced: 25-Feb-49

Constituted: 4TH Pur Sqdn (intcp)/20-Nov-40
Activated: 15-Jan-41
Redesignated: 4TH Ftr Sqdn/15-May-42

5TH Ftr Sqdn

Sobriquet: 'Spitten Kittens'
Insignia/Replaced: 16-Jan-51

Constituted: 5TH Pur Sqdn (intcp)/20-Nov-40
Activated: 15-Jan-41
Redesignated: 5TH Ftr Sqdn/15-May-42

• Twelfth USAAF •

Supermarine 'Spitfire'
circa: Jul-42 thru Apr-44

Nose Markings:
By early 1944 many of the 52dFG's Spitfires were displaying Insignia Red propeller spinners. Individual squadron insignia were often applied to both sides of the forward fuselage cowling area.

Fuselage:
Squadron codes and individual call letters were applied with Insignia White, RAF Sky or equivalent light grey.

• Fifteenth USAAF •

North American P-51 'Mustang'
circa: Apr-44 thru V-E Day

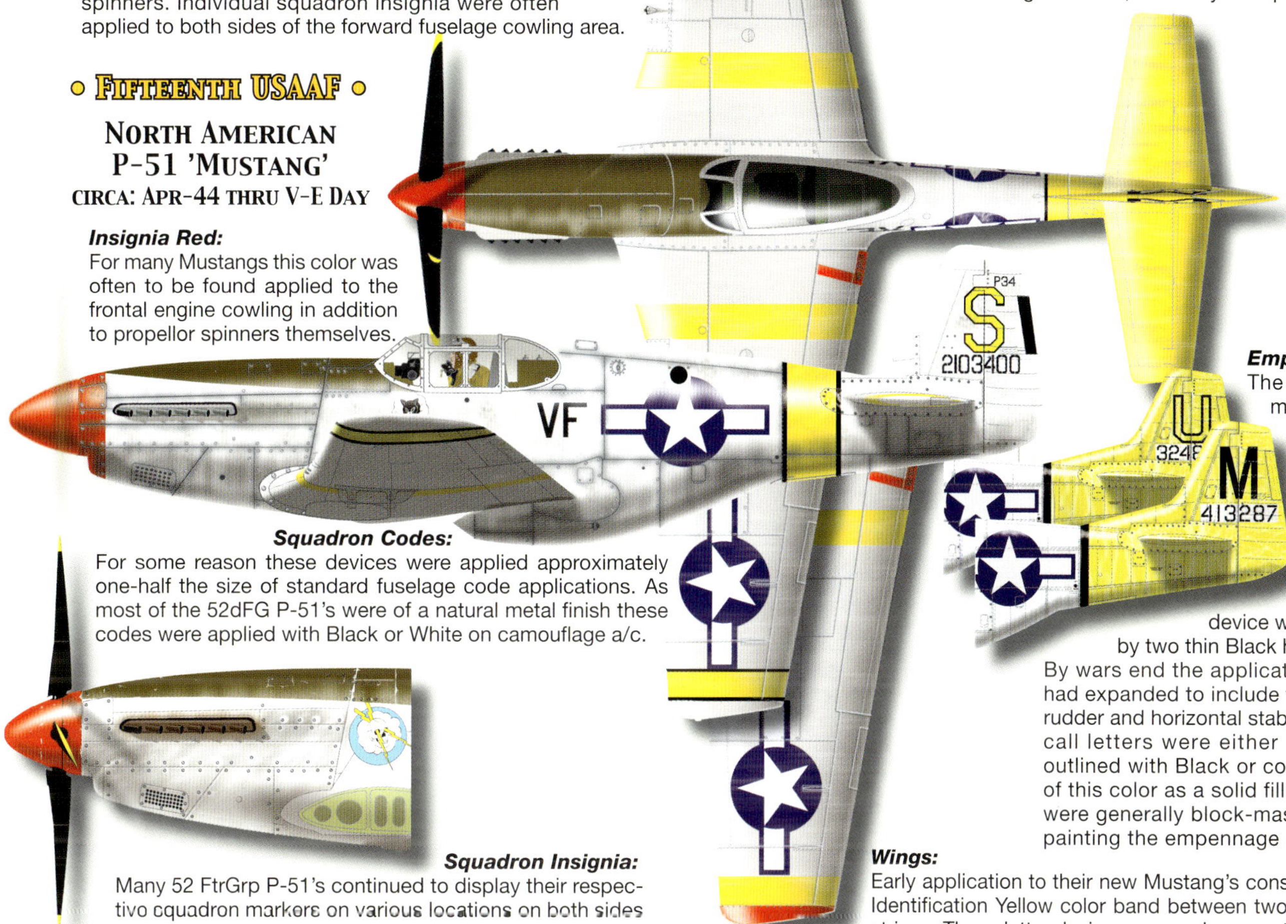

Insignia Red:
For many Mustangs this color was often to be found applied to the frontal engine cowling in addition to propellor spinners themselves.

Empennage:
The original tactical markings on most 52dFG's P-51's consisted of a vertical band of Yellow encircling the rear of the fuselage, aft the national insignia. This device was accompanied by two thin Black horizontal stripes. By wars end the application of this color had expanded to include the entire tail fin, rudder and horizontal stabilizers. Individual call letters were either Insignia Yellow outlined with Black or comprised entirely of this color as a solid fill. Serial numbers were generally block-masked out prior to painting the empennage proper.

Squadron Codes:
For some reason these devices were applied approximately one-half the size of standard fuselage code applications. As most of the 52dFG P-51's were of a natural metal finish these codes were applied with Black or White on camouflage a/c.

Squadron Insignia:
Many 52 FtrGrp P-51's continued to display their respective squadron markers on various locations on both sides of the engine cowling or forward fuselage surfaces.

Wings:
Early application to their new Mustang's consisted of an Identification Yellow color band between two thin Black stripes. These latter devices were subsequently dropped in favor of the addition of Insignia Red wing tips.

• Assigned: Desert Air Force, Jul-42 ; Ninth AAF, Nov-42 ; Twelfth AAF, Aug-43 thru V-E Day •

XII
Bomber Command

IX
Fighter Command

57th
Bomb Wing
1943- 1944

87th
Fighter Wing
1944

57th Fighter Group

Insignia/Approved: 2-Feb-50 (from WWII Design)
Motto: 'First In The Blue'
Sobriquet: 'America's Flying Circus'
Constituted: 57th Pur Grp (Intep)/20-Nov-40
Activated: 15-Jan-41
Redesignated: 57th Ftr Grp/May-42

64thFS Insignia:
This image appeared in many varying configurations, with and without a disc enclosure. The Pyramid was actually a late addition to the design and used to indicated the squadrons prior area of operations subsequent to a permanent departure from North Africa for duty in other parts of the Mediterranean.

64th Ftr Sqdn

Sobriquet: 'The Black Scorpions'
Insignia/Revised: 17-Jul-56

Constituted: 64th Pur Sqdn (Intcp)/20-Nov-40
Activated: 15-Jan-41
Redesignated: 64th Ftr Sqdn/15-May-42

(Number-In-Squadron)
No Color Assigned
10-39

65th Ftr Sqdn

Sobriquet: 'The Fighting Cocks'
Insignia/Approved: 18-Dec-41

Constituted: 65th Pur Sqdn (Intcp)/20-Nov-40
Activated: 15-Jan-41
Redesignated: 65th Ftr Sqdn/15-May-42

(Number-In-Squadron)
No Color Assigned
40-69

66th Ftr Sqdn

Sobriquet: 'The X-terminators'
Insignia/Approved: 2-Jan-42

Constituted: 66th Pur Sqdn (Intcp)/20-Nov-40
Activated: 15-Jan-41
Redesignated: 66th Ftr Sqdn/15-May-42

(Number-In-Squadron)
No Color Assigned
70-99

Squadron Insignia: Each squadron comprising the 57thFG not only made extensive use of their respective insignia but they left an abundance of photographic evidence to prove it. From personal clothing to mobile canteens, these unit images were very much a part of the everyday lives of America's Flying Circus.

30.) Grosseto Main, Italy
25-Sep-44

31.) Villafranca di Verona, Italy
28-Apr-45

27.) Arcola, Italy
16-Jan-44

28.) Alto, Corsica
24-Mar-44

29.) Ombrone, Italy
17-Sep-44

23.) Gioia del Colle, Italy
25-Sep-43

24.) Foggia #8, Italy
2-Oct-43

25.) Foggia #1, Italy
6-Oct-43

26.) Amendola, Italy
22-Oct-43

18 & 19.) Gozo, Malta
13-Jul-43

20.) Pachino, Sicily
20-Jul-43

21.) Scordia, Sicily
31-Jul-43

22.) Rocco Bernardo, Italy
18-Sep-43

17.) Causeway, Tunisia
19-Jun-43

16.) Cape Bon, Tunisia
6-Jun-43

15.) Hani, Tunisia
21-Apr-43

13.) El Djem, Tunisia
14-Apr-43

12.) Hasbub, Tunisia
4-Apr-43

11.) Soltane, Tunisa
20-Mar-43

10.) Ben Gardane, Tunisa
9-Mar-43

1.) L/G # 174, Egypt
16-Sep-42

2.) L/G #172, Egypt
5-Nov-42

3.) L/G #75, Egypt
9-Nov-42

4.) Gambut, Libya
13-Nov-42

5.) Martuba, Libya
16-Nov-42

6.) Belandah, Libya
2-Dec-42

7.) Hamraiet, Libya
5-Jan-43

8.) Bur Dufan (R)-R6045SW, Libya
19-Jan-43

9.) Zuara, Libya
23-Feb-43

• USAFMEAF/DAF •
• Ninth USAAF •
Curtiss P-40 'Warhawk'
circa: Jan-42 thru Aug-43

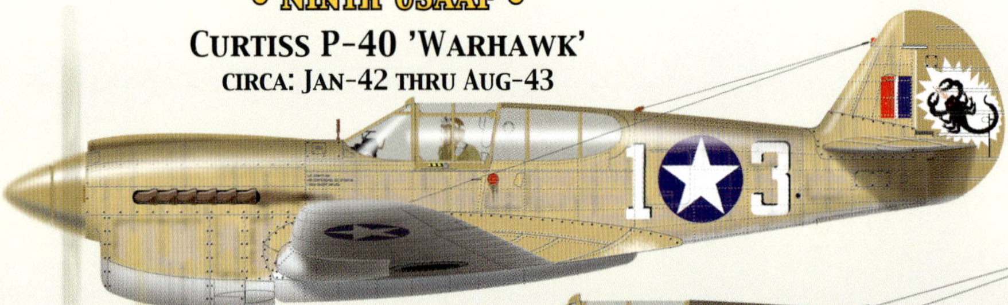

Tactical Markings:
Upon arrival in the Middle East one of the first orders of business was the application of the Allied Recognition Flash to the fins of the newly assigned P-40's. The existing a/c serial numbers were either simply over painted or, for the most part, removed entirely. The 64thFS quickly seized on this opportunity and applied their newly designed unit insignia to the rudder surfaces of their aircraft. Placement of all squadron soon became standardized to the lower front engine cowling area.

Squadron Codes:
These markings were applied on either side of the national insignia using Insignia White. To help with legibility the numerals were either outlined in Black or backed by a Black drop-shadow.

National Insignia:
An additional 'friendly forces' aircraft recognition aid was the application of the two-inch Identification Yellow surround to the national insignia beginning Sep-42.

Serial Numbers:
As operations gradually evolved into a pattern, aircraft serial numbers began to re-appear on 57thFG combat aircraft. These markings however were confined to the rudder surface area as opposed to the original Fin/Rudder surfaces, and were often applied using Black instead of the original Identification Yellow paint.

Airframe Finishes:
As originally delivered the P-40's of the 57thFG consisted of a two-color camouflage paint scheme, Middle Stone over Azure Blue, with the propeller spinners being sprayed with the former. It wasn't long however before these aircraft were quickly adorned with the standard RAF tri-color desert camouflage which entailed adding a random pattern of Dark Earth to the upper fuselage and control surfaces. At about this same time the Group also adopted the non-standard, but widely used, Insignia Red spinners with a matching color band applied to the leading six-inches of the cowling.

• Twelfth USAAF •
Curtiss P-40 'Warhawk'
circa: Aug-43 thru Feb-44

Spinners / Cowling:
The first six inches of the engine cowlings and the propeller spinners of the reassigned P-40's comprising the 57th Fighter Group continued to be painted with Insignia Red.

Fuselage / Empennage Markings:
The introduction of the new 'Star & Bars' aircraft insignia in June 1943 created something of a copy-fitting problem for the 57thFG. As opposed to tucking a second digit of the two-digit squadron codes under the rear horizontal stabilizer, it was decided to combine the numbers, which had previously been separated by the earlier 'Circle & Star' pattern. As with previous applications of this devise however, the numerals were applied with Insignia White with a Black contour outline or drop-shadow. By this time pressure from Wing saw to it that virtually all of the group's P-40's again displayed an individual serial number. These reinstated numbers were directed be applied using the original Identification Yellow paint. The Allied 'Friendly Forces' recognition flash was still displayed on both sides of the fin, thus the reinstated serial numbers continued to be positioned entirely on the upper rudder surfaces.

Airframe:
By the time the 57thFG reached the Twelfth AAF virtually all of the Groups combat aircraft bore a tri-color desert camouflaged paint scheme consisting of Sand and Dark Earth with a Sky under-frame.

• TWELFTH USAAF •

REPUBLIC P-47 'THUNDERBOLT'

CIRCA: JAN-44 THRU V-E DAY

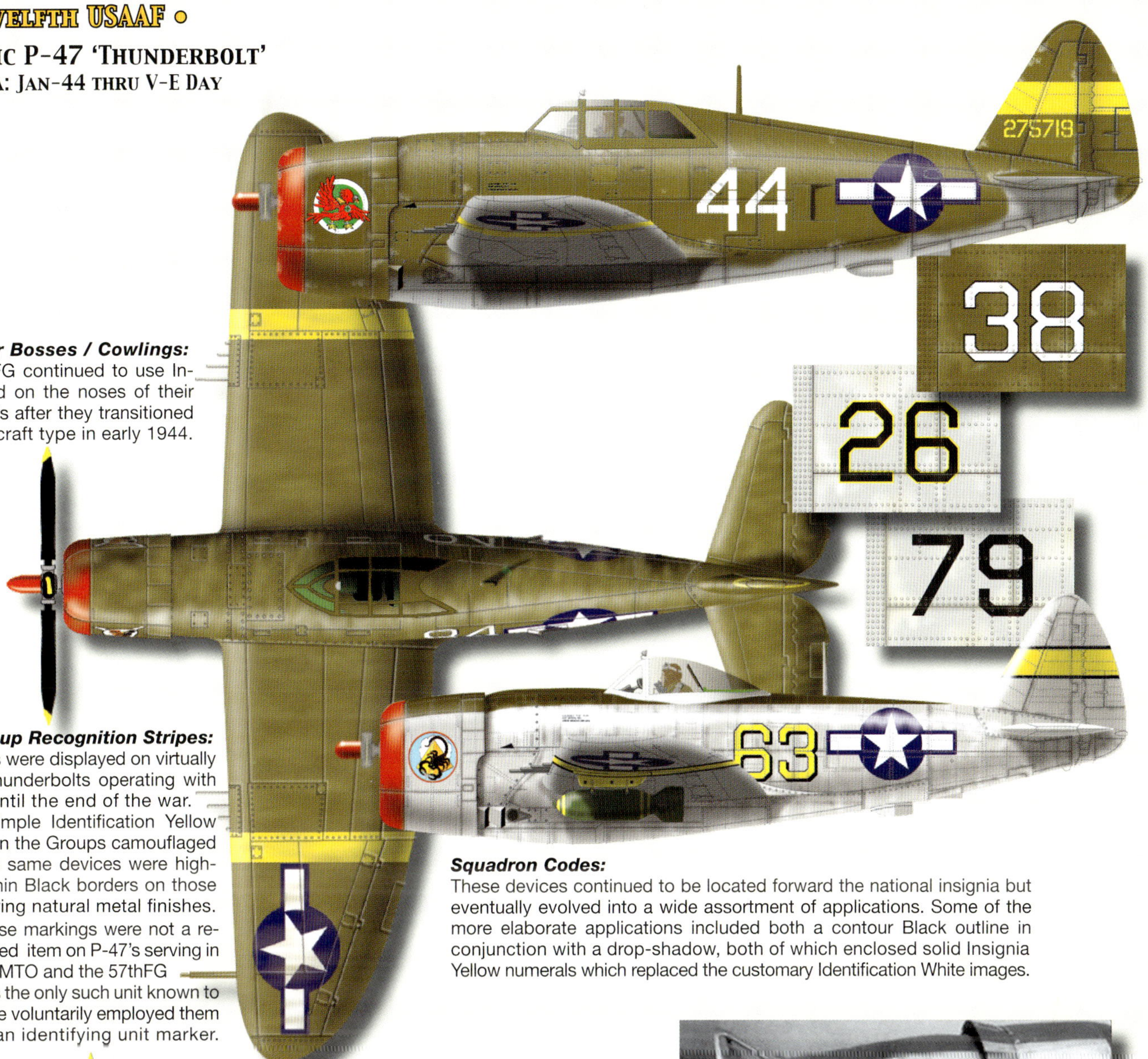

Propeller Bosses / Cowlings:
The 57thFG continued to use Insignia Red on the noses of their new P-47's after they transitioned to this aircraft type in early 1944.

Group Recognition Stripes:
These devices were displayed on virtually all combat Thunderbolts operating with the 57thFG until the end of the war. Applied as simple Identification Yellow color bands on the Groups camouflaged aircraft, these same devices were highlighted with thin Black borders on those aircraft featuring natural metal finishes. These markings were not a required item on P-47's serving in the MTO and the 57thFG was the only such unit known to have voluntarily employed them as an identifying unit marker.

Squadron Codes:
These devices continued to be located forward the national insignia but eventually evolved into a wide assortment of applications. Some of the more elaborate applications included both a contour Black outline in conjunction with a drop-shadow, both of which enclosed solid Insignia Yellow numerals which replaced the customary Identification White images.

Insignia:
Perhaps more than any other fighter unit serving in the MTO during WWII, the 57thFG utilized their insignia to the fullest extent imaginable. This high profile imagery contributed in no small degree to this outfit being selected to be featured in William Wylers classic wartime documentary 'Thunderbolt'. Normally squadron insignia were centered on both sides of the engine cowling. The photos at right are that of Lt.Col. William J. Yates personal ship. Col. Yates was Commanding Officer of the 57th at wars end.

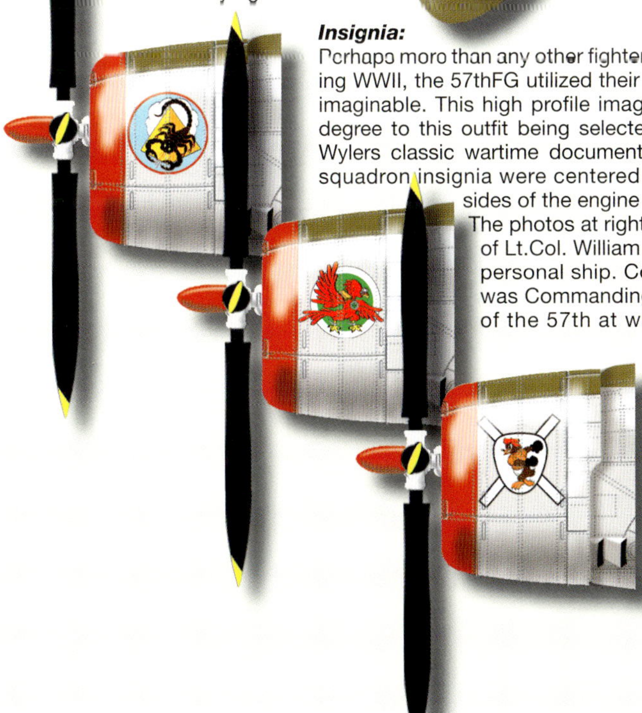

• Assigned Ninth AAF, Oct-1942 ; Twelfth AAF, Aug-1943 thru V-E Day •

57TH BOMB WING 1943-1944

XII TACTICAL AIR COMMAND

87TH FIGHTER WING 1944

XXII TACTICAL AIR COMMAND

87TH FIGHTER WING 1944-V-E DAY

8TH FIGHTER WING 1943

IX FIGHTER COMMAND

79TH FIGHTER GROUP

INSIGNIA/(UNOFFICIAL)
MOTTO: (NONE)
SOBRIQUET: 'FALCONS'
CONSTITUTED: 79TH PUR GRP (INTEP)/13-JAN-42
ACTIVATED: 9-FEB-42
REDESIGNATED: 79TH FTR GRP/MAY-42

Western Desert Air Force

On-the-job-trainning took on a whole new meaning to the pilots and ground crews of the 57thFG. This unit flew numerous combat operations in support of the British offensive against Rommel's Afrika Korps. Officially however, the 57thFG did not enter combat as a full unit until March of 1943.

85TH FTR SQDN

INSIGNIA/REPLACED: 7-AUG-53
SOBRIQUET: 'FLYING SKULLS'

CONSTITUTED: 85TH PUR SQDN (INTCP)/13-JAN-42
ACTIVATED: 9-FEB-42
REDESIGNATED: 85TH FTR SQDN: 15-MAY-42

86TH FTR SQDN

INSIGNIA/REVISED: 20-JAN-59
SOBRIQUET: 'COMANCHES'

CONSTITUTED: 86TH PUR SQDN (INTCP)/13-JAN-42
ACTIVATED: 9-FEB-42
REDESIGNATED: 86TH FTR SQDN/15-MAY-42

87TH FTR SQDN

INSIGNIA/REPLACED: 16-JUL-56
SOBRIQUET: 'SKEETERS'

CONSTITUTED: 87TH PUR SQDN (INTCP)/13-JAN-42
ACTIVATED: 9-FEB-42
REDESIGNATED: 87TH FTR SQDN/15-MAY-42

• Ninth USAAF •

Curtiss P-40 'Warhawk'
circa: Nov-42 thru May-44

Squadron Codes:
All numerical designations were positioned on either side of the U.S. roundel and preceded with the letter 'X', painted Insignia White and, as a rule, outlined in Black. With the introduction of the 'star & bars' insignia in June 1943, the entire three-digit code was grouped together and located forward the new insignia design.

Insignia:
These images were prevalent on all 79thFG / P-40 combat aircraft.

• Twelfth USAAF •

Republic P-47 'Thunderbolt'
circa: Jun-44 thru V-E Day

Empennage Group Marker:
Serial numbers were obliterated, replaced with a striking medium blue fin and rudder, further adorned with three Identification Yellow, (sometimes orange) lightning bolts. Many, but not all, horizontal stabilizers also received a full coat of blue.

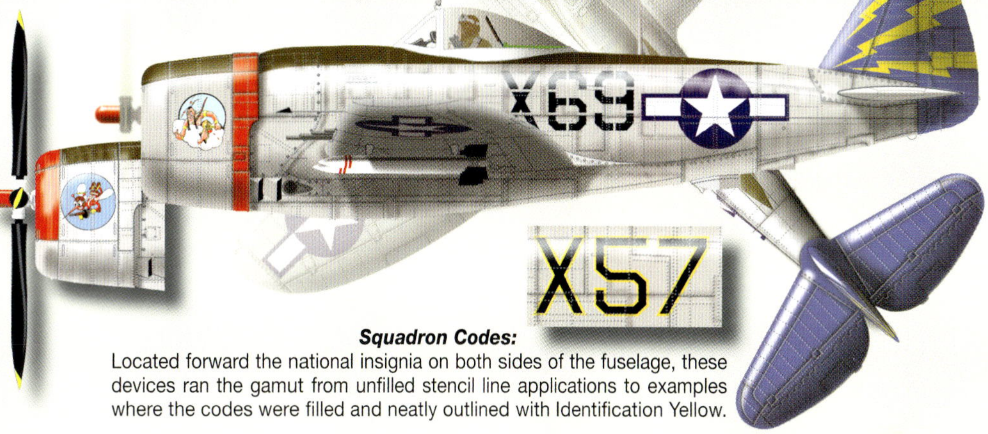

Propeller Bosses & Cowlings:
Like most AAF fighter units serving in the MTO, the 79thFG voluntarily elected to apply Insignia Red to the noses of their aircraft. In some instances the rear cowling flaps received a treatment of this color, on others, it appeared only on the top two-thirds of the outer cowling ring.

Insignia:
The use of insignia on their aircraft cowlings continued to be widespread within all of the 79thFG squadrons.

Squadron Codes:
Located forward the national insignia on both sides of the fuselage, these devices ran the gamut from unfilled stencil line applications to examples where the codes were filled and neatly outlined with Identification Yellow.

86thFS
Although the 'Comanche' insignia is most often associated with the 86th, this 'Fighting Bulldog' design appeared representing the unit on page 174 of the National Geographic Society's *'Insignia and Decorations of the U.S. Armed Forces'* (Revised Edition: 1-Dec-44). Numerous attempts to clarify this additional image have to date been unsuccessful.

87thFS
The 'Skeeter' image appeared on occasional applications enclosed by either a white (or sometimes black) bordered medium blue cloud. This configuration appears to have been virtually interchangeable at times with its circular counterpart, but seems to have been confined mainly to aircraft, rather than uniform applications (patches, etc).

- 1.) L/G 174, Egypt 18-Nov-42
- 2.) L/G 150, Gazala, Libya 23-Jan-43
- 3.) Darraugh North L/G, Libya 7-Feb-43
- 4.) Castel Benito L/G, Libya 27-Feb-43
- 5.) Causeway L/G, Tunisia 11-Mar-43
- 6.) Sidi el Hani L/G, Tunisia 17-Apr-43
- 7.) El Houaria L/G, Tunisia 2-Jun-43
- 8.) Bou Grara, Tunisia 6-Jun-43
- 9.) Causeway L/G, Tunisia 14-Jun-43
- 10.) Syracuse, Sicily 16-Jun-43
- 11.) Cassibile L/G, Sicily 26-Jul-43
- 12.) Palagonia L/G, Sicily 32-Jul-43
- 13.) Isole L/G, Crotone, Sicily 13-Sep-43
- 14.) Firmo L/G, Italy (det) 24-Sep-43
- 15.) Pisticci L/G, Italy 24-Sep-43
- 16.) Penny Post L/G, Italy 26-Sep-43
- 17.) Foggia #3, Salsola, Italy 4-Oct-43
- 18.) Madna L/G, Italy 19-Nov-43
- 19.) Capodichino A/F, Italy 17-Jan-44
- 20.) Pomigliano A/F, Italy 1-May-44
- 21.) Serragia A/F, Corsica 11-Jun-44
- 22.) Y-12 St. Raphael/Frejus, FR 22-Aug-44
- 23.) Y-23 Valence A/F, France 1-Sep-44
- *24.) Y-6 Lyon/Bron A/F, FR (det) 15-Sep-44
- *25.) Y-18 Le Vallon A/F, FR (det) 22-Sep-44
- 26.) Iesi L/G, Italy 3-Oct-44
- 27.) Fano L/G, Italy 5-Dec-44
- 28.) Cesenatico L/G, Italy 20-Mar-45

*Stations not depicted on map

• Assigned Twelfth AAF, Jan-1943 ; Fourteenth AAF, May-1944 thru V-J Day •

XXII Tactical Air Command — 47th Bomb Wing 1942-1943 — XII Bomber Command

62d Fighter Wing 1943 - 1944

81st Fighter Group

Insignia/Approved:2-Mar-43
Motto: 'The Name, The Arms And Loyalty'
Constituted: 81st PurGrp(Intep)/13-Jan-42
Activated: 9-Feb-42
Redesignated: 81st FtrGrp/May-42

No Known Squadron Insignia

91st Ftr Sqdn

Insignia/(unknown)

Constituted: 91st Pur Sqdn (intep)/13-Jan-42
Activated: 9-Feb-42
Redesignated: 91st Ftr Sqdn/15-May-42

No Color Assigned — Squadron Codes Unknown

92d Ftr Sqdn

Insignia/Approved: 30-Jun-45

Constituted: 92d Pur Sqdn (intep)/13-Jan-42
Activated: 9-Feb-42
Redesignated: 92d Ftr Sqdn/15-May-42

No Color Assigned — Squadron Codes Unknown

No Known Squadron Insignia

93d Ftr Sqdn

Insignia/(unknown)

Constituted: 93d Pur Sqdn (intep)/13-Jan-42
Activated: 9-Feb-42
Redesignated: 93d Ftr Sqdn/15-May-42

No Color Assigned — Q

• Twelfth USAAF •

Bell P-39 'Airacobra'
c. Jun-42 thru c. Mar-44

Fuselage:
The 93dFS split its aircraft codes, the squadron was positioned to the left of the national insignia, call letter to the right. Due to the low degree of contrast between the yellow fuselage band and the white code letters, these latter devices were sometimes accompanied with a Black contour outline which enhanced legibility significantly.

Tactical Markings:
For some unfortunate reason there is precious little photographic evidence or written material to mark the service of this unit during the course of the war. Aircraft operating with the 93dFS could be identified by a 36in. (approx) tall, insignia White upper case letter 'Q' located just forward the national insignia. One of the other squadrons used a 10in (approx) letter 'X' followed by a hyphen which in turn was followed by the individual aircraft call letter, all of which were applied with Insignia White paint. Unfortunately, to date no records have surfaced that indicate which of the remaining two squadrons utilized this code. Of the third squadron markings absolutely nothing is currently known.

Spinners:
As was the case with most Allied fighter Groups operating within the MTO, the 81stFH adopted the voluntary use of Insignia Red on this portion of their aircraft.

Wings:
Beginning in late 1942 and early '43 a number of Airacobra's within the 81stFG developed the practice of painting 18in.wide (approx.) wrap-around Identification Yellow bands on the outboard section of both wings. These, along with the corresponding fuselage bands, were designed as 'friendly forces' tactical markings. Such devices were known to be highly effective in reducing Allied aircraft losses due to friendly fire mishaps, mainly caused by inexperienced gun crews manning both navel and land based AA batteries. With the introduction of the replacement 'star & bars' insignia, these were more often than not simply applied directly over the existing yellow bands.

Insignia:
When the new 'star & Bars' insignia was introduced in June 1943, this new device quickly replaced the previous 'star & circle' pattern on the wing surfaces. It was immediately apparent to the ground crews however, that there was going to be a fitting problem when it came to applying this new insignia to the fuselage of their P-40's. The 'bars' inherent with the new design were going to overlap the existing Identification Yellow tactical marking band. It was perhaps because of a reluctance to do anything to detract from this now familiar 'friendly forces' indicator, that for some time during the summer of 1943 the combat aircraft of the 81stFG could be seen concurrently displaying both the old and new insignia patterns.

• Assigned Twelfth AAF, Dec-1942 ; Fifteenth AAF, Nov-1943 thru V-E Day •

47th Bmb Wng
1943

North African
Stratigic A/F

XII
Bomber Command

305TH Ftr Wng (P)
1943-1944

5TH Ftr Wng
1944

306TH Ftr Wng
1944-1945

NO KNOWN GROUP INSIGNIA

82D Fighter Group

Insignia: (unknown)
Motto: (unknown)
Sobriquet: 'Kraut Exterminators, Inc.'
Constituted: 82D PurGrp(Intep)/13-Jan-42
Activated: 6-Feb-42
Redesignated: 82D FtrGrp/May-42

97thFS Insignia: Although the rectangular format of this insignia was the officially approved design configuration, the vast majority of individual applications adopted a more common circular disc pattern.

95TH Ftr Sqdn

Insignia/Approved: 4-Feb-54
(from WWII design)
Sobriquet: 'Boneheads'

Constituted: 95TH Pur Sqdn (Intep)/13-Jan-42
Activated: 9-Feb-42
Redesignated: 95TH Ftr Sqdn/15-May-42

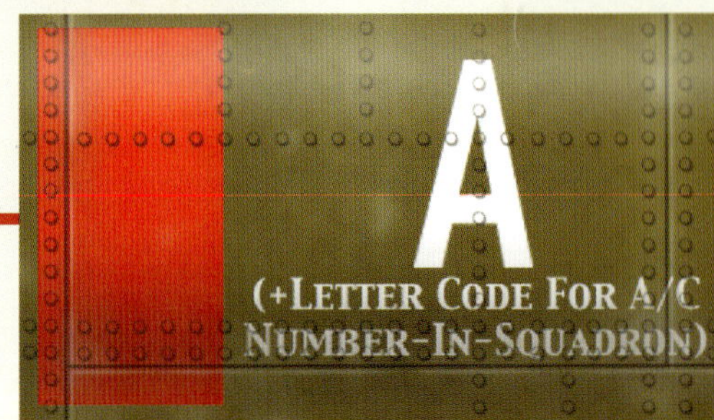

96TH Ftr Sqdn

Insignia/Approved: 18-Aug-42
Sobriquet: (unknown)

Constituted: 96TH Pur Sqdn (Intep)/13-Jan-42
Activated: 9-Feb-42
Redesignated: 96TH Ftr Sqdn/15-May-42

97TH Ftr Sqdn

Insignia/Approved: 30-Oct-42
Sobriquet: 'Devil-Cats'

Constituted: 97TH Pur Sqdn (Intep)/13-Jan-42
Activated: 9-Feb-42
Redesignated: 97TH Ftr Sqdn/15-May-42

• Twelfth / Fifteenth USAAF •

Lockheed P-38 'Lightning'

circa : Oct-42 thru V-E Day

Squadron Codes:
These were applied to outer radiator housing surfaces with 24in. letters using primarily Insignia White, but in some instances Identification Yellow was substituted. With the introduction of NMF aircraft to the Groups inventory, these same outer radiator housings were painted Black and the individual squadron codes were then applied over this area using Insignia White paint. Numerous early applications to camouflaged aircraft received an additional drop-shadow treatment. When squadron inventories ultimately exceeded twenty-six, numerals, beginning with '1', substituted as the aircraft call letter.

Color Markings:
Most combat aircraft assigned to the 82dFG early on adopted the use of MTO 'friendly-forces' Insignia Red propeller spinners. Individual squadron colors first appeared on the extreme nose areas of the Groups P-38's, and this practice was soon expanded to include the entire nacelle frontal nose area. Squadron colors were soon being similarly applied to the propeller spinners as an additional tactical marking.

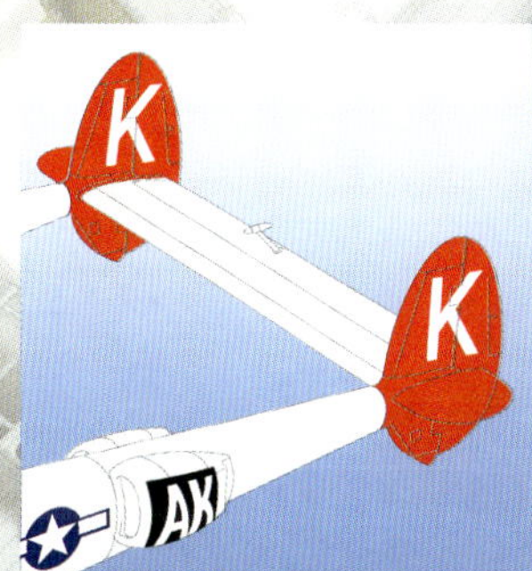

Color Notes:
The specific shade of blue selected for use by the 87thFS is currently unclear. Additionally, with the introduction of NMF aircraft, the 96thFS adopted Identification Yellow as the replacement squadron for their original Insignia White.

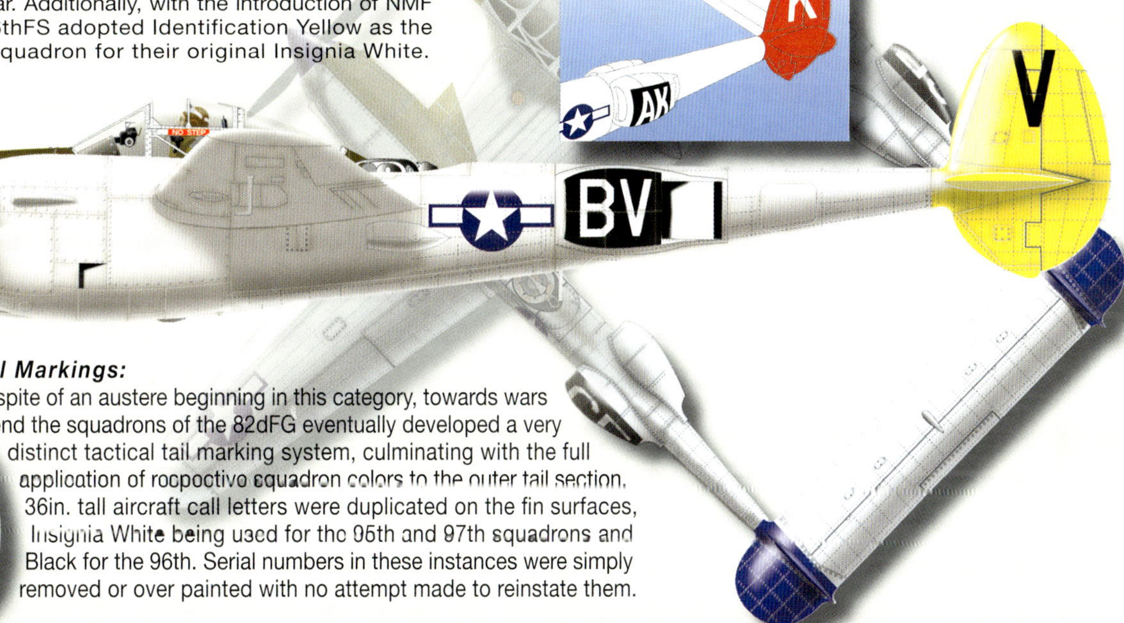

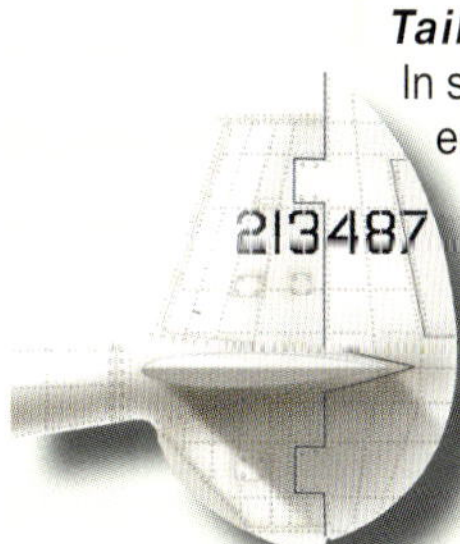

Tail Markings:
In spite of an austere beginning in this category, towards wars end the squadrons of the 82dFG eventually developed a very distinct tactical tail marking system, culminating with the full application of respective squadron colors to the outer tail section. 36in. tall aircraft call letters were duplicated on the fin surfaces, Insignia White being used for the 95th and 97th squadrons and Black for the 96th. Serial numbers in these instances were simply removed or over painted with no attempt made to reinstate them.

• Twelfth AAF, Mar-1943 thru Feb-1945 • First TAC/AF(Prov) Feb-1945 thru V-E Day •

XXII Tactical Air Command — XII Tactical Air Command — Northwest African Tactical Air Force — XXII Air Support Command

64th Ftr Wng 1943

87th Ftr Wng 1944

64th Ftr Wng 1945

86th Fighter (Bmr) Group

Insignia/Approved: 17-Oct-42
Motto: 'Courage Will Endure'
Sobriquet: 'The Invaders'
Constituted: 86th BombGrp(Lt)/13-Jan-42
Activated: 10-Feb-42
Redesignated: 86th BombGrp(Dive)/Sep-42
Redesignated: 86th Ftr-BmrGrp/Aug-43
Redesignated: 86thFtrGrp/May-43

311th Bomb Squadron (Dive)
This unit was originaly assigned to the 86th BG on 10-Feb-42 but was attached to Northwest Training Command from 20-Jun-43 until 1-Oct-43 when the squadron was disbanded. This 'Blue Duck' insignia of the 311th was officially approved 27-Oct-42.

525th Ftr Sqdn

Insignia/Replaced: 29-Sep-55

Constituted: 309thBmb Sqdn (Lt)/13-Jan-42
Activated: 10-Feb-42
Redesignated: 309th Bomb Sqdn (Dive)/3-Sep-42
Redesignated: 525th Ftr-Bmr Sqdn/23-Aug-43
Redesignated: 525th Ftr Sqdn/30-May-44

No color assigned
A
A-36's Sq. Letter Code + Letter For A/C Assignment-In-Squadron
1-39
P-47's Aircraft Number-In-Squadron

526th Ftr Sqdn

Insignia/Replaced: 6-Sep-55

Constituted: 310thBmb Sqdn (Lt)/13-Jan-42
Activated: 10-Feb-42
Redesignated: 310th Bomb Sqdn (Dive)/3-Sep-42
Redesignated: 526th Ftr-Bmr Sqdn/23-Aug-43
Redesignated: 526th Ftr Sqdn/30-May-44

No color assigned
B
A-36's Sq. Letter Code + Letter For A/C Assignment-In-Squadron
40-69
P-47's Aircraft Number-In-Squadron

527th Ftr Sqdn

Insignia/approved: 11-Jan-43

Constituted: 312thBmb Sqdn (Lt)/13-Jan-42
Activated: 10-Feb-42
Redesignated: 312th Bomb Sqdn (Dive)/3-Sep-42
Redesignated: 527th Ftr-Bmr Sqdn/23-Aug-43
Redesignated: 527th Ftr Sqdn/30-May-44

No color assigned
C
A-36's Sq. Letter Code + Letter For A/C Assignment-In-Squadron
70-99
P-47's Aircraft Number-In-Squadron

• Twelfth USAAF •

North American A-36 'Apache'
circa: May'43 thru V-E Day

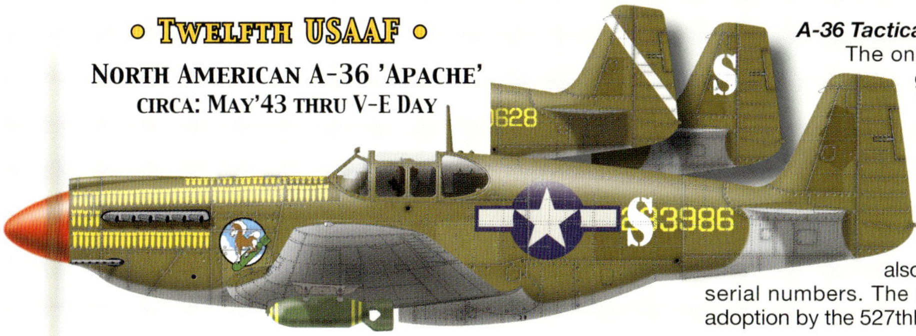

A-36 Tactical Markings:
The only distinguishing markings adopted within the group was relocating the serial numbers from the tail section. These were reapplied, in a larger version to the fuselage aft the national insignia. In a radical departure from standard AAF markings, the squadrons of the group adopted a rounded, bold serif type style which were originally applied with Insignia White to the upper fin area. For reasons uncertain today, these call letters were also soon relocated to the fuselage, over painting the serial numbers. The only other known distinctive marking was the adoption by the 527thFBS of a diagonal white stripe over the fin/rudder.

Curtuss P-40 'Warhawk'
circa: Jan thru May-'44

P-40 Tactical Markings:
Other than Insignia Red applied to the a/c spinners, no additional group or squadron markings appear to have been applied. The specific roll these played within the 86th is uncertain today. All Warhawks received by this group were well worn hand-me-downs from various other units. According to the group's war diary, all losses of these aircraft during their brief tenure with the 86thFBG were landing or take-off related, indicating that these a/c were utilized for training or other support purposes.

Republic P-47 'Thunderbolt'
circa: May'44 thru V-E Day

P-47 Tactical Markings:
With the addition of Thunderbolts to the groups inventory came an apparent change of attitude towards the use of color as a tactical marking device. Horizontal Insignia Red stripes soon adorned the new arrivals, each stripe with an approximate width measuring 6in., with a similar 6in. wide area of metal surface showing between each painted stripe. On most of the Groups P-47's, seven slightly narrower wrap-around stripes were applied chord-wise to each of the rear horizontal stabilizers. With the addition of these distinctively new group markings, the existing a/c tail serial numbers were removed or over-painted, the former being the dominate case. Either way, these numbers were reapplied in Black mid-fuselage, forward the Number-In Squadron code, similarly applied in Black, and approximately 30in. over-all height. The vast majority of both the fuselage codes were affixed with the stencil lines un-filled.

Tactical Color:
Propeller hubs and cowling noses received a customary coat of the NA/MTO Allied recognition color, Insignia Red. Additionally, a large majority of the P-47's assigned to the 86thFBG had their cowling flaps similarly adorned. Unlike similar applications within other groups however, these color bands did not over-paint the anti-glare panel but terminated at the intersection point of the two colors.

1.) La Senia A/F, Algeria 12-May-43
2.) Marnia, French Morroco 3-Jun-43
3.) Tafaraouri A/F, Algeria 11-Jun-43
4.) Korba L/G, Tunisia 30-Jun-43
5.) Gela L/G, Sicily 20-Jul-43
6.) Barcelona L/G, Sicily 27-Aug-43
7.) Sele A/F, Italy 22-Sep-43
8.) Serretelle A/F, Italy 12-Oct-43
9.) Pomigliano A/F, Italy 19-Nov-43
10.) Marcianise A/F, Italy 30-Apr-43
11.) Ciampino A/F, Italy c.12-Jun-44
12.) Orbetello A/F, Italy c.19-Jun-44
13.) Poretta A/F, Corsica c.12-Jul-44
14.) Grosseto A/F, Italy c.17-Sep-44
15.) Pisa A/F, Italy 23-Oct-44
16.) Y-1 Tantonville A/F, France 20-Feb-45
17.) Y-72 Braunschardt A/F, Germany c.18-Apr-45

• Assigned Ninth AAF, Dec-1942 ; Twelfth AAF, Aug-1943 thru V-E Day •

XII Tactical Air Command

XII Air Support Command

IX Fighter Command

64th Ftr Wng 1944

324th Fighter Group

Insignia/Replaced: 1-May-53
Motto: 'To Dare'
Constituted: 324th FtrGrp/24-Jun-42
Activated: 6-Jul-42

Original 315thFS Insignia

This patch was the original combat insignia for this unit until March 1943. At that time the new SQ/CO deemed the replacement Crusader image as being more appropriate to the mission and accomplishments of the squadron. Whether this 'Bugs-on-a-cloud' insignia was originally a Warner Bros. generated design is unknown at this time.

314th Ftr Sqdn

Sobriquet: 'The Hawks'
Insignia/Approved: 8-Jul-44

Constituted: 314th Ftr Sqdn/24-Jun-42
Activated: 6-Jul-42

P-40's Number-In-Squadron
Y10-Y39
P-47's Number-In-Squadron
10-39

315th Ftr Sqdn

Sobriquet: 'The Crusaders'
Insignia/unofficial

Constituted: 315th Ftr Sqdn/24-Jun-42
Activated: 6-Jul-42

P-40's Number-In-Squadron
Y40-Y69
P-47's Number-In-Squadron
40-69

316th Ftr Sqdn

Sobriquet: 'Hell's Belles'
Insignia/Approved: 2-Sep-43

Constituted: 316th Ftr Sqdn/24-Jun-42
Activated: 6-Jul-42

P-40's Number-In-Squadron
Y70-Y99
P-47's Number-In-Squadron
70-99

• Ninth / Twelfth USAAF •

Curtuss P-40 'Warhawk'
circa: Oct'42 thru Jul'44

Tail Markings:
Although virtually all P-40's assigned to the 325thFG bore an Allied Recognition Flash located in the standard location on the fin, these devices had all but disappeared by late 1943.

Colors:
Relatively small horizontally elongated diamonds in respective squadron colors were affixed to both sides of the forward lower fuselage, and vertically aligned with the leading edge of the exhaust cut-out. Propeller spinners were universally painted red in keeping with existing fighter policy.

Insignia:
The 316thFS was known to have frequently replaced the starboard 'diamond' with their own 'Hell's Belle's' insignia.

Squadron Codes:
Initially all squadrons utilized a 'Y' prefix followed by a two-digit 'number-in-squadron' identification code. Sizes varied with these applications, but the prefix was always approximately 2/3 the height of the numerals. The 'Y' prefix and first digit of the code were located to the left side of the national insignia while the second digit was situated to the right. This positioning was consistent on both sides of the fuselage. After the introduction of the new 'star-and-bars' national insignia in June 1943, it was not uncommon to see 325thFG P-40's displaying the new insignia on the wings while retaining the older roundel on the fuselage. This was due to a fitting problem created by the addition of the new 'bars'. By late 1943 however the 'Y' prefix had been discarded and 'number-in-squadron' designators were unilatterially placed forward the fuselage insignia.

Repbublic P-47 'Thunderbolt'
circa: Jul'42 thru V-E Day

Group Marker:
In a departure from the norm the 324thFG adopted a distinctive lightning bolt design that was applied to the upper, forward fuselage, emanating almost directly behind the cowling flaps and terminating approximately mid-cockpit. Most applications were of a red bolt which was often accompanied by a drop-shadow or contour outline in either black or a squadron color. In a few known cases these 'bolts' were themselves applied in a squadron color.

Tail Markers:
A black horizontal stripe at the upper third of the vertical stabilizer became a standard feature within the Group. Added to this device was a 'half-diamond' in respective squadron color, aligned with the leading edge of the fin.

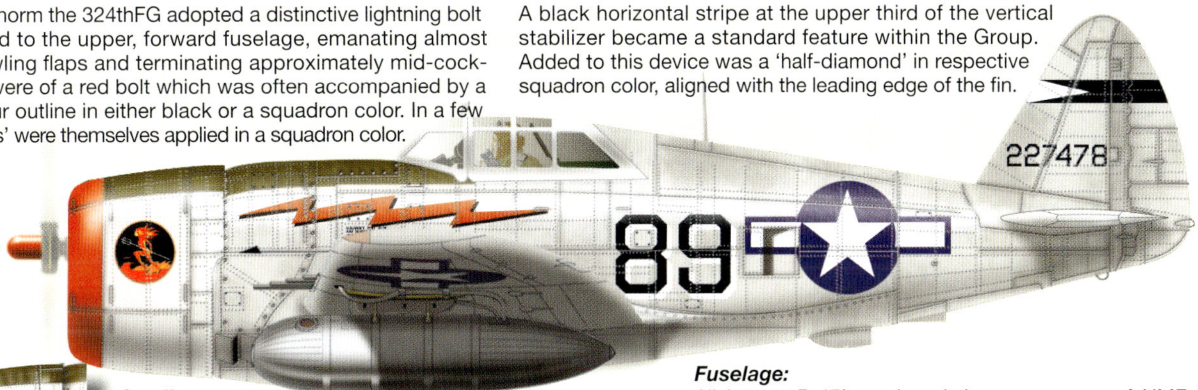

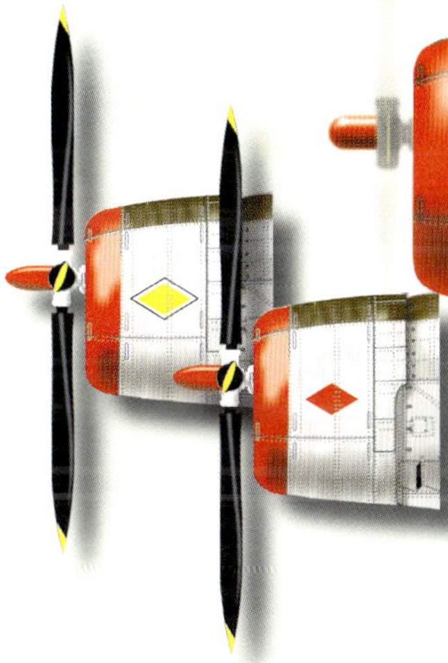

Cowlings:
The 314th and 315 FS's continued to employ a diamond shape in squadron colors on each side of the aircraft cowling, the 314th frequently incorporating a black contour outline with their pattern. The 316thFS revised its previous P-40 policy but reversed the locations of their diamond and 'Hell's Belle's' insignia. The later was now affixed on the left center cowling while the diamond was relocated to the right. All squadrons painted the leading edges of their cowlings in a standard solid red.

Fuselage:
All known P-47's assigned the group were of NMF with squadron codes applied in black paint and located forward the national insignia on both sides of the fuselage. Some of the applications stood alone while others received either a drop-shadow or full contour outline in respective squadron color.

1.) L/G-91 El Amiriya, Egypt
Dec-42

2.) L/G-99 El Kabrit, Egypt
2-Feb-43

3.) Kairouan A/F, Tunisia
2-Jun-43

4.) El Haouaria, Tunisia
c.18-Jun-43

5.) Men-zel Heurr, Tunisia
3-Oct-43

6.) Cercola, Italy
25-Oct-43

7.) Pignataro Maggiore, Italy
6-May-44

8.) Le Banca A/F, Italy
6-Jun-44

9.) Montalto di Castro, Italy
14-Jun-44

10.) Ghisonaccia A/F, Corsica
19-Jul-44

11.) Le Luc L/G, France
25-Aug-44

12.) Y-17 Istres / Le Tube, France
2-Sep-44

13.) Y-5 Amberieu, France
2-Sep-44

14.) Y-7 Dole / Tavaux, France
20-Sep-44

15.) Y-2 Luneville, France
4-Jan-45

• Assigned ; Twelfth AAF, Jan-1943 ; Fifteenth AAF, Dec-1943 thru V-E Day •

XII Bomber Command — Northwest African Strategic Air Force — 42D Bomb Wing

XV Fighter Command (Prov)

306TH Fighter Wing

325TH Fighter Group

Insignia/Replaced: 1-Oct-51
Motto: 'Plan-Contest'
Sobriquet: 'The Checkertail Clan'
Constituted: 325TH FtrGrp/24-Jun-42
Activated: 3-Aug-42

317TH Ftr Sqdn

Insignia/Replaced: 13-Dec-51

Constituted: 24-Jun-42
Activated: 3-Aug-42

Number-In-Squadron
10-39

318TH Ftr Sqdn

Insignia/Revised: 9-Nov-55

Constituted: 24-Jun-42
Activated: 3-Aug-42

Number-In-Squadron
40-69

319TH Ftr Sqdn

Insignia/Replaced: 28-May-57

Constituted: 24-Jun-42
Activated: 3-Aug-42

Number-In-Squadron
70-99

○ Twelfth USAAF ○

Curtuss 'Warhawk'

circa: Jan-Dec 1943

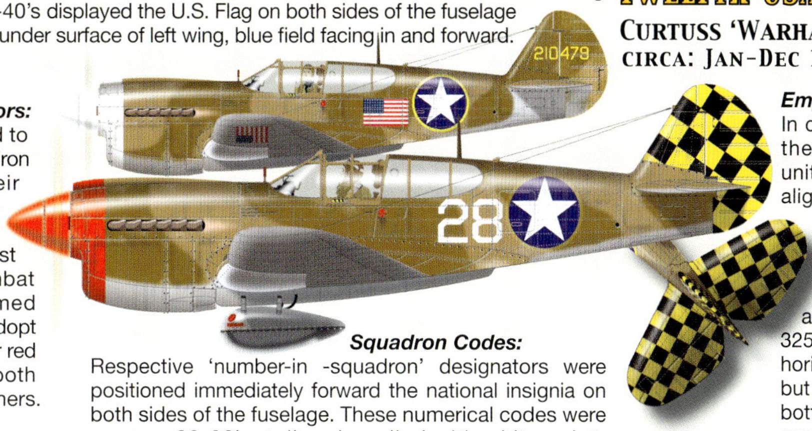

National Colors:
Original P-40's displayed the U.S. Flag on both sides of the fuselage and on the under surface of left wing, blue field facing in and forward.

Squadron Colors:
When initially deployed to North Africa each squadron applied a coat of their respective color to both spinner and cowling as depicted. Within the first several weeks of combat however, it was deemed prudent to unilaterally adopt a standard MTO theater red as a replacement on both cowling and prop spinners.

Squadron Codes:
Respective 'number-in -squadron' designators were positioned immediately forward the national insignia on both sides of the fuselage. These numerical codes were approx. 28-30in. tall and applied with white paint.

Empennage:
In compliance with the request from HQ/NAAF, the 325thFG developed a striking tactical unit marking devise. A checkerboard pattern aligned at 90° to the leading edges of the P-40 vertical and horizontal tail planes was developed, incorporating an alternating motif of 12in. yellow and black squares. By the end of June, 1943 this pattern had been applied to nearly all Warhawks assigned to the 325th. Initially only the upper surfaces of the horizontal stabilizers received this treatment, but this policy was quickly amended to include bottom surfaces as well. This pattern would be carried over onto the group's P-47's with an identical 12in. rectangular checkerboard configuration.

○ Twelfth / Fifteenth USAAF ○

Republic 'Thunderbolt'

circa: Dec-44 thru May-44

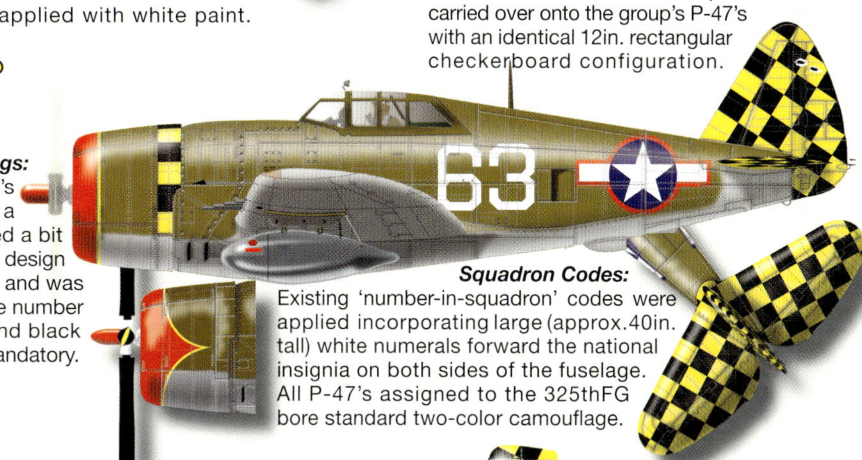

Cowlings:
All prop bosses and leading cowling edges of the groups P-47's were painted Insignia Red, the later being further treated with a 2-3in. wide band of Identification Yellow. The 318thFS added a bit of flourish by adding a scallop to each side of the cowling. This design element swept back to the leading edge of the cowling flaps, and was also accented with a similar yellow border. Additionally, a large number of the groups Thunderbolts displayed alternating yellow and black cowling flaps and were apparently discretionary rather than mandatory.

Squadron Codes:
Existing 'number-in-squadron' codes were applied incorporating large (approx.40in. tall) white numerals forward the national insignia on both sides of the fuselage. All P-47's assigned to the 325thFG bore standard two-color camouflage.

○ Fifteenth USAAF ○

North American 'Mustang'

circa: May-44 thru V-E Day

Colors:
Mustangs operated by the group were in NMF. Red spinners and cowlings were standard. An assortment of wing tip applications were present within all squadrons and included motifs from solid yellow to yellow with red tips, and in some examples, included a miniature checkerboard pattern.

Squadron Codes:
Now applied using black paint, the original two-digit codes were retained as was the placement forward the national insignia, again, on both sides of the fuselage.

Note:
Allied Recognition wing stripes were not applied to later replacement aircraft.

Group Marker:
Early adaptations of the Groups distinctive yellow / black checkerboard tail marking encompassed the fin, rudder and horizontal stabilizers (*1st Pattern*). By wars end this design had been expanded to include the entire empennage area (*2nd Pattern*).

• Assigned Twelfth AAF, Feb-1944 ; Fifteenth AAF, May-1944 thru V-E Day •

62d Ftr Wng 1944

XII Fighter Command

306th Ftr Wng 1944

332d Fighter Group

Insignia/Approved: 15-Jan-43
Motto: 'Spit Fire'
Sobriquet: 'Red Tails'
and
'The Tuskegee Airmen'
Activated: 13-Oct-42

99th Ftr Sqdn

Insignia/Approved: 24-Jun-44

Constituted:
99th Pur Sqdn/19-Mar-41
Activated: 22-Mar-41
Redesignated:
99th Ftr Sqdn/15-May-42

A-00
A-35

100th Ftr Sqdn

Insignia/Approved: 25-Nov-44

Constituted:
100th Pur Sqdn/27-Dec-41
Activated: 19-Feb-42
Redesignated:
100th Ftr Sqdn/15-May-42

1-39
91-99

301st Ftr Sqdn

Insignia/Approved: 29-Jun-45

Constituted: 4-Jul-42
Activated: 13-Oct-42

40-69

302d Ftr Sqdn

Insignia/Approved: 2-Nov-44

Constituted: 4-Jul-42
Activated: 13-Oct-42

70-90

• Twelfth USAAF •

Bell P-39 'Airacobra'
circa: Feb thru May-1944

P-39 Tactical Markings:
The P-39's flown by the Group were hand-off's from other units and were flown with existing markings.

Curtuss P-40 'Warhawk'
circa: Feb thru May-1944

P-40 Tactical Markings:
When the Group began operating with P-40's received from other units, squadron codes were quickly applied using white paint letters & numerals accented with a thin red contour outline. The two digit numerals were positioned on either side of the national insignia. No additional squadron or group markings were applied to these aircraft.

Republic P-47 'Thunderbolt'
circa: Apr thru Jun-1944

P-47 Tactical Markings:
The 322dFG operated only for a short time with P-47's, mostly Razorback's, turned over from the 325thFG while awaiting delivery of replacement P-51's. Existing tail markings were over painted with either red or Olive Drab, and the majority of trim tabs were painted in respective squadron colors. The existing 325thFG code and cowling tactical markings remained unchanged.

• Fifteenth USAAF •

North American P-51 'Mustang'
circa: May-44 thru V-E Day

Cowlings:
Each squadron employed its own distinctly different nose pattern. Propeller spinners were universally painted red.

Group Marker:
The policy of painting the tail plane of their aircraft red, beginning with the units P-47's, was carried over when the Group received its consignment of P-51's. What would become known as the *1st Pattern* entailed applying paint to the fin, rudder and wing root. The subsequent *2nd Pattern* encompassed most of the empennage and envolved applying the paint on a 20° diagonal line eminating from the antenne base and decending to intersect the the leading bottom edge of the rudder.

1st Pattern

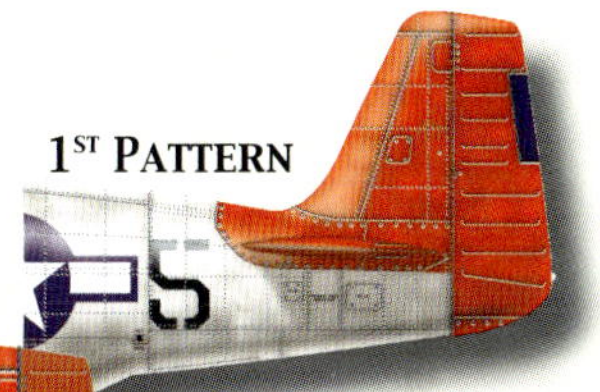

99th FtrSqdn

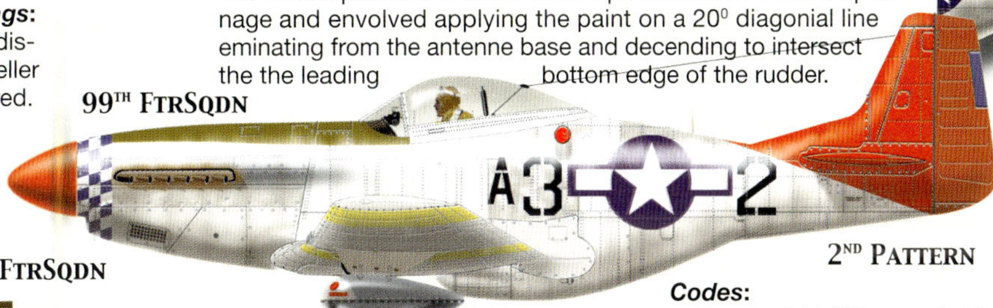

2nd Pattern

Trim Tabs:
Frequently painted with the designated squadron colors.

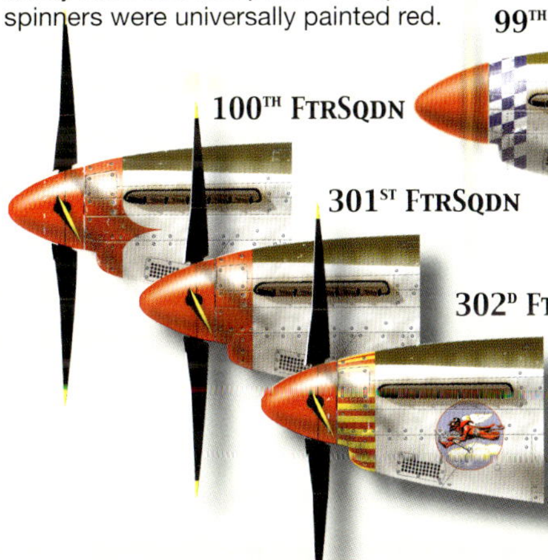

Codes:
All Mustangs operated by the 322dFG were in NMF and squadron codes were applied in a similar manner as employed with the Groups Warhawks. The two-digit numbers were relegated to each side of the national insignia and applied with black paint. The letter 'A' integrated as part of the 99thFS code was approximately 2/3 smaller size than that of the numerals. Stencil lines on the fuselage squadron code applications often remained unfilled.

Insignia:
Only one combat aircraft from the 322dFG is known to have ever displayed a squadron insignia; No.75 belonging to the 302dFS.

Wings:
With one exception all squadrons comprising the 332dFG displayed red wing tips. The 99thFS opted for a 15in. Orange/Yellow stripe set-in 10in. from the outside wing tip edge and running parallel with the fuselage.

• Assigned: Eighth AAF Oct-1942 / Twelfth AAF, Jan-1943 thru V-E Day •

XII Fighter Command

Northwest African Costal Air Force

XXII Air Support Command

63D Ftr Wng 1944

XXII Tactical Air Command

62D Ftr Wng 1944-1945

350TH Fighter Group

Insignia/Replaced: 10-Sep-54
Motto: 'Boldness And Vigor'
Activated: 1-Oct-42
Constituted: 350TH FtrGrp/2-Oct-42

1ST Brazilian Ftr Sqdn

Call Sign: 'Jambock'

This was the official insignia adopted by the *1º Grupo de Aviacao de Caca (1º GAvCa)*. This contingent of the Brazilian Expeditionary Force was attached to the 350thFG and served in combat for seven months with the AAF from October, 1944 through V-E Day.

345TH Ftr Sqdn

Insignia/(unofficial)
Sobriquet: 'Devil Hawks'
Call Sign: 'Lifetime'

Activated: 1-Oct-42
Constituted: 345TH Ftr Sqdn/2-Oct-42

346TH Ftr Sqdn

Insignia/(unofficial)
Sobriquet: 'Checkerboard Squadron'
Call Sign: 'Minefield'

Activated: 1-Oct-42
Constituted: 346TH Ftr Sqdn/2-Oct-42

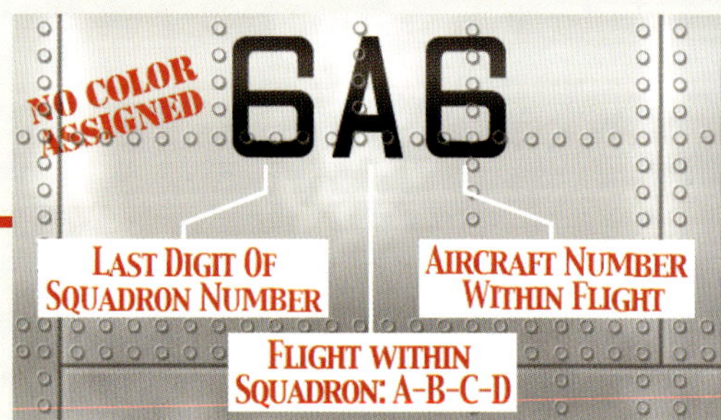

347TH Ftr Sqdn

Insignia/(unofficial)
Sobriquet: 'Screaming Red Ass Squadron'
Call Sign: 'Midwood'

Activated: 1-Oct-42
Constituted: 347TH Ftr Sqdn/2-Oct-42

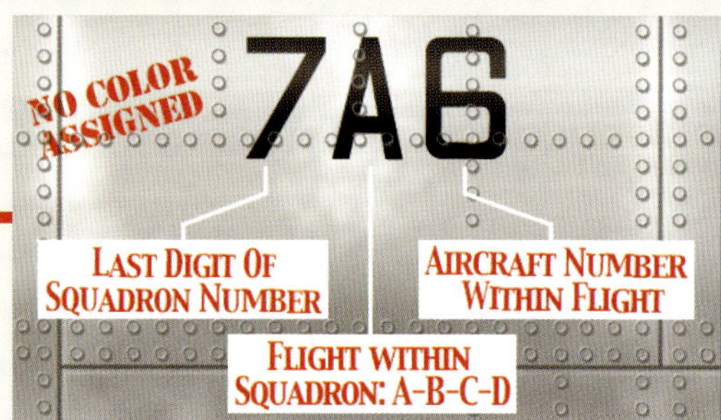

• Twelfth USAAF •

Bell P-400/P-39 'Airacobra'
circa: Jun-42 thru Apr-44

Tactical Markings:
The 350thFG flew over 3,800 defensive sorties using the Airacobra. Unlike the Groups later P-47's however, very few of these aircraft were adorned with squadron insignia. The last two digits of each aircraft's serial number was affixed to both sides of the cockpit using Identification Yellow. In addition a vertical band of the same color was affixed to the rear fuselage. Insignia Red spinners were standard except for a few early applications, again using yellow, but these were soon replaced with the standard MTO red.

346thFS Insignia (Variation):
Although the differences for the most part are subtle, this variation to the 346thFS insignia has turned up enough times in researching this squadron to warrant inclusion herein.

Lockheed P-38 'Lightning'
circa: Jun-42 thru Sep-43

Tactical Markings:
Between June and September of 1943 each squadron received two P-38 Lightnings. The P-38's operated by the 350thFG were hand-off's from other outfits. Existing unit markings were painted over and it appears that the only attempt at assigning group/squadron markings was in the sporadic application of a single digit to both outfacing radiator housings. This at least applied to those Lightnings assigned to the 347thFS. It is uncertain at this time whether the other squadrons utilized similar devices.

Early 346thFS Insignia :
This design was the original insignia representing the 346th Fighter Squadron during that units deployment to North Africa early in the war. The image was subsequently replaced by the 'Jugs' design when the entire Group converted from the P-39 Airacobra to the P-47 Thunderbolt in the late summer of 1944. The motto translates to 'Swift-Deadly' but with typical American style humor, some individual jacket patches were reportedly altered to read 'Slow-Easy' in direct reference to the Airacobras limited aerial dogfighting skills.

• Stations Not Depicted On Map •

A.) HQ & 345thFS: Stn.357-Duxford, England /Oct-42 thru Jan-43
B.) 346thFS: Stn.355-Coltishall, England/Oct-42 thru Jan-43
C.) 347thFS: Stn.361-Snailwell, England/Oct-42 thru Nov-42
D.) 347thFS: Stn.367-Kingscliffe, England/ Dec-42
E.) 347thFS: Stn.121-Bassingborne, England/Jan thru Feb-43

1.) Oujda, French Morocco (HQ) 6-Jan-43
2.) Oran / La Senia, Algeria (HQ) 14-Feb-43
3.) Feriana / Thelepte L/G, Tunisia (Det) c.Feb-43
4.) Orleansville / Warnier A/F, Algeria (Det) c.Mar/Apr-43
5.) Le Sers, Tunisia (Det) c.Apr-43
6.) Maison Blanche, Algeria (HQ) c.May/Jul-43
7.) Jijal / Taher, Algeria (Det) c.May/Dec-43
8.) Monistir, Tunisia (Det) c.Jun-43
9.) Annaba (Bone), Algeria (Det) c.Jul-43
10.) Rorhaia, Algeria (HQ) 17-Jul-43
11.) Cagliari / Elmas, Sardinia (HQ) 5-Nov-43
12.) Alghero / Fertilla, Sardinia (Det) c.Nov/Aug-43
13.) Ghisonaccia, Corsica (HQ) 6-Feb-44
14.) Naples / Capodichino, Italy (Det) c.Feb/Mar-44
15.) Sidi Amor, Tunisia (Det) c. Feb/Jun-44
16.) Aghione, Corsica (Det) c.May/Jul-44
17.) Naples / Pomigliano, Italy (Det) c.Jun/Aug-44
18.) Anzio / Tre Concello, Italy (Det) c.Jun-44
19.) Ajaccio / Compo del Ora, Corsica (Det) c.Jul/Sep-44
20.) Tarquinia, Italy (HQ) 8-Sep-44
21.) Piombino, Italy (Det) c.Jul/Aug-44
22.) Livorno / Rosignano, Italy (Det) c.Aug/Sep-44
23.) Pisa, Italy (HQ) 2-Dec-44

345th Fighter Squadron

General Background:
With the exception of 1° CAvCahe the vast majority of P-47's serving with the 350thFG were of a NMF variety. While this itself does not render the Group unique, what did make it stand out was the fact that this was the only fighter group serving with the Twelfth AAF that displayed individual squadron tactical markings, rather than the usual single group marker.

Squadron Marker:
The 345thFS could be recognized by the presence on the tail plane of a diagonal blue rectangle. This device extended upwards from the top edge of the horizontal stabilizer wing root and angled back at approximately 58° to terminate at the top outside edge of the rudder. Emanating from this same upper rudder edge and descending back down to the wing root was an Orange-Yellow three pronged lightning bolt.

Squadron Nose Markings:
The first three flaps on both sides of the cowling were painted with alternating colors of blue and yellow as depicted. For reasons unknown today, unlike the other squadrons comprising the 350thFG, no combat insignia was ever known to have been displayed on a single 347thFS Thunderbolt. These cowling markings appear to have been a low priorty and are absent from a number of photos taken towards wars end.

Fuselage:
Standard three digit squadron codes were approximately 30in. in height and were positioned forward the national insignia on both sides of the fuselage. Applied with white paint on the squadrons few camouflaged aircraft, black was the color selected for applications on metal surfaces. A select few P-47's displaying these codes within the 347th received a full red contour outline.

346th Fighter Squadron

Squadron Codes:
35-36in. tall, three-digit codes were located on both the engine cowling and forward fuselage area. Most of these applications to painted airframes consisted of Orange-Yellow characters with a thin Insignia White contour outline. Those applications to metal surfaces consisted of solid black characters of similar size affixed to identical locations on each side of the airframe.

Squadron Marker:
Rudders were decorated with a checkerboard motif as the 346th squadron recognition devise. The rectangles comprising this pattern were aligned at 90° to the trailing edge of the fin, and painted b&w on camouflaged surfaces, black only on metal finishes.

Squadron Insignia:
Virtually every combat aircraft assigned to operational status within the 346thFS was eventually adorned with the ever-present 'Jug' insignia. In all instances these images were located immediately forward the national insignia on either side of the fuselage. Although unquestionably bearing a strong resemblance to Walt Disney's Goofy cartoon character, this design was not in fact the creation of Disney Studios, but the brainchild of one of the men assigned to the 346 Fighter Squadron after converting to the P-47. Ground crew often painted pilot names directly above the insignia image.

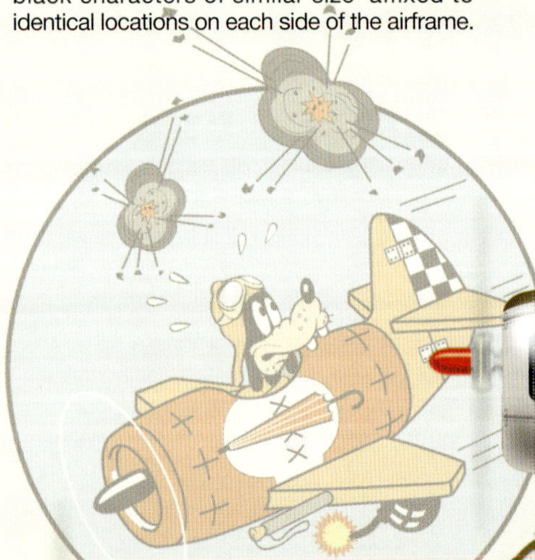

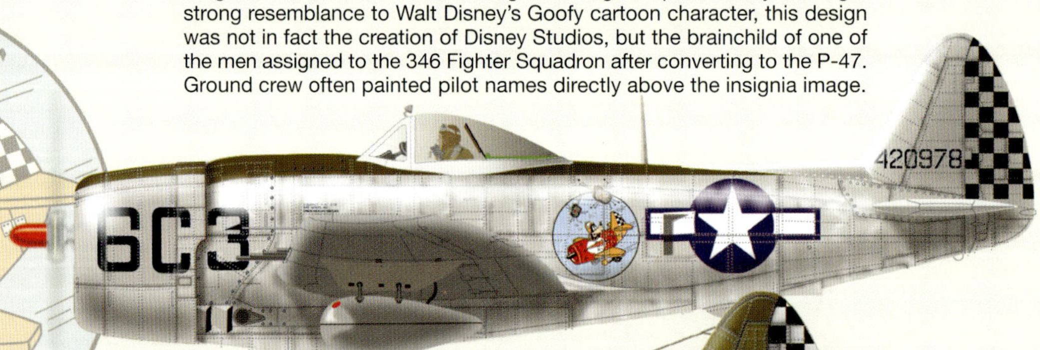

'Oh Johnnie' P-47D-27-RE s/n 42-26785:
This particular a/c is included herein for two distinct reasons. This was the only 'Bubble-Top' P-47 known to have served with the 350thFG and was piloted by Medal of Honor recipient, 1st. Lt. Raymond L. Knight. After leading repeated successful attacks in the region of the Po Valley, Lt. Knight was KIA when his badly shot-up Thunderbolt went down in the Appennines Mountains while attempting to return to base after concluding his mission.

• 347th Fighter Squadron •

Squadron Insignia:
Located on either side of the engine cowling, these images underwent subtle changes which primarily concerned the lightning bolts. The original design contained no lightning bolts whatsoever. Soon after its introduction however, two of these devices were added. Near wars end this number was increased to four bolts. All three patterns can be seen in numerous wartime photos. With all applications however, the 'Red Ass' image always faced towards the leading surface edge of the engine cowling.

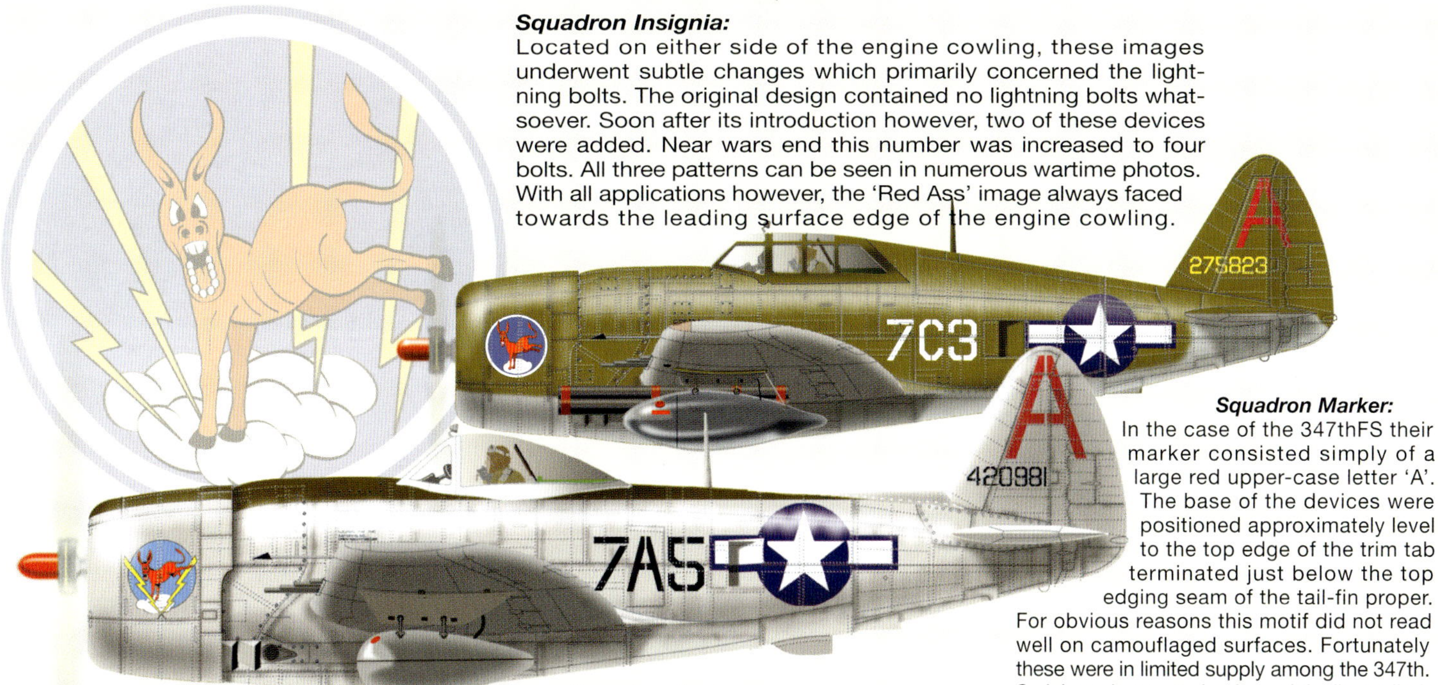

Squadron Marker:
In the case of the 347thFS their marker consisted simply of a large red upper-case letter 'A'. The base of the devices were positioned approximately level to the top edge of the trim tab terminated just below the top edging seam of the tail-fin proper. For obvious reasons this motif did not read well on camouflaged surfaces. Fortunately these were in limited supply among the 347th. Serial numbers remained as originally applied.

Squadron Codes:
These devices were applied forward the national insignia on both sides of the airframe, white on camouflaged surfaces, black on NMF. Overall size was generally the same height as the intercooler vent.

• 1st Brazilian Fighter Squadron •

Squadron Codes:
A two-digit code system was developed by this squadron. These were large collegiate style letters, very similar to those used by the USAAF, and were positioned on the upper third of the engine cowling. These devices were painted black on NMF and white on camouflaged aircraft surfaces.

Squadron Insignia:
These designs were located on the upper third of the forward fuselage, just aft the cowling flaps and applied to both sides

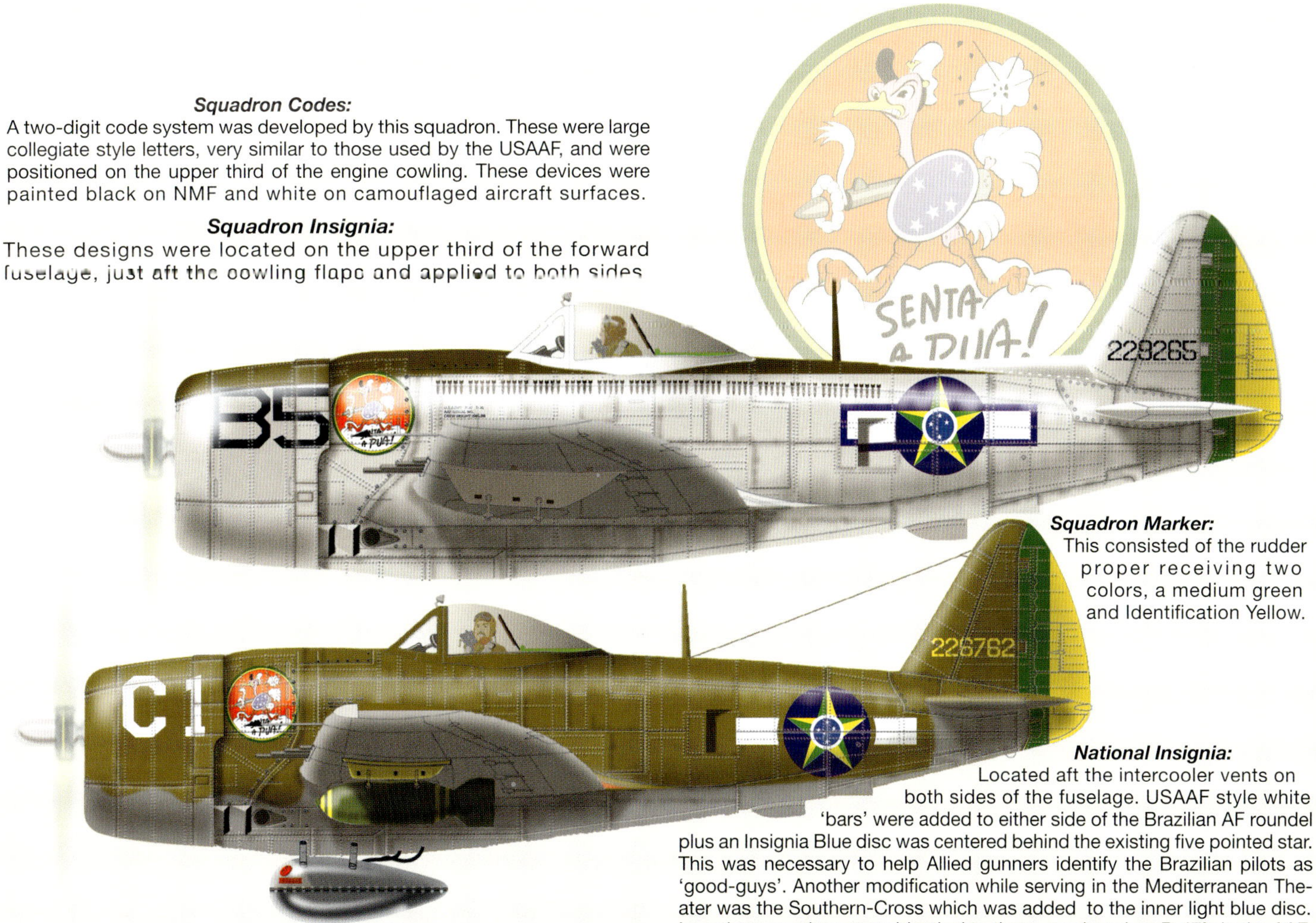

Squadron Marker:
This consisted of the rudder proper receiving two colors, a medium green and Identification Yellow.

National Insignia:
Located aft the intercooler vents on both sides of the fuselage. USAAF style white 'bars' were added to either side of the Brazilian AF roundel plus an Insignia Blue disc was centered behind the existing five pointed star. This was necessary to help Allied gunners identify the Brazilian pilots as 'good-guys'. Another modification while serving in the Mediterranean Theater was the Southern-Cross which was added to the inner light blue disc. Locations on wings were identical to those employed on P-47's in the AAF.

U.S.A.A.F. NIGHT FIGHTER SQDNS.

MEDITERRANEAN THEATER OF OPERATIONS

• Assigned : Twelfth AAF, 10-May-43 thru V-E Day •

63D Fighter Wng

63D Fighter Wng

Northwest African Costal Air Force

62D Fighter Wng

XXII Tactiacl Air Command

414TH Night Ftr Sqdn

Insignia/unofficial

Constituted: 414TH Night Ftr Sqdn/21-Jan-43
Activated: 26-Jan-43

Bristol 'Beaufighter'
circa: May-43 thru 1945

Aircraft Inventory:
The 414thNFS reportedly operated with Douglas A-20 'Havoc' and P-70 '*Nighthawks' in addition to the Lockheed P-38 'Lightning' and North American P-51 'Mustang'. Specific data pertaining to the actual combat operations conducted by the 414thNFS using the above aircraft is somewhat sketchy. In spite of the fact that the 414thNFS received their allotment of P-61's earlier than its sister squadrons, the Black Widow arrived to late in the Mediterranean to have much overall impact.
* *Working title for Douglas A-20's modified as night fighters.*

Northrop P-61 'Black Widow'
circa: Dec-44 thru V-E Day

1.) La Senia, Algeria
10-May-43

2.) Rerhaia, Algeria
c.11-Jun-43

3.) Protville, Tunisia (Det.)
23 to 29-Jul-43

4.) Elmas, Sardinia
c.11-Nov-43

5.) Ghisonaccia, Corsica (Det.)
9-Jan-44

6.) Borgo, Corsica
5-Feb-44

7.) Alghero, Sardinia
11-May thru 22-Jun '44

9.) Borgo, Corsica
5-Sep-44

10.) Pisa, Italy
13-Oct-44

11.) Pontedera, Italy
c.25-Nov-44

*12.) Florennes, Belgium (Det.)
c.27-Jan thru 3-Apr-45

*13.) Strossfeld, Germany
3-Apr-45

• Assigned : Twelfth AAF, 12-May-43 thru V-E Day •

XII Fighter Command — 62D Fighter Wng — 1ST Air Defence Wng — Northwest African Costal Air Force

87TH Fighter Wng (TDY) — 64TH Fighter Wng — XII Air Support Command — 64TH Fighter Wng (TDY)

415TH Night Ftr Sqdn

Insignia/Approved: 4-Dec-43

Constituted: 415th Night Ftr Sqdn/8-Feb-43
Activated: 10-Feb-43

Bristol 'Beaufighter'

circa: May-43 thru Apr-45

Primary Combat Aircraft:
The reliable 'Beau' was the squadrons mainstay throughout the vast majority of the units entire deployment from North Africa to Germany.

Northrop P-61 'Black Widow'

circa: Apr-45 thru V-E Day

Replacement Inventory:
Shortly after transferring to Braunschardt A/F the squadron was reequipped with the Black Widow. By the time the unit had completed transitional training however, only a few actual sorties were flown with their new aircraft before the war in Europe reached its conclusion.

***Additional Stations Not Depicted On Map**

17.) *Station Y-18*: Le Vallon, France, c. 1-Sep-44
18.) Station Y-9: Dijon/Longvic, France, c. 15-Sep-44
19.) Station A-96: Toul/Ochey, France, c. 30-Nov-44
20.) Station A-64: St. Dizier, France, c. 18-Mar-45
21.) Y-72: Braunschardt, Germany, c. 17-Apr-45

1.) La Senia, Algeria 12-May-43
2.) La Sebala, Tunisia 22-Jun-43
3.) Monastir, Tunisia 25-Jun-43
4.) Protville, Tunisia (Det.) 23 / 29-Jul-43
5.) La Sebala, Tunisia 20-Jul-43
6.) Cassibile, Sicily 3-Sep-43
7.) Catania, Sicily 5-Nov-43
8.) Pietra Montecorvino, Italy (Det.) 29-Nov / 26-Dec-43
9.) Gaudo A/F, Italy 6-Dec-43
10.) Pietra Montecorvino, Italy 26-Dec-43
11.) Marcainise, Italy 30-Jan-44
12.) Pomigliano di'Arco, Italy 25-Mar-44
13.) La Banca, Italy c. 11-Jun-44
14.) Voltone, Italy c. 17-Jun-44
15.) Solonzara, Corsica c. 19-Jul-44
16.) Piombino, Italy (Det.) c. 25-Jul / 5-Aug-44

• Assigned : Twelfth AAF, 8-Aug-43 thru V-E Day •

63D Fighter Wng — 62D Fighter Wng — Northwest African Costal Air Force

XXII Tactiacl Air Command

416TH Night Ftr Sqdn

Insignia/Unofficial

Constituted: 416TH Night Ftr Sqdn/17-Feb-43
Activated: 20-Feb-43

Bristol 'Beaufighter'
circa: Aug-43 thru V-E Day

De Havilland 'Mosquito'
circa: Aug-43 thru V-E Day

Combat Inventory:
It would appear that the 416thNFS has the distinction of being the only USAAF unit in WWII to have conducted combat operations entirely with foreign aircraft operating with both the Beaufighter and Mosquito.

1.) Algiers, Algeria
c. 8-Aug-43

2.) Bone (Annaba), Algeria
17-Aug-43

3.) Bizerte, Tunisia
15-Sep-43

4.) Catania, Sicily
21-Sep-43

5.) Lecce, Italy
27-Sep-43

6.) Grottaglie, Italy
30-Sep-43

7.) Rerhaia, Algeria (Det.)
27-Dec-43/25-Jan-44

8.) Pomigliano, Italy
C. 28-Jan-44

9.) Tre Cancello L/G (Det.)
Jun/Jul-44

10.) Tarquinia, Italy
8-Jul-44

11.) Borgo, Corsica
14-Aug-44

12.) Rosignano, Italy
c. 1-Sep-44

13.) Pomigliano, Italy (Det.)
1-Sep-44

14.) Pisa, Italy
c. 1-Oct-44

*15.) Etain, France (Det.)
c. 1-Oct-44

16.) Pontedera, Italy
27-Mar-45

*Station No. 15 not depicted on map
Indicates TDY / Detachment Assignment

• ASSIGNED : TWELFTH AAF, 8-AUG-43 THRU V-E DAY •

XII FIGHTER COMMAND

63D FIGHTER WNG

64TH FIGHTER WNG

417TH NIGHT FTR SQDN

INSIGNIA/UNOFFICIAL

CONSTITUTED: 417TH NIGHT FTR SQDN/17-FEB-43
ACTIVATED: 20-FEB-43

BRISTOL 'BEAUFIGHTER'
CIRCA: MAY-43 THRU MAR-45

Combat Inventory:
The story of P-61's in the 417thNFS is almost identical to that of the 415thNFS. The 417th received their Black Widows in March of 1945 and immediately underwent transitional training. The first combat mission flown with their new aircraft took place on 3-May-45, five days before V-E Day.

NORTHROP P-61 'BLACK WIDOW'
CIRCA: MAR-45 THRU V-E DAY

5.) Bogro, Corsica
c. 25-Apr/7-Sep-44

4.) Borgo, Corscia
(ground echelon) Feb/Apr-44

3.) La Senia, Algeria
10-Jan-44

2.) Ghisonaccia, Corcica
(ground echelon) Jan/Feb-44

1.) Tafaraoui, Algeria
8-Aug-43

*6.) La Vallon, France
12-Sep-44

*7.) A-78 Florennes, Belgium
(ground echelon) 5/22-Jan-45

*8.) A-64 St. Dizer, France
5-Apr-45

*9.) Y-90 Giebelstadt, Germany
24-Apr-45

*Station No's.6 thru 9 not depicted on map
Indicates TDY / Detachment Assignment

U.S.A.A.F. TROOP CARRIER GROUPS

MEDITERRANEAN THEATER OF OPERATIONS

• Assigned Twelfth AAF, Nov-1942 thru V-E Day •

51st Tr Carr Wng
1942

60th Tr Crr Group

Insignia: unknown
Constituted:
60th Transport Group/20-Nov-40
Activated: 1-Dec-40
Redesignated:
60th Troop Carrier Group/Jul-42

Insignia unknown

10th Tr Crr Sqdn

No color assigned — No squadron codes issued

Insignia/Approved: 30-Oct-52
(from WWII design)
Constituted: 10th Trsp Sqdn/1-Jan-38
Activated: 1-Dec-40
Redesignated: 10th Trp Carr Sqdn/5-Jul-42

11th Tr Crr Sqdn

No color assigned — No squadron codes issued

Insignia/Approved: 14-Jul-45
Constituted: 11th Trsp Sqdn/1-Jan-38
Activated: 1-Dec-40
Redesignated: 11th Trp Carr Sqdn/5-Jul-42

12th Tr Crr Sqdn

No color assigned — No squadron codes issued

Insignia/Approved: 11-Sep-44
Constituted: 12th Trsp Sqdn/1-Jan-38
Activated: 1-Dec-40
Redesignated: 12th Trp Carr Sqdn/5-Jul-42

28th Tr Crr Sqdn

No color assigned — No squadron codes issued

Insignia/Approved: 14-Jul-45
Constituted: 28th Trsp Sqdn
(Mail and Cargo)/19-Jan-42
Activated: 1-Feb-42
Redesignated: 28th Trsp Sqdn/19-May-42
Redesignated: 28th Tr Carr Sqdn/5-Jul-42

Douglas C-47 'Skytrain'
Nov-42 thru V-E Day

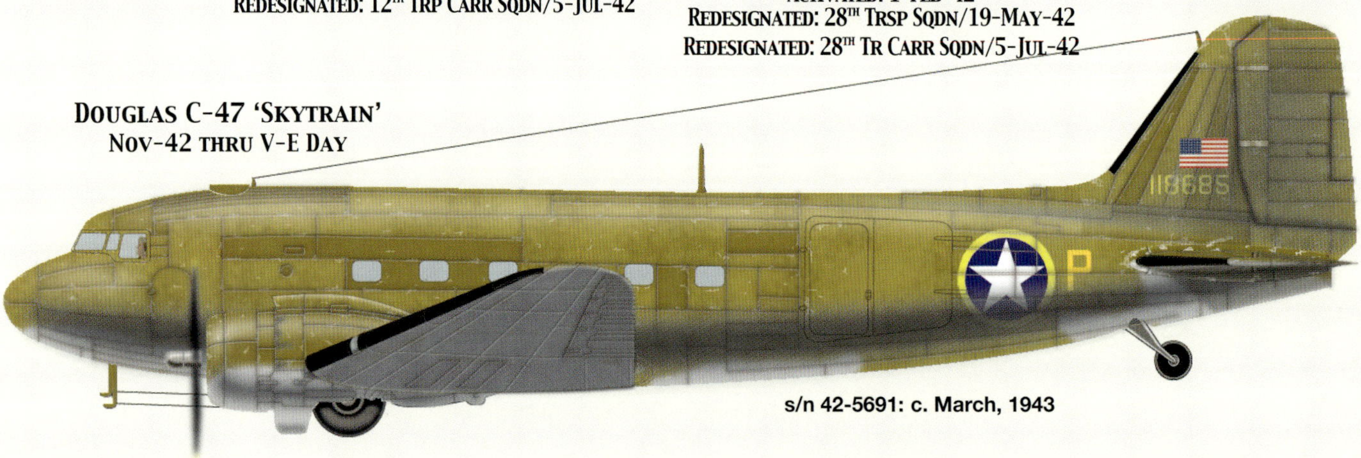

s/n 42-5691: c. March, 1943

• Assigned Twelfth AAF, May-1943 : Ninth AAF, Feb-1944 thru V-E Day •

52D Tr Carr Wng
1943

61ST Tr Crr Group

Insignia: unknown
Constituted:
61ST Trns Grp/20-Nov-40
Activated: 1-Dec-40
Redesignated:
61ST Tr Carr Grp/Jul-42

Insignia Unknown

13TH Tr Crr Sqdn

Insignia Unknown

No color assigned — No squadron codes issued

Insignia/unknown
Constituted: 13TH Trsp Sqdn/20-Nov-40
Activated: 1-Dec-40
Redesignated: 13TH Tr Carr Sqdn/4-Jul-42

14TH Tr Crr Sqdn

No color assigned — No squadron codes issued

Insignia/Approved: 28-Dec-42
Constituted: 14TH Trsp Sqdn/20-Nov-40
Activated: 4-Dec-40
Redesignated: 14TH Tr Carr Sqdn/4-Jul-42

15TH Tr Crr Sqdn

Insignia Unknown

No color assigned — No squadron codes issued

Insignia/unknown
Constituted: 15TH Trsp Sqdn/20-Nov-40
Activated: 4-Dec-40
Redesignated: 15TH Tr Carr Sqdn/4-Jul-42

53D Tr Crr Sqdn

No color assigned — No squadron codes issued

Insignia/Approved: 10-Sep-53
(modified from this WWII design)
Constituted: 53D Trsp Sqdn/30-Mar-42
Activated: 1-Jun-42
Redesignated: 53D Trp Carr Sqdn/4-Jul-42

Douglas C-47 'Skytrain'
May-43 thru V-E Day

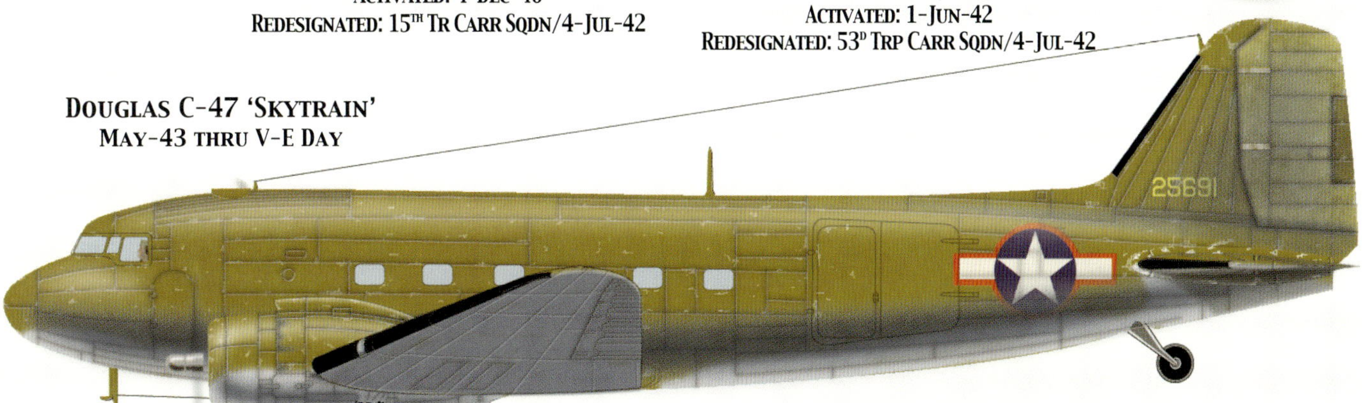

s/n 42-5691: c. June, 1943

• Assigned Twelfth AAF, Nov-1943 thru V-E Day •

51st Tr Carr Wng 1943

62d Tr Crr Group

Insignia: Approved/18-Aug-55
(possibly of WWII origin)
Constituted:
62d Trns Grp/20-Nov-40
Activated: 11-Dec-40
Redesignated:
62d Tr Carr Grp/Jul-42

4th Tr Crr Sqdn

No Color Assigned | No Squadron Codes Issued

Insignia/Approved: 17-Sep-42
Constituted: 4th Prov Trsp Sqdn/1-Mar-35
Redesignated: 4th Trns Sqdn/25-Jun-35
Activated: 8-Jul-35
Redesignated: 4th Tr Carr Sqdn/4-Jul-42

7th Tr Crr Sqdn

No Color Assigned | No Squadron Codes Issued

Insignia/Approved: 19-Aug-44
Constituted: 7th Trns Sqdn/1-Oct-33
Activated: 14-Oct-39
Redesignated: 7th Tr Carr Sqdn/4-Jul-42

8th Tr Crr Sqdn

No Color Assigned | No Squadron Codes Issued

Insignia/Approved: 12-Jun-43
Constituted: 8th Trns Sqdn/1-Oct-33
Activated: 1-Feb-40
Redesignated: 8th Tr Carr Sqdn/4-Jul-42

51st Tr Crr Sqdn

No Color Assigned | No Squadron Codes Issued

Insignia/Approved: 30-Apr-44
Constituted: 51st Trns Sqdn/30-May-42
Activated: 1-Jun-42
Redesignated: 51st Tr Carr Sqdn/4-Jul-42

Douglas C-47 'Skytrain'
Nov-42 thru V-E Day

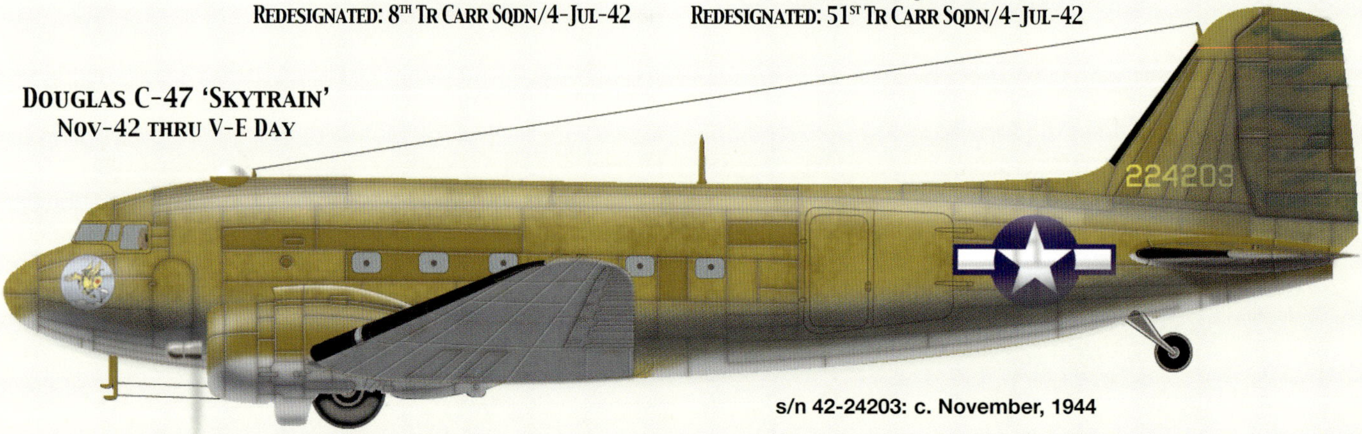

s/n 42-24203: c. November, 1944

• Assigned Twelfth AAF, Nov-1942 thru V-E Day •

51st Tr Carr Wng
1943

64th Tr Crr Group

Insignia: Approved/16-Jun-42
Constituted:
64th Trns Grp/20-Nov-40
Activated: 4-Dec-40
Redesignated:
64th Tr Carr Grp/Jul-42

16th Tr Crr Sqdn

INSIGNIA UNKNOWN

NO COLOR ASSIGNED

NO SQUADRON CODES ISSUED

Insignia/unknown
Constituted: 16th Trns Sqdn/20-Nov-40
Activated: 11-Dec-40
Redesignated: 16th Tr Carr Sqdn/4-Jul-42

17th Tr Crr Sqdn

NO COLOR ASSIGNED

NO SQUADRON CODES ISSUED

Insignia/unofficial
Constituted: 17th Trns Sqdn/20-Nov-40
Activated: 11-Dec-40
Redesignated: 17th Tr Carr Sqdn/4-Jul-42

18th Tr Crr Sqdn

INSIGNIA UNKNOWN

NO COLOR ASSIGNED

NO SQUADRON CODES ISSUED

Insignia/unknown
Constituted: 18th Trns Sqdn/20-Nov-40
Activated: 11-Dec-40
Redesignated: 18th Tr Carr Sqdn/4-Jul-42

35th Tr Crr Sqdn

NO COLOR ASSIGNED

NO SQUADRON CODES ISSUED

INSIGNIA UNKNOWN

Insignia/unknown
Constituted: 35th Trns Sqdn/2-Feb-42
Activated: 14-Feb-42
Redesignated: 35th Tr Carr Sqdn/4-Jul-42

Douglas C-47 'Skytrain'
Nov-42 thru V-E Day

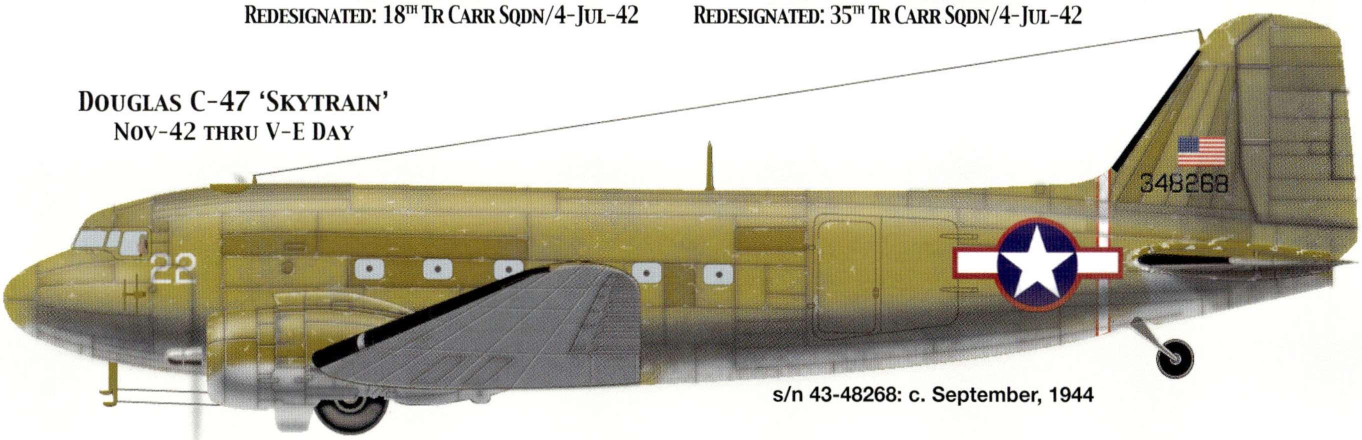

s/n 43-48268: c. September, 1944

• Assigned Twelfth AAF, Apr-1943 : Ninth AAF, Feb-1944 thru V-E Day •

52d Tr Carr Wng 1943

313th Tr Crr Group

Insignia: Approved/3-Feb-43
Constituted:
313th Trns Grp/28-Jan-42
Activated: 2-May-42
Redesignated:
313th Tr Carr Grp/Jul-42

29th Tr Crr Sqdn

No color assigned — No squadron codes issued during this period

Insignia/Approved: 24-Aug-43
Constituted: 29th Trns Sqdn/28-Jan-42
Activated: 2-Mar-42
Redesignated: 29th Tr Carr Sqdn/4-Jul-42

47th Tr Crr Sqdn

No color assigned — No squadron codes issued during this period

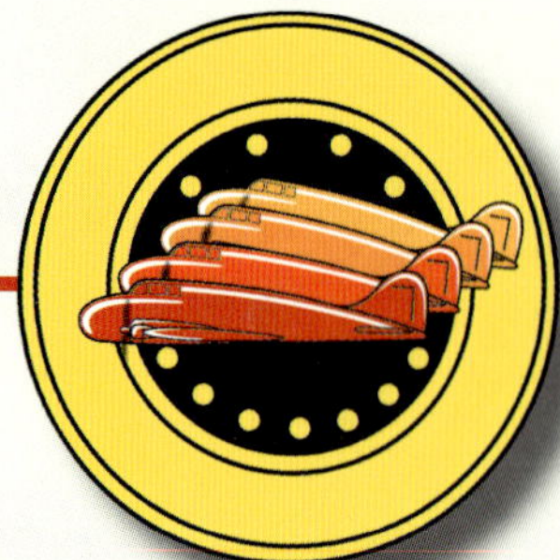

Insignia/Approved: 27-Feb-43
Constituted: 47th Trns Sqdn/30-May-42
Activated: 15-Jun-42
Redesignated: 47th Tr Carr Sqdn/4-Jul-42

48th Tr Crr Sqdn

Insignia Unknown

No color assigned — No squadron codes issued during this period

Insignia/unknown
Constituted: 48th Trns Sqdn/30-May-42
Activated: 15-Jun-42
Redesignated: 48th Tr Carr Sqdn/4-Jul-42

49th Tr Crr Sqdn

No color assigned — No squadron codes issued during this period

Insignia/Approved: 13-Jan-43
Constituted: 49th Trns Sqdn/30-May-42
Activated: 15-Jun-42
Redesignated: 49th Tr Carr Sqdn/4-Jul-42

Douglas C-47 'Skytrain'
Apr-43 thru V-E Day

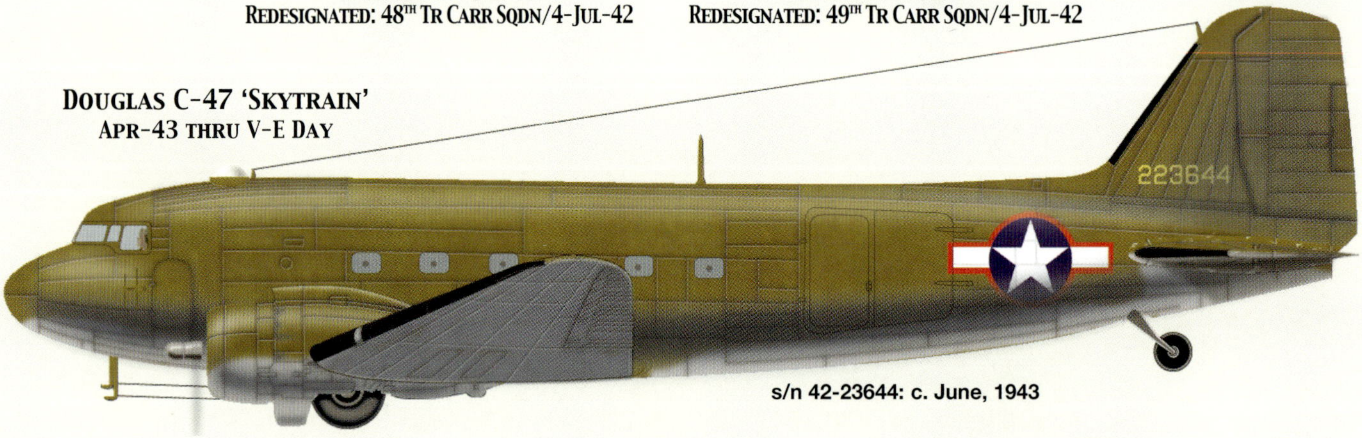

s/n 42-23644: c. June, 1943

• Assigned Twelfth AAF, May-1943 : Ninth AAF, Feb-1944 thru V-E Day •

52D Tr Carr Wng 1943

314TH Tr Crr Group

Insignia: Approved/17-Aug-42
Constituted:
314TH Trns Grp/28-Jan-42
Activated: 2-Mar-42
Redesignated:
314TH Tr Carr Grp/Jul-42

32D Tr Crr Sqdn

Insignia Unknown

No Color Assigned — No Squadron Codes Issued During This Period

Insignia/unknown
Constituted: 32D Trns Sqdn/28-Jan-42
Activated: 2-Mar-42
Redesignated: 32D Tr Carr Sqdn/4-Jul-42

50TH Tr Crr Sqdn

Insignia Unknown

No Color Assigned — No Squadron Codes Issued During This Period

Insignia/unknown
Constituted: 50TH Trns Sqdn/30-May-42
Activated: 15-Jun-42
Redesignated: 50TH Tr Carr Sqdn/4-Jul-42

61ST Tr Crr Sqdn

Insignia Unknown

No Color Assigned — No Squadron Codes Issued During This Period

Insignia/unknown
Constituted: 61ST Tr Carr Sqdn/13-Oct-42
Activated: 26-Oct-42

62D Tr Crr Sqdn

No Color Assigned — No Squadron Codes Issued During This Period

Insignia/replaced: 24-Apr-43
Constituted: 62D Tr Carr Sqdn/27-Nov-42
Activated: 5-Dec-42

Douglas C-47 'Skytrain'
May-43 thru V-E Day

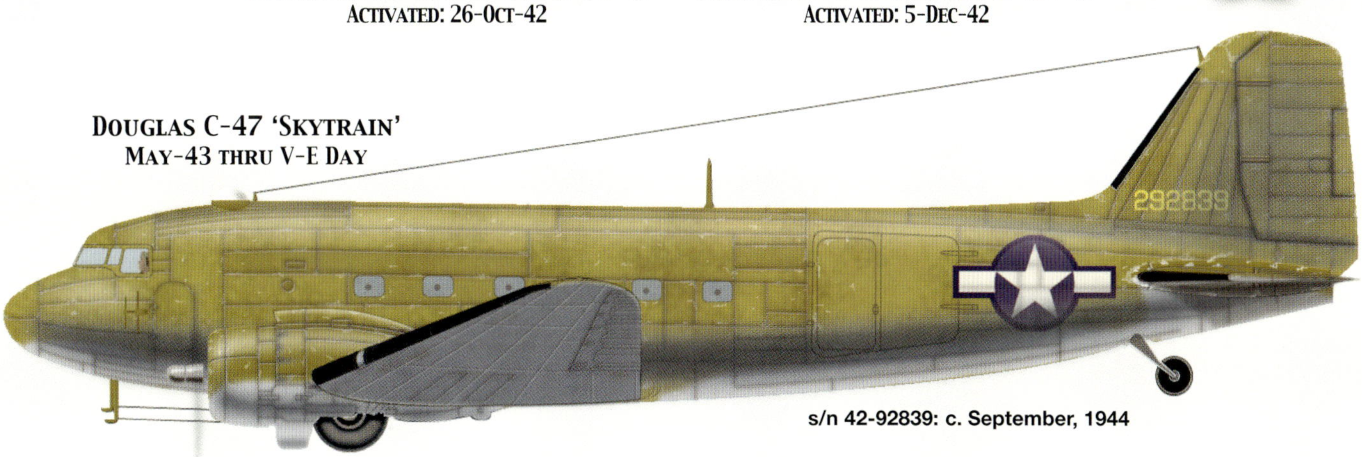

s/n 42-92839: c. September, 1944

• Assigned Ninth AAF, Nov-1942 : Twelfth AAF, Sep-1943 : Ninth AAF, Feb-1944 thru V-E Day •

52d Tr Carr Wng
1943

316th Tr Crr Group

Insignia: unknown
Constituted:
316th Trns Grp/2-Feb-42
Activated: 14-Feb-42
Redesignated:
316th Tr Carr Grp/Jul-42

Insignia Unknown

36th Tr Crr Sqdn

No color assigned **6E**

Insignia Unknown

Insignia/unknown
Constituted: 36th Trns Sqdn/2-Feb-42
Activated: 14-Feb-42
Redesignated: 36th Tr Carr Sqdn/4-Jul-42

37th Tr Crr Sqdn

No color assigned **W7**

Insignia/replaced: 6-Jul-51
Constituted: 37th Trns Sqdn/2-Feb-42
Activated: 14-Feb-42
Redesignated: 37th Tr Carr Sqdn/4-Jul-42

44th Tr Crr Sqdn

No color assigned **4C**

Insignia Unknown

Insignia/unknown
Constituted: 44th Trns Sqdn/30-May-42
Activated: 15-Jun-42
Redesignated: 44th Tr Carr Sqdn/4-Jul-42

45th Tr Crr Sqdn

No color assigned **T3**

Insignia Unknown

Insignia/unknown
Constituted: 45th Trns Sqdn/30-May-42
Activated: 15-Jun-42
Redesignated: 45th Tr Carr Sqdn/4-Jul-42

Douglas C-47 'Skytrain'
Nov-42 thru V-E Day

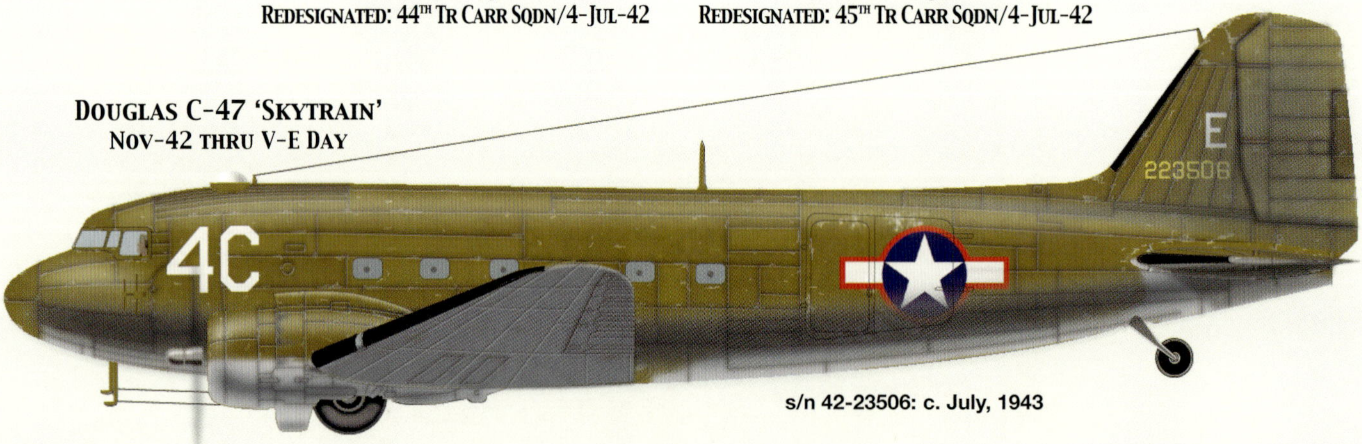

s/n 42-23506: c. July, 1943

•TROOP CARRIER TACTICAL MARKINGS•

The U.S. 'Stars-and-Stripes' national colors were a standard tactical marking affixed to transport aircraft tails originally arriving in North Africa from England. Other than this there was little effort made to identify group/squadron assignments outside the occasional application of a squadron insignia to the nose section of individual aircraft. Such applications however appear to have been random with no official unit policy being established.

The 60th and 64th Troop Carrier Squadrons affixed individual aircraft letters to the sides of the rear fuselage using RAF 'Sky' or Identification Yellow. Units involved in the airborne assault during 'Operation Husky' in the summer of 1943 were known to have applied identification numbers to the forward fuselage of their transports with either white or yellow paint. These were the only known official TCG markings utilized within the MTO.

•TEMPORARY DUTY UNITS•

Occasionally Troop Carrier squadrons with permanent duty assignments to the Ninth AAF were attached TDY to the Twelfth AAF for special operations within the MTO. This was especially true when the Allies began planning for 'Operation Dragoon', the invasion of southern France which launched 15-Aug-44.

'Rugby Force' was the designation for the airborne element of this assault, with 'Operation Dove' the assigned code name for the glider infantry phase of the operation. The squadrons listed below represent those outfits that participated in, and received official campaign recognition for 'Operation Dragoon'.

435th Tr Crr Group

75th TCS

76th TCS

78th TCS

436th Tr Crr Group

79th TCS

NO KNOWN SQUADRON INSIGNIA

80th TCS

NO KNOWN SQUADRON INSIGNIA

82d TCS

NO KNOWN SQUADRON INSIGNIA

437th Tr Crr Group

83d TCS

NO KNOWN SQUADRON INSIGNIA

84th TCS

NO KNOWN SQUADRON INSIGNIA

85th TCS

86th TCS

NO KNOWN SQUADRON INSIGNIA

438th Tr Crr Group

87th TCS

88th TCS

NO KNOWN SQUADRON INSIGNIA

89th TCS

NO KNOWN SQUADRON INSIGNIA

439th Tr Crr Group

91st TCS

NO KNOWN SQUADRON INSIGNIA

92d TCS

NO KNOWN SQUADRON INSIGNIA

94th TCS

NO KNOWN SQUADRON INSIGNIA

440th Tr Crr Group

95th TCS

96th TCS

97th TCS

441st Tr Crr Group

99th TCS

NO KNOWN SQUADRON INSIGNIA

100th TCS

NO KNOWN SQUADRON INSIGNIA

302d TCS

NO KNOWN SQUADRON INSIGNIA

442d Tr Crr Group

303d TCS

NO KNOWN SQUADRON INSIGNIA

304th TCS

NO KNOWN SQUADRON INSIGNIA

305th TCS

NO KNOWN SQUADRON INSIGNIA

U.S.A.A.F. BOMBARDMENT GROUPS

MEDITERRANEAN THEATER OF OPERATIONS

"I could see omens of the war's end almost every day in the blue southern sky when, flying provocatively low, the bombers of the American Fifteenth Air Force crossed from their Italian bases to attack German industrial targets."
Albert Speer; Third Reich Minister for Armaments

It is probably safe to say that overall regulations governing the marking of combat aircraft within the European-African-Middle Eastern Theater were more relaxed than for similar units stationed in Great Britain. This was especially true during the earlier phases of this campaign, and a great deal of the inconsistencies can invariably be attributed to the transitory conditions to which AAF units were subjected. Until the Allies occupied southern Italy, combat air units were in a constant state of flux, always moving from one temporary airfield to another.

Ground maintenance crewmen were stretched to their physical limits between moves and keeping the combat aircraft in their charge air worthy. Considering these factors it is small wonder that when viewing wartime photographs of both fighter and bomber units one is immediately aware of the variations in marking placement, sizes, shapes and even colors. All things considered, it was quite an accomplishment, especially in the early stages of the desert war, that these aircraft were marked as well as they were.

In addition to the standard group/squadron markings, there were special purpose devices that were likewise subject to a wide range of applications in the field. One such device was the vertical fuselage stripe used to denote a lead, or Mickey ship. Adopted primarily by the medium bomb groups, it appears that the use of these markings, though commonly used and measuring anywhere from 12' to 18' in width, were never officially adopted at any organizational level. At least no written directive pertaining to these markings has been located to date.

As previously noted in the introduction to the Fighter section, AAF combat units serving within the MTO were not shy about displaying their respective group/squadron insignia on the sides of their aircraft. Decision makers within the Twelfth and Fifteenth AAF's apparently realized what their counterparts in England did not. The only way to keep the enemy from recognizing any given unit sortied against them was to use no fuselage markings whatsoever, and that the need for inter group/squadron recognition far outweighed the risk of your enemy knowing who you were. Consequently, as long as the aircraft bore tactical designations, there was little harm done if the men flying the missions wanted to do so with a squadron insignia affixed to their aircraft.

As with the fighter units, combat aircraft finishes within the AAF bomb groups reflected the state of Allied dominance in the air throughout the campaign in the Mediterranean area. Initial inventories of bombers consisted of a three-color camouflage surface pattern, applied in England prior to disbursement to North Africa. As the threat of aerial attacks on their forward airfields began to diminish, the three-color was replaced with a standard AAF two-color camouflage pattern.

By the time the Allied armies had secured bases of operation on the southern Italian mainland, virtually all replacement bombers received by both the Twelfth and Fifteenth AAF's bore a natural metal finish. Control of the air over the Luftwaffe was firmly in Allied hands and with this control came the benefits of eliminating the need for camouflaged airframes on all combat aircraft with the exception of those few 'special operations' aircraft.

• Assigned Twelfth AAF, Mar-1943 : Fifteenth AAF, Dec-1943 thru V-E Day •

5TH Bomb Wng
1943-1945

5TH Bomb Wng
1943

2D Bombardment Group (H)

Insignia: Approved: 19-Jan-24
Organized: 1ST Day Bmb Grp/10-Sep-18
Reconstituted, reorganized: 18-Sep-19
Redesignated: 2D Bmb Grp/1921
Redesignated: 2D Bmb Grp (H)/1939

20TH Bomb Sqdn (H)

Insignia; Arrroved/12-Jun-24

Organized:
20TH Aero Sqdn/26-Jun-17
Redesignated:
20TH Sqdn/14-Mar-21
20TH Bomb Sqdn/25-Jan-23
20TH Bomb Sqdn (H)/9-Dec-39

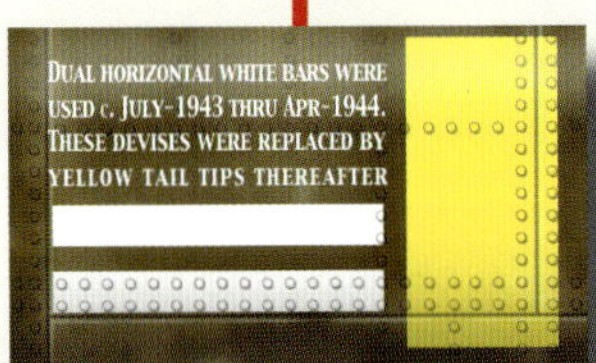

49TH Bomb Sqdn (H)

*Insignia; Approved/3-Mar-24

Organized:
49TH Aero Sqdn/6-Aug-17
Redesignated:
49TH Sqdn/14-Mar-21
49TH Bomb Sqdn/25-Jan-23
49TH Bomb Sqdn (H)/6-Dec-39

*Original 49th Aero Sqdn WWI Insignia.

96TH Bomb Sqdn (H)

*Insignia; Arrroved/3-Mar-24

Organized:
96TH Aero Sqdn/20-Aug-17
Redesignated:
96TH Sqdn/14-Mar-21
96TH Bomb Sqdn/25-Jan-23
49TH Bomb Sqdn (H)/6-Dec-39

*Original 96th Aero Sqdn WWI Insignia.

429TH Bomb Sqdn (H)

Insignia; Arrroved/12-May-30

Organized:
41ST Aero Sqdn/16-Jun-17
Reconstituted:
41TH Sqdn/10-Jun-22
Redesignated:
41ST Sch Sqdn/25-Jan-23
41ST Obs Sqdn (LR,A)/1-Mar-35
41ST Rcn Sqdn/1-Sep-36
41ST Rcn Sqdn (LR)/22-Dec-39
41ST Rcn Sqdn (H)/20-Nov-40
429TH Bomb Sqdn (H)/22-Apr-42

◦ Twelfth AAF & Fifteenth AAF ◦

Boeing B-17 'Flying Fortress'

circa: Mar-43 thru V-E Day

circa: July, 1943

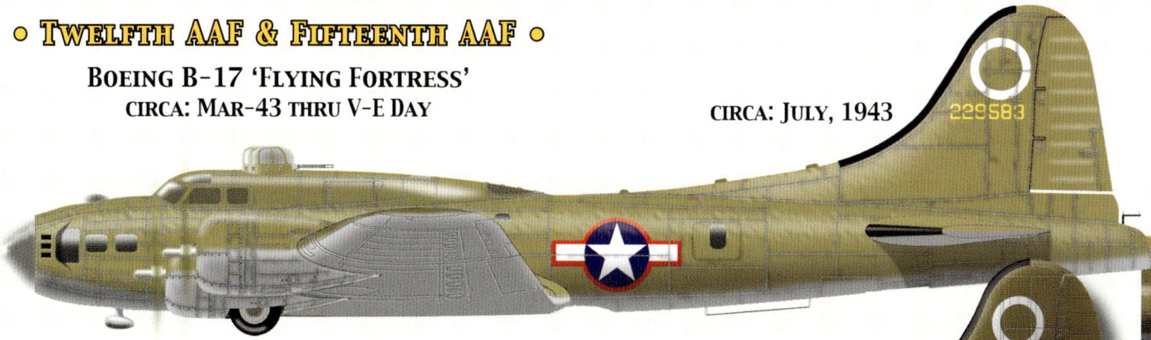

circa: August, 1943

circa: December, 1943

Tactical Markings:
The 2dBG began developing tactical unit markings shortly after deployment to North Africa. These devises were confined to the fin area of their aircraft, with a simple circular disc serving as a group designator. Virtually all Fortresses assigned to the 2dBG at this time displayed a standard two-color camouflage paint scheme. The group (and later squadron) symbols were applied with white paint and varied discernibly in size, line weight and shape as can be evidenced by comparing wartime photos.

20th Bomb Squadron:
Early 20th Bomb Squadron 'twin-bar' tactical marking.

When properly applied the tactical markings for the 2dBG consisted of a 48in. geometric circle positioned directly above the ASN. When squadron symbols were eventually added (late 1943) these consisted of 36in tall letters for the 49th and 96th Bomb Squadrons and a 'half-arrow' for the 429th, all positioned directly below and centered on the ASN.

Rudders:
In the closing months of the war the 2dBG adopted the practice of painting the entire rudder surface area of their aircraft, black on NMF while white was used on camouflaged surfaces. A further modification was the addition of a horizontal stripe. These devises were theoretically 24in. in height and aligned directly aft the ASN, but this varied somewhat from one application to another. There are some researchers that maintain that the 429thBS used Insignia Blue as opposed to black for their applications, however, no documentation nor wartime photographic evidence has surfaced that firmly supports this contention.

circa: March, 1945

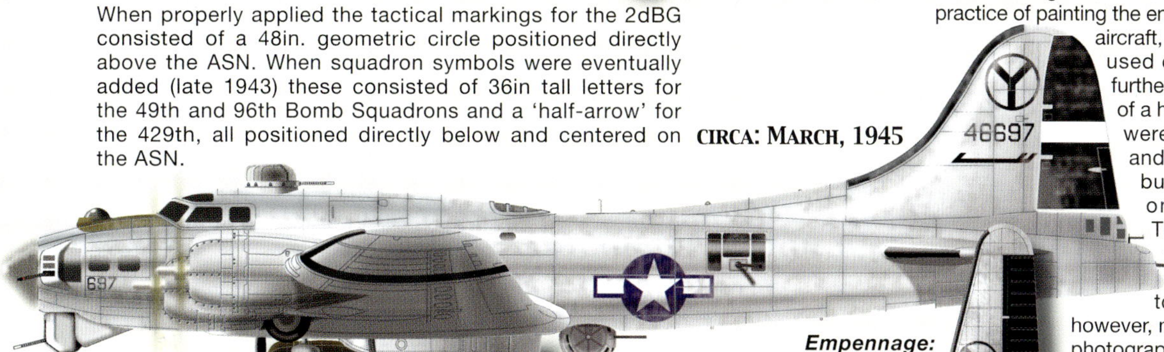

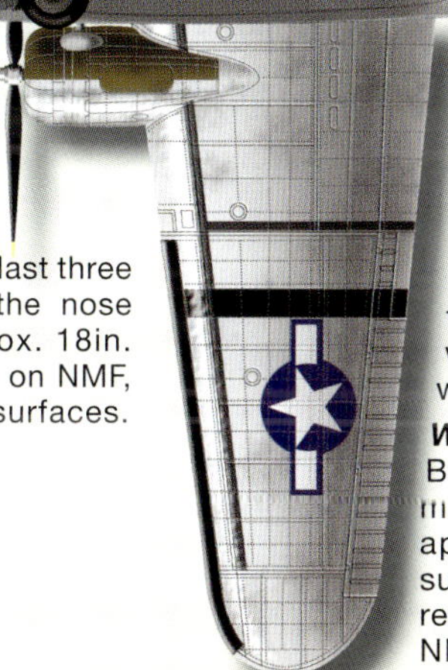

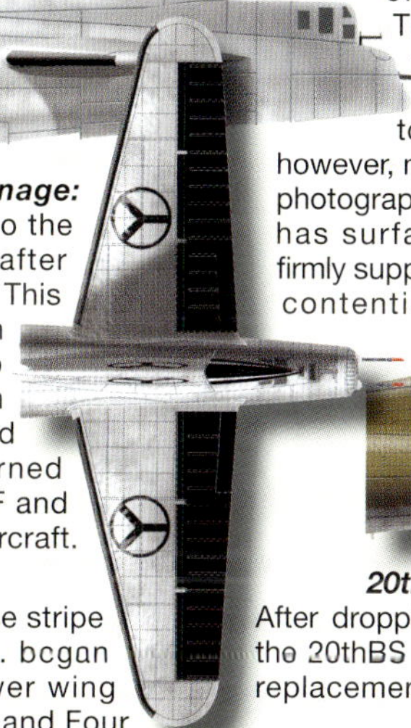

Nose Markings:
After assignment to the Fifteenth AAF all four squadrons adopted the practice of applying the last three digits of the ASN to the nose area. These were approx. 18in. in height, painted black on NMF, white on camouflaged surfaces.

Empennage:
A **'Y'** symbol was added to the circular group marker shortly after transferring to the Fifteenth AAF. This devise was later carried over in slightly reduced dimensions to the upper central surfaces of both horizontal stabilizers. By wars end the elevator surfaces were adorned with a coat of black paint on NMF and white on remaining camouflaged aircraft.

Wings:
Beginning in early 1945 a chord-wise stripe measuring approximately 10-20in. began appearing on both upper and lower wing surfaces, outboard of engines One and Four respectively. These markings were black on NMF and white on camouflaged surfaces.

20th Bomb Squadron:
After dropping the use of the twin-bars, the 20thBS adopted a yellow fin tip as a replacement tactical squadron marker.

• Assigned Ninth AAF, Jul-1942 : Twelfth AAF, Aug-1943 : Tenth AAF, Feb-1943 thru V-J Day •

IX Bomber Command

Northwest African Tactical Air Force

57th Bomb Wng 1944

12th Bombardment Group (M)

Insignia: Approved: 3-Feb-42
Motto: ' The Spirt Conquers All '
Sobriquet: ' Earthquakers '
Constituted: 12th Bmb Grp (L)/20-Nov-40
Activated: 15-Jan-41
Redesignated: 12th Bmb Grp (M)/Dec-41

81st Bomb Sqdn (M)

Insigni; Arroved/6-Jan-42
Sobriquet: 'Battering Rams'

Constituted:
81st Bomb Sqdn (L)/20-Nov-40
Activated: 15-Jan-41
Redesignated:
81st Bomb Sqdn (M)/30-Dec-41

Aircraft Number-In-Squadron
1-25
No Color Assigned

82d Bomb Sqdn (M)

Insignia; Replaced/22-May-51
Sobriquet: 'Bulldogs'

Constituted:
82d Bomb Sqdn (L)/20-Nov-40
Activated: 15-Jan-41
Redesignated:
82d Bomb Sqdn (M)/30-Dec-41

Aircraft Number-In-Squadron
26-51
No Color Assigned

83d Bomb Sqdn (M)

Insignia; Arroved/8-Aug-44
Sobriquet: 'Black Angles'

Constituted:
83d Bomb Sqdn (L)/20-Nov-40
Activated: 15-Jan-41
Redesignated:
83d Bomb Sqdn (M)/30-Dec-41

Aircraft Number-In-Squadron
52-75
No Color Assigned

434th Bomb Sqdn (M)

Insignia; Approved/18-Feb-42
Sobriquet: 'Cyclones'

Constituted:
19th Rcn Sqdn (L)/20-Nov-40
Activated: 15-Jan-41
Redesignated:
94th Bomb Sqdn (L)/14-Aug-41
94th Rcn Sqdn (M)/30-Dec-41
434th Bomb Sqdn (M)/22-Apr-42

Aircraft Number-In-Squadron
76-99
No Color Assigned

• Ninth AAF, Twelfth AAF & Tenth AAF •

North American B-25 'Mitchell'

circa: Jul-42 thru V-J Day

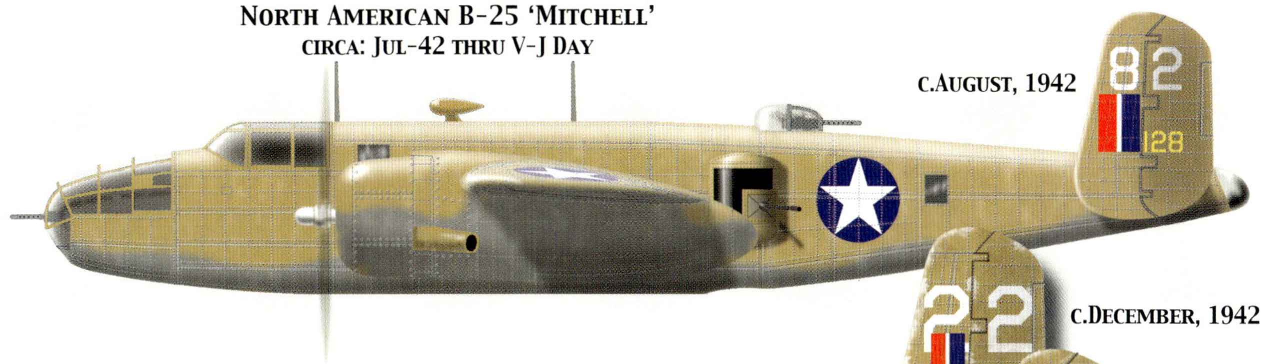

Tactical Markings:

There were no unit markings that distinguished the 12thBG as a whole, and in fact the only such devises were the 'number-in-squadron' numerals applied to the outfacing surfaces of both vertical stabilizers. To say that there was no standard application of these tail markings would be a gross understatement, except to say that they were all applied using white paint. Other than that, the numeral size and locations were varied and inconsistent, as can be evidenced by the accompanying, albeit it small sampling of marking examples.

The problem was not due to carelessness nor indifference on behalf of the ground crews, but rather the constant movement from one landing ground after another to which the 12thBG was subjected during their grueling eighteen month long combat tour in the Mediterranean.

*Stations not depicted on map: c.October, 1942-April, 1943

During the North African Campaign elements of the 12thBG(M) utilized any number of hastily organized Advanced Landing Grounds in both the Egyptian and Libyan deserts. Often these L/G's were little more than a flat spot sufficient for landing and take-off's. The Mitchell's would be met by ground crews manning utility trucks loaded with 50gal. drums of aviation gas and munitions. The aircraft would be quickly re-fueled, re-armed and made ready for a speedy return to combat against Erwin Rommel's Afrikakorps.

• Assigned Twelfth AAF, Jun-1942 : Fifteenth AAF, Nov-1943 : Twelfth AAF, Jan-1944 : 1stTAF(P), Dec-1944 thru V-E Day •

42d Bomb Wng
August-1943

47th Bomb Wng
February-1943

42d Bomb Wng
August-1943

17th Bombardment Group (M)

Insignia: Approved: 2-Nov-37
Motto: 'Ever Into Danger'
Authorized: 17th Obs Grp/18-Oct-27
Redesignated: 17th Pur Grp: 1929
Activated: 15-Jul-31
Redesignated: 17th Atk Grp/1939
Redesignated: 17d Bmb Grp (M)/1939

Early 17th Bomb Group:
As near as can be determined the above design represents the first official version of the 17thBG's insignia which received official approval for use on 19-Jan-34.

34th Bomb Sqdn (M)

Insignia; Arrroved/18-Jun-32
Sobriquet: 'Thunderbirds'

Organized:
34th Aero Sqdn/11-Jun-17
Reconstituted & Redesignated:
34th Pur Sqdn/24-Mar-23
Activated: 15-Jul-31
Redesignated:
34th Atk Sqdn/1-Mar-35
34th Bomb Sqdn (M)/17-Oct-39

Group Color | Aircraft Number-In-Squadron | 1-24

37th Bomb Sqdn (M)

Insignia; Arrroved/25-Jul-34
Sobriquet: 'Lions'

Organized:
37th Aero Sqdn/13-Jun-17
Reconstituted & Redesignated:
37th Pur Sqdn/24-Mar-23
Activated: 1-Sep-33
Redesignated:
37th Atk Sqdn/1-Mar-35
37th Bomb Sqdn (M)/6-Dec-39

Group Color | Aircraft Number-In-Squadron | 25-49

95th Bomb Sqdn (M)

Insignia; Arrroved/4-Mar-24
Sobriquet: 'Kicking Mules'

Organized:
95th Aero Sqdn/20-Aug-17
Redesignated:
95th Pur Sqdn/14-Mar-21
95th Pur Sqdn/25-Jan-23
95th Atk Sqdn/1-Mar-35
95th Bomb Sqdn (M)/17-Oct-39

Group Color | Aircraft Number-In-Squadron | 50-74

432d Bomb Sqdn (M)

Insignia; Arrroved/30-Jan-41
Sobriquet: 'Winged Helmet Of Mercury'

Organized:
89th Aero Sqdn/19-Aug-17
Reconstituted:
89th Obs Sqdn/14-Mar-21
Redesignated:
89th Rcn Sqdn/24-Oct-36
89th Rcn Sqdn (MR)/22-Dec-39
89th Rcn Sqdn (M)/20-Nov-40
432d Bomb Sqdn (M)/22-Apr-42

Group Color | Aircraft Number-In-Squadron | 75-99

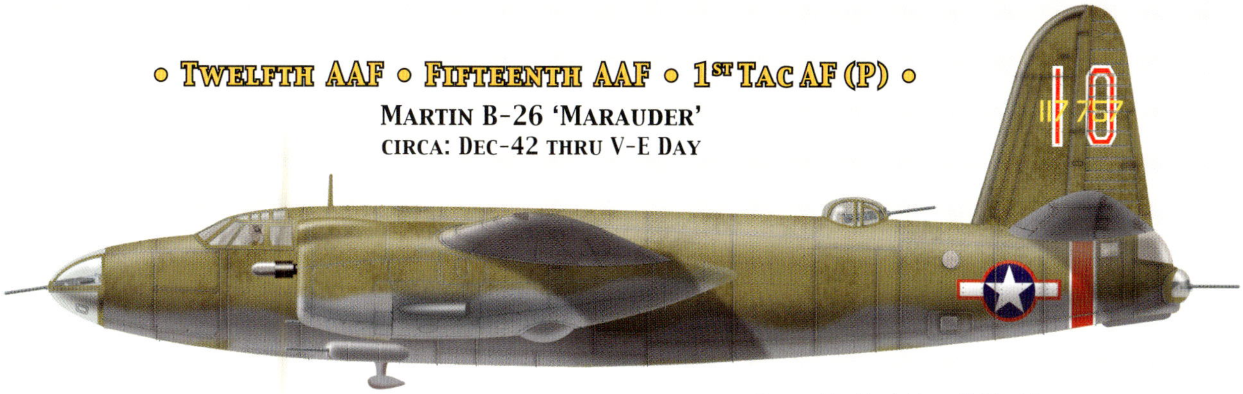

• Twelfth AAF • Fifteenth AAF • 1st Tac AF (P) •

Martin B-26 'Marauder'

circa: Dec-42 thru V-E Day

Group Tactical Aircraft Markings:
Sometime in July of 1943 Insignia Red was adopted as the unit recognition color for the 17th Bomb Group. Large aircraft-in-squadron numbers were applied to the fin and rudder areas utilizing this color and were generally outlined with white paint in order to increase legibility. Serial numbers were reapplied with Identification Yellow over these aircraft-in-squadron designators. An Insignia Red vertical stripe was additionally applied to the rear fuselage area below the horizontal stabilizers, just forward the gunners station. These stripes were also outlined with white, however precise measurement and positioning of these devices varied considerably, especially on early applications. During the initial period of the 17thBG's deployment to the MTO, virtually all Marauders within their inventory displayed a standard USAAF two-color camouflage paint scheme.

Insignia Anomalies:
The images of the 37th and 95th Bomb Sqdns depicted on the facing page both appeared in the 1944 National Geographic special edition on U.S. military insignia as representing these units. The contention that there was often a disparity between 'official' and 'applied' applications of unit insignia is evidenced by these two photos showing very typical design applications as worn by Lt.Col.Jimmy Doolittle's Tokyo Raiders in April, 1942.

With the gradual appearance of NMF aircraft as the war progressed, the white outlines disappeared from the tail designators and serial numbers were reapplied with black paint in place of the earlier yellow applications on the camouflaged surfaces. Similarly, the white outline was dropped from the groups vertical red marker stripe. A few examples of these later applications were known to have been outlined with a thin black border, but this practice with not widespread within the squadrons of the 17thBG.

• Assigned Twelfth AAF, Oct-1942 thru V-E Day •

XXII Tactiacl Air Command — XII Tactiacl Air Command — XII Air Support Command

47th Bombardment Group (L)

Insignia: (unknown)
Motto: (Unknown)
Consituted:
47th Bomb Grp (L)/20-Nov-40
Activated: 15-Jan-41

Wartime Insignia Unknown

Early 86thBS Insignia:
The above image was the original insignia of the 86thBS(L) and was displayed by this unit throughout its deployment in both North Africa and Sicily. Shortly after relocating to Italy however, a replacement design was submitted (see below) which ultimately brought to a close the service of this original *'Death thumbing its nose'* image.

84th Bomb Sqdn (L)

Insignia; Approved/9-Sep-42

Constituted:
84th Bmb Sqdn (L)/20-Nov-40
Activated: 15-Jan-41

No color assigned — Aircraft Number-in-Squadron: 01-24

85th Bomb Sqdn (L)

Insignia; Approved/9-Sep-44

Constituted:
85th Bmb Sqdn (L)/20-Nov-40
Activated: 15-Jan-41

No color assigned — Aircraft Number-in-Squadron: 25-49

86th Bomb Sqdn (L)

Insignia; Approved/8-Mar-45
Sobriquet: The Knightly Intruders'

Constituted:
86th Bmb Sqdn (L)/20-Nov-40
Activated: 15-Jan-41

No color assigned — Aircraft Number-in-Squadron: 50-74

97th Bomb Sqdn (L)

Insignia; Approved/9-Sep-44

Constituted:
20th Rcn Sqdn (L)/20-Nov-40
Activated: 15-Jan-41
Redesignated:
97th Bmb Sqdn (L)/14-Aug-41

No color assigned — Aircraft Number-in-Squadron: 75-99

Douglas A-20/DB-7 'Havoc/Boston'
circa: Nov-42 thru V-E Day

Early Group Markings:
A number of the original combat aircraft assigned to the 47thBG displayed the American flag on both sides of the tail fin in addition to the under surface of the port side wing. The group quickly adopted the use of a 'number-in-squadron' method of identification, these being originally applied with white paint on the upper forward fuselage area. Squadron insignia were known to have been applied just aft of these markings but the extent of this practice is uncertain.

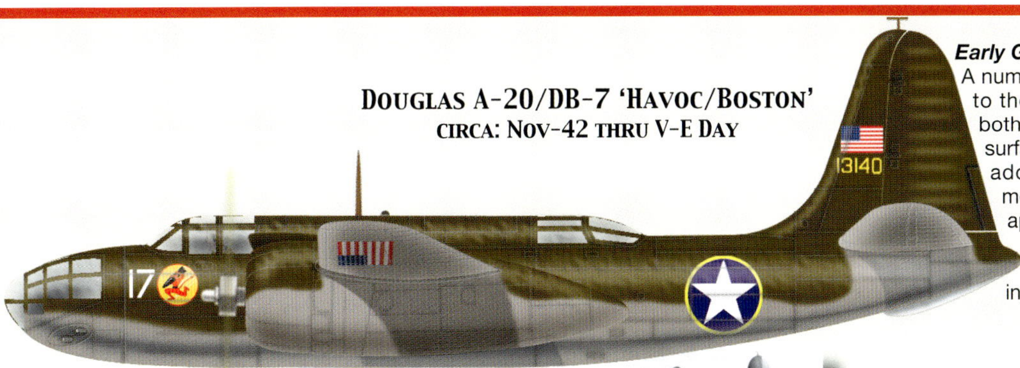

Early Nose Art:
This interesting photo of 'Lady Jean' provides an excellent shot of squadron insignia application, in this case the original design of the 86thBS. Note the U.S. flag located on mid tail fin.

Modifications To Tactical Markings:
A variety of paint schemes were employed by this group varying from a standard USAAF two-color O.D. over Neutral Grey to an R.A.F. tri-color disruptive temperate zone land pattern. In early 1943 all squadrons were directed to relocate their respective 'number-in-squadron' markings to the tail section of the aircraft. These were to be enlarged and appliedusing white paint above the existing aircraft serial number. Applications of these markings varied considerably in both style as well as location but the one constant was the inclusion of both fin and rudder surface areas. No additional unit markings were employed by the 47thBG for the remainder of the war.

Douglas A-26 'Invader'
circa: Jan-45 thru V-E Day

Late Group Markings:
When the 47thBG began receiving these aircraft in the final months of the war they consisted of two surface types; all natural metal finishes or with an overall black paint scheme. The same method of affixing tactical markings were employed with the new A-20's as existed with the groups existing inventory A-20's, albeit with a greater degree of uniformity. The 'number-in-squadron' designators were affixed to both the fin and rudder areas using black paint on NMF's, white on those aircraft painted with ANA-515 Gloss Black.

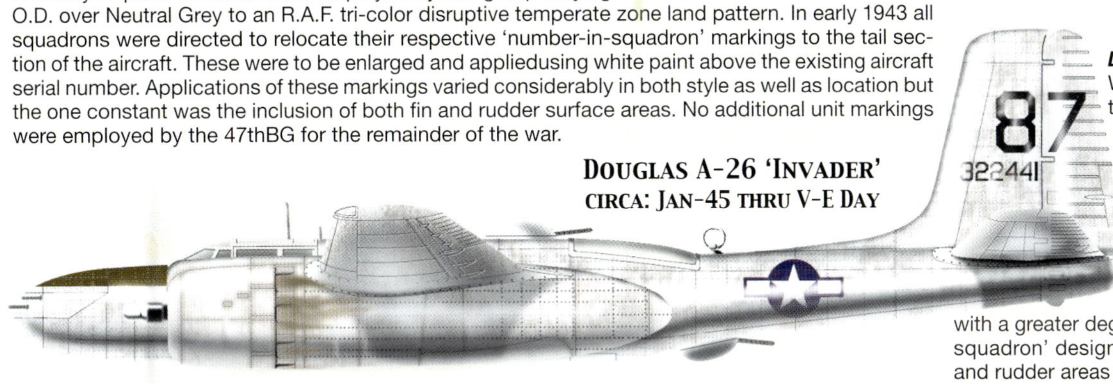

1.) Mediouna, French Morocco
18-Nov-42

2.) Youks-les-Bains, Algeria
7-Jan-43

3.) Canrobert, Algeria
6-Mar-43

4.) Thelepte, Tunisia
30-Mar-43

5.) Souk-el-Arba, Tunisia
13-Apr-43

6.) Soliman, Tunisia
c.1-Jul-43

7.) Gozo Island, Malta
21-Jul-43

8.) Torrente Comunelli, Sicily
9-Aug-43

9.) Gerbini, Sicily
20-Aug-43

10.) Grottaglie, Italy
23-Sep-43

11.) Vincenzo A/F, Italy
15-Oct-43

12.) Vesuvius A/F, Italy
c.10-Jan-44

13.) Capodichino, Italy
22-Mar-44

14.) Vesuvius A/F, Italy
25-Apr-44

15.) Ponte Galeria, Italy
c.10-Jun-44

16.) Ombrone A/F, Italy
27-Jun-44

17.) Poretta, Corsica
11-Jun-44

18.) Salon, France
7-Sep-44

19.) Follonica, Italy
18-Sep-44

20.) Rosignano, Italy
Oct-44

21.) Grosseto, Italy
11-Dec-44

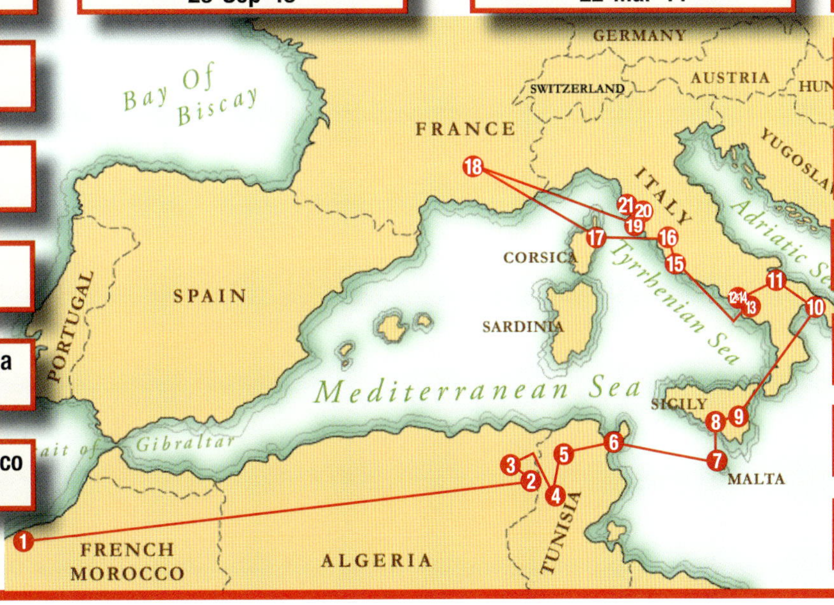

• Assigned Eighth AAF, May-1942 : Twelfth AAF, Nov-1942 : Fifteenth AAF, Nov-1943 thru V-E Day •

5th Bomb Wng 1944

5th Bomb Wng 1943

9th Bmr Comd 1942

97th Bombardment Group (H)

Insignia: Approved: 5-Mar-43
Motto: 'The Hour Has Come'
Constituted:
97th Bmb Grp (H)/28-Jan-42
Activated: 3-Feb-42

340th Bomb Sqdn (H)

Insignia; Replaced/16-Mar-56

Constituted:
340th Bomb Sqdn (H)/28-Jan-42
Activated: 3-Feb-42

341st Bomb Sqdn (H)

Insignia; Replaced/6-Aug-57

Constituted:
341st Bomb Sqdn (H)/28-Jan-42
Activated: 3-Feb-42

342d Bomb Sqdn (H)

Insignia; Replaced/9-Nov-51

Constituted:
341st Bomb Sqdn (H)/28-Jan-42
Activated: 3-Feb-42

414th Bomb Sqdn (H)

Insignia; Arrroved/24-Jun-44

Constituted:
24th Rcn Sqdn (H)/28-Jan-42
Redesignated:
414th Bomb Sqdn (H)/22-Apr-42

Boeing B-17 'Flying Fortress'
circa: May-42 thru V-E-Day

Empennage Markings:
When the 97thBG initially arrived from England its aircraft bore no distinctive tactical markings of any kind. This quickly changed when the Group adopted a triangle upon assignment to the Twelfth AAF, a symbol that it would continue to display throughout the war. Virtually all tactical markings adopted by the 97th BG were confined to both sides of the tail fin and upper surfaces of the horizontal stabilizers. Early applications of the 97th's adopted triangle symbol on their inventory of camouflaged B-17's consisted simply of a linear white outline of this geometric symbol. These were positioned directly above, and centered upon, the existing aircraft serial number. Each squadron was assigned a numerical designator which was in turn positioned directly below the serial number and likewise applied with white paint.
When all heavy bombers serving within the MTO were transferred to the Fifteenth AAF, the B-17's were consolidated into the 5th Bomb Wing which was identified by the use of an uppercase sans serif 'Y'. The 97th's previous outlined white triangle became a solid image with the 5thBW 'Y' centered therein. Each squadrons numerical designator were retained, albeit now in black and centered upon a newly adopted white circle. The location of both of these devices in relationship to the A/C serial number remained unchanged. A new addition to the Groups markings however was the application of the Triangle 'Y' motif to the upper mid- surface areas of both horizontal stabilizers.

Early 342d Bomb Squadron insignia:
As previously noted in Vol.I of the Battle Colors series, the Disney Studios 'kicking donkey' insignia was originally developed for the 342dBS while this unit was still in garrison stateside. It was replaced once the squadron had been shipped overseas and replaced with what was considered a more intimidating image.
The lower image was apparently an interim or proposed design, the black pyramid obviously representing the 97th Bomb Group with the two yellow bombs standing in for the numerical '2' squadron tail marking designator. In any event, this design was superseded by the officially adopted insignia depicted on the facing page.

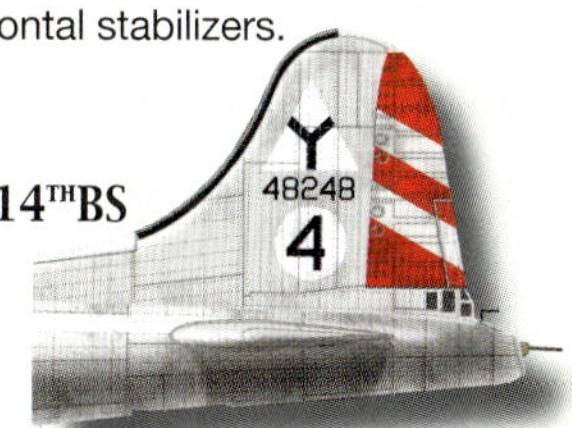

414ᵀᴴBS

342ᴰBS

Group Tactical Marking:
The 97thBG's Triangle 'Y' designator was known to have been applied using both Insignia White and Identification Yellow for the geometric symbol, with the letter 'Y' configuration consistently applied in black on camouflaged surfaces. On natural metal finished surfaces the triangle was applied in black with the 'Y' masked out during the painting process.

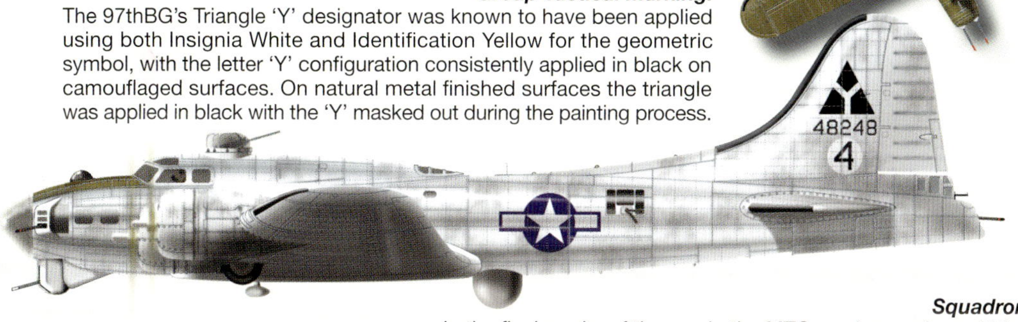

341ˢᵀBS

340ᵀᴴBS

Squadron Markings:
In the final weeks of the war in the MTO, each squadron within the 97thBG began adopting a distinctive rudder pattern as an improved means of unit identification. Numorouc aircraft within all squadrons additionally began applying solid color to the fin center panel. The full extent to which these eleventh-hour rudder markings and paint modifications to fins were used by the squadrons comprising the 97thBG is today an unresolved issue.

• Assigned Ninth AAF, Nov-42 : Twelfth AAF, Sep-1943 : Fifteenth AAF, Nov-1943 thru V-E Day •

47TH Bomb Wng 1943

5TH Bomb Wng 1943

9TH Bmr Comd 1942

98TH Bombardment Group (H)

Insignia: Approved: 29-Jul-42
Motto: 'Force For Freedom'
Constituted:
98TH Bomb Grp/28-Jan-42
Activated: 3-Feb-42
Redesignated:
98TH Bomb Grp (VH)/May-1945

FORCE FOR FREEDOM

343D Bomb Sqdn (H)

Insignia; (unknown)

No Known Squadron Insignia

Constituted:
343D Bomb Sqdn (H)/28-Jan-42
Activated: 3-Feb-42
Redesignated:
343D Bomb Sqdn (VH)/23-May-45

No Color Assigned
No Squadron Codes Issued

344TH Bomb Sqdn (H)

Insignia; (unknown)

No Known Squadron Insignia

Constituted:
344TH Bomb Sqdn (H)/28-Jan-42
Activated: 3-Feb-42
Redesignated:
344TH Bomb Sqdn (VH)/23-May-45

No Color Assigned
No Squadron Codes Issued

345TH Bomb Sqdn (H)

Insignia; (unknown)

No Known Squadron Insignia

Constituted:
345TH Bomb Sqdn (H)/28-Jan-42
Activated: 3-Feb-42
Redesignated:
345TH Bomb Sqdn (VH)/23-May-45

No Color Assigned
No Squadron Codes Issued

415TH Bomb Sqdn (H)

Insignia; (unknown)

No Known Squadron Insignia

Constituted:
25TH Rcn Sqdn (H)/28-Jan-42
Activated: 3-Feb-42
Redesignated:
415TH Bomb Sqdn (H)/22-Apr-42

No Color Assigned
No Squadron Codes Issued

• Ninth USAAF • Twelfth USAAF • Fifteenth USAAF •

Concolidated B-24 'Liberator'

circa: Nov-42 thru V-E Day

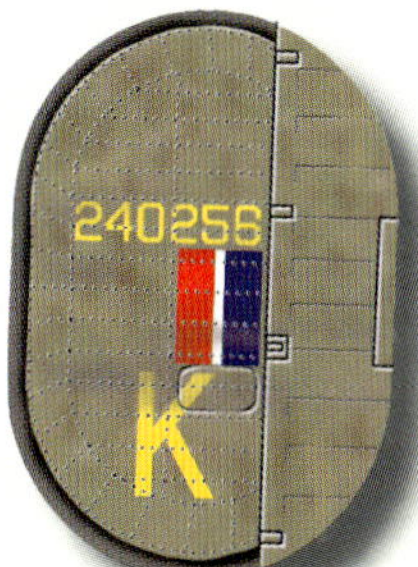

Circa November 1942:
The Groups original overseas deployment tactical markings consisted of nothing more than the application of an assigned letter to the lower portion of each vertical fin. An RAF tri-colored Recognition Flash was the only additional marking and these were located on both inward and outward facing surfaces of both vertical fins. These RAF flashes gradually began to disappear with the passing of time as they were generally not reinstated when an aircraft was repaired and/or repainted.

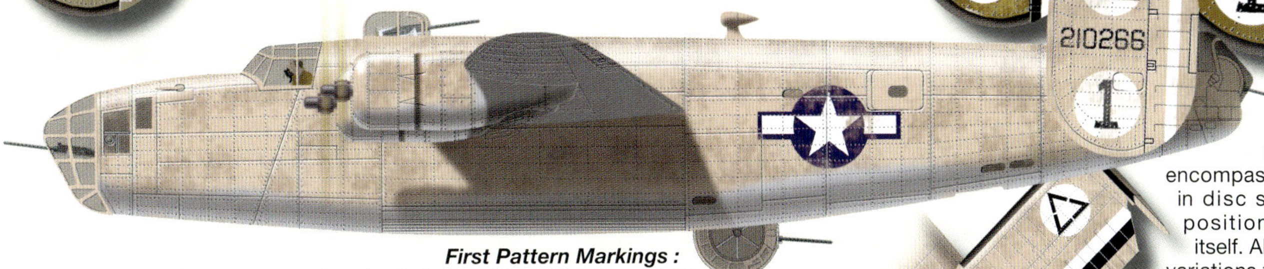

Variations:
These were numerous and encompassed differences in disc size as well as positioning on the fin itself. Also evident were variations to the thickness (weight) of the disc's internal graphics, and even the presence or absence of an a/c call letter.

First Pattern Markings :
The need for an improved method of aircraft identification quickly became apparent, compounded by the assignment of additional heavy bomb groups to the Fifteenth AAF. The 47thBW triangle was directed applied within a white disc to the upper area of all B-24's fins. A newly assigned 98thBG designator (a numerical '**1**') was to occupy a similar disc at the lower fin area. A narrow vertical white stripe was directed to be applied to the rudder surface areas. These symbols were soon adapted for use on the upper surface areas of the tail plane as depicted.

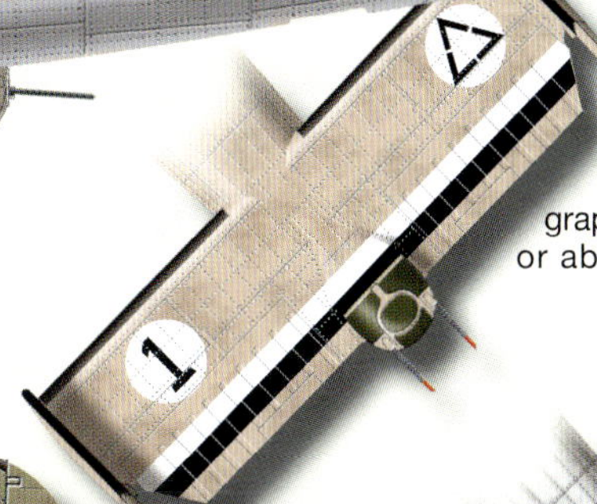

Second Pattern Markings:
As the war progressed the need for a quicker and more accurate method of tactical markings arose. The replacement markings selected involved dividing the outward tail plane approximately in half diagonally. The lower leading portion was additionally divided into six equal horizontal sections and, beginning at the lower section, painted with alternating colors of black and yellow. This configuration eliminated the need for the this device was subsequently eliminated entirely from the tail fin itself although its use was continued, albeit sporadically, on tail plane surfaces.

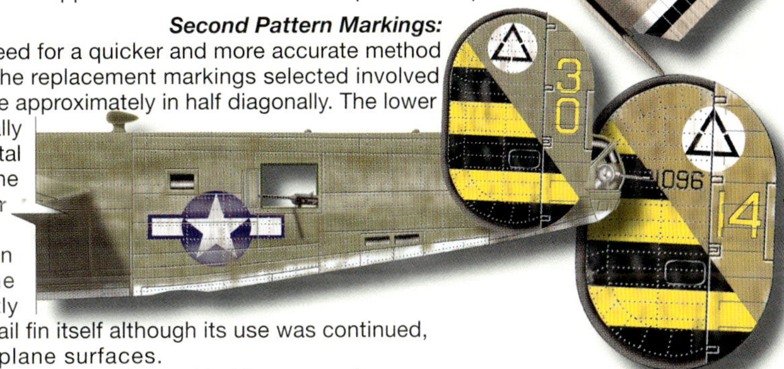

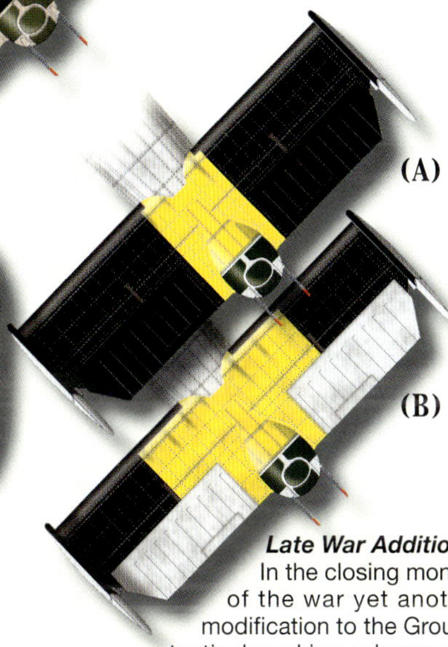

The treatment of individual a/c serial numbers with this new marker was erratic, and ran the gambit from total removal to full restoration. It was not uncommon for these numbers to simply be left in place and over painted. Individually assigned a/c numbers began appearing on the outfacing tail rudder surfaces about this same time, applied in both a stacked or in-line method with the numerals often displaying a thin black outline. The 98thBG's Triangle/Circle unit designator continued to be employed on the upper tail surface, but positioning of this device varied significantly from one application to another.

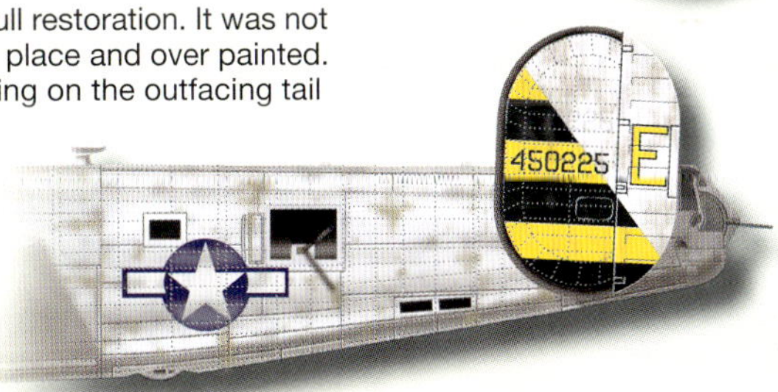

Late War Additions:
In the closing months of the war yet another modification to the Group's tactical marking scheme was ordered. The circular devises were directed to be replaced with a black & yellow paint pattern. The top image **(A)** represents the official upper tail surface pattern as directed while the lower image **(B)** depicts the vast majority of actual field applications to 98thBG combat aircraft.

• Assigned Twelfth AAF, Feb-1943 : Fifteenth AAF, Nov-1943 thru V-E Day •

5TH Bomb Wng 1943

5TH Bomb Wng 1943

99TH Bombardment Group (H)

Insignia: Approved/3-Nov-43

Motto: ' Sight With Might '

Sobriquet: ' The Diamondbacks '

Constituted:

99TH Bomb Grp (H)/28-Jan-42

Activated: 1-Jun-42

Mystery Insignia!

There is considerable confusion concerning the above image. Some sources maintain that it was intended as a late war replacement for the original ***348thBS*** insignia, while others claim it was a runner-up design for the ***346thBS***. Either premise seems plausible but to date the final answer has eluded all efforts to establish its precise origins.

346TH Bomb Sqdn (H)

Insignia; Approved/18-Feb-44

Constituted:

346TH Bomb Sqdn (H)/28-Jan-42

Activated: 1-Jun-42

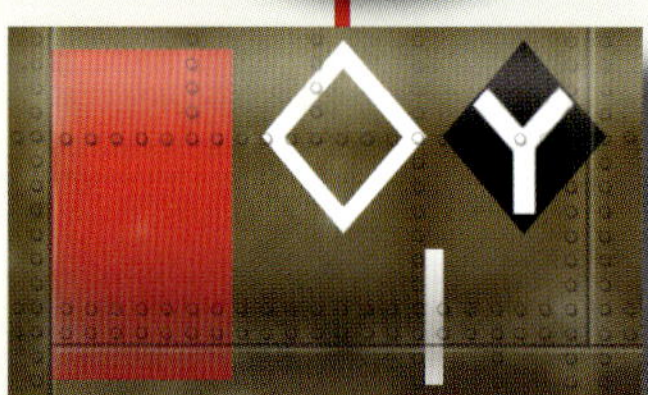

347TH Bomb Sqdn (H)

Insignia; Approved/18-Feb-44

Constituted:

347TH Bomb Sqdn (H)/28-Jan-42

Activated: 1-Jun-42

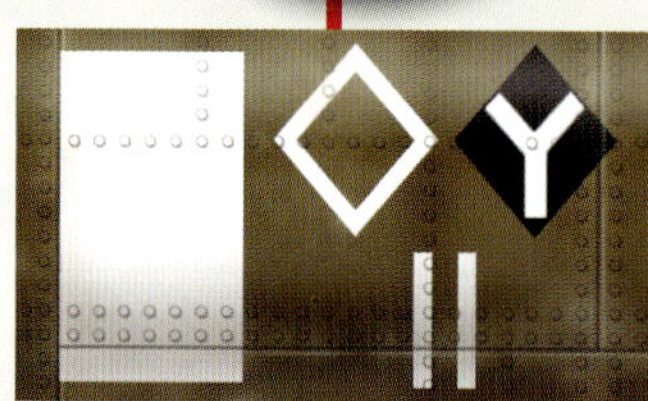

348TH Bomb Sqdn (H)

Insignia; Approved/18-Feb-44

Constituted:

348TH Bomb Sqdn (H)/28-Jan-42

Activated: 1-Jun-42

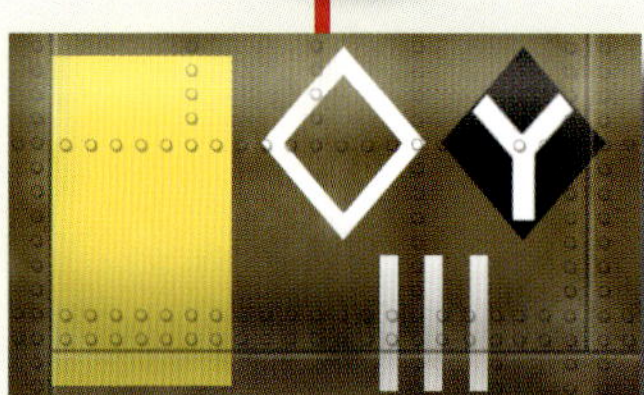

416TH Bomb Sqdn (H)

Insignia; Approved/11-Jan-43

Constituted:

26TH Rcn Sqdn (H)/28-Jan-42

Redesignated:

416TH Bomb Sqdn (H)/22-Apr-42

Activated: 1-Jun-42

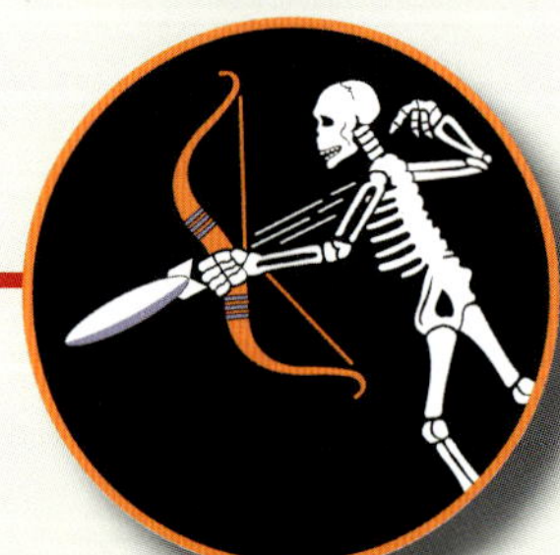

• Twelfth USAAF • Fifteenth USAAF •

Boeing B-17 'Flying Fortress'

circa: Feb-43 thru V-E Day

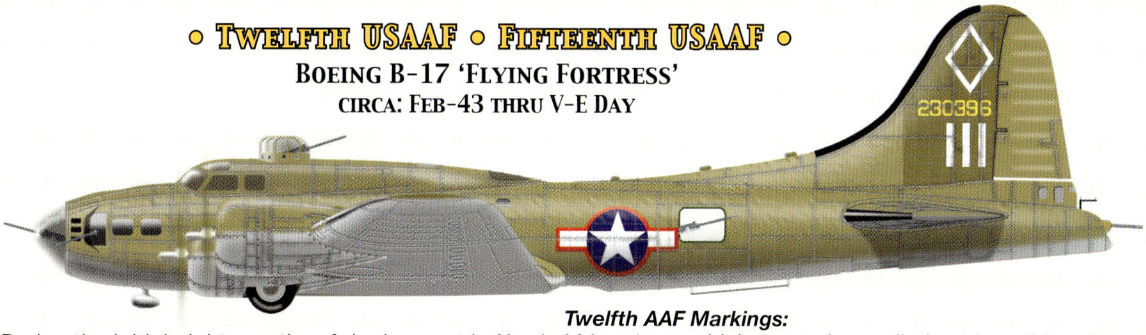

Twelfth AAF Markings:

During the initial eight months of deployment in North Africa the 99thBG displayed virtually no individual unit tactical markings. In mid-summer of 1943 all heavy bomber groups were instructed to develop their own distinctive markers. The symbol selected to represent the 99thBG consisted of a simple white outlined diamond shape which was to be applied on the tail fin, directly above the existing aircraft serial number. Later that same year, individual squadron designators were adopted via large Roman numerals similarly affixed to the tail fin, albeit in this case positioned directly below the serial number and centered on the designated Group tactical marker.

Fifteenth AAF Markings:

The existing geometric diamond symbol was retained in a modified form subsequent to the 99thBG's transfer to the Fifteenth AAF. The outline configuration was replaced with a solid white or black pattern depending upon surface finish, i.e., camouflaged vs. natural metal finish. An addition to this symbol was the inclusion of the 47thBW's upper case 'Y' which was applied using white paint on black backgrounds and white paint on NMF's. In many of the latter cases, the 'Y' was masked out upon symbol application with the metal surface area allowed to show through in place of the white paint. Black or white paint was also used when applying the squadron Roman numerical designators. New to the tactical marking scheme was the addition of the 99thBG symbol to the top surfaces of both horizontal stabilizers, and these were applied in a like manner as those similar devices on the tail fin surfaces.

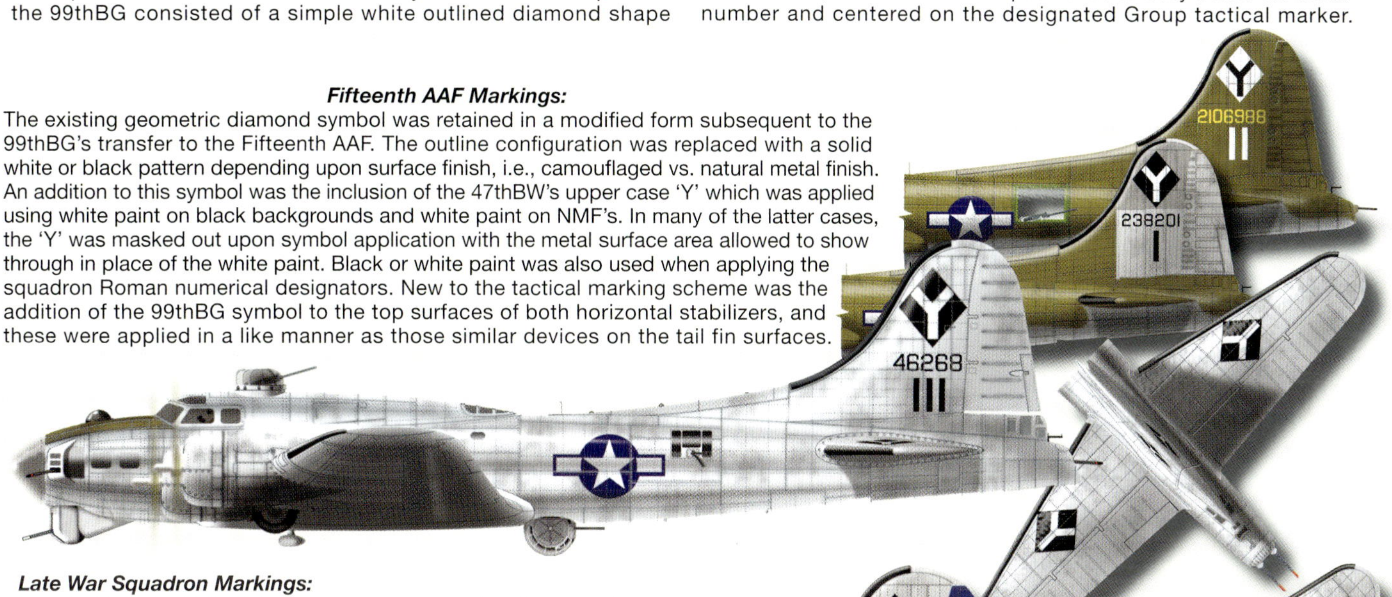

Late War Squadron Markings:

In early 1945 the 98thBG began a program of enhancing squadron recognition of its combat aircraft by means of a series of color bands applied to the rear area of the aircraft fuselage in respective squadron colors. The location of these color bands were fairly consistent however the widths varied considerably. Some aircraft assigned to the 416thBS were reported as displaying engine cowlings similary adorned with their respective color.

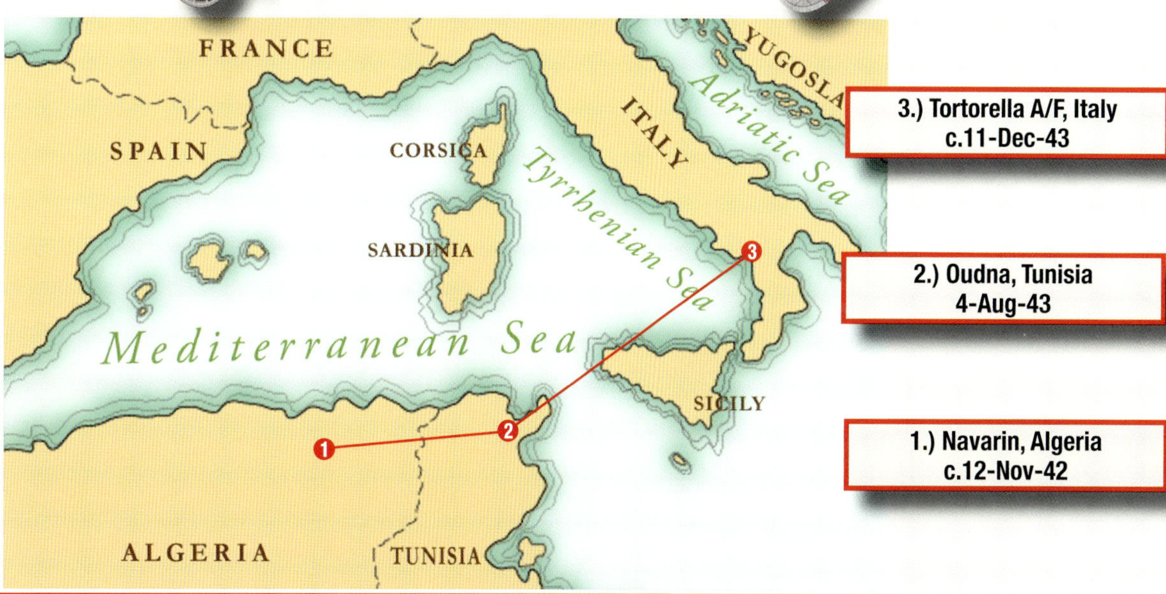

• Assigned Eighth AAF, Jul-1942 : Twelfth AAF, Nov-1942
Fifteenth AAF, Nov-1943 thru V-E Day •

5th Bomb Wng
1942

5th Bomb Wng
1942

'I Wanted Wings'

Many will recognize this famous Disney design, but that this image had its roots in the 301stBG is not as well known. It all started with Lt. Emmet Cook, a USAAF Bombardier assigned to the 352dBS who became a POW on 22-Mar-43, when shot down on his 32nd mission over Palermo, Sicily. His original hand drawn 'I Wanted Wings' post card was mailed to Ft. Worth Texas on 8-Jun-43 informing his mother of his recent 'Kriegie' status in Stalag Luft III.

301st Bombardment Group (H)

Insignia: Approved/11-Aug-42
Constituted:
301st Bomb Grp (H)/28-Jan-42
Activated: 3-Feb-42
Redesignated:
301st Bomb Grp (VH)/Aug-45

32d Bomb Sqdn (H)

Insignia; Approved/21-Nov-36

Organized:
32d Aero Sqdn (M)/13-Jun-17
Redesignated:
32d Bomb Sqdn/24-Mar-23
Activated: 24-Jun-32
Redesignated:
32d Bomb Sqdn (H)/6-Dec-39
32d Bomb Sqdn (VH)/5-Aug-45

352d Bomb Sqdn (H)

Insignia; (unknown)

Constituted:
352d Bomb Sqdn (H)/28-Jan-42
Activated: 3-Feb-42
Redesignated:
352d Bomb Sqdn (VH)/5-Aug-45

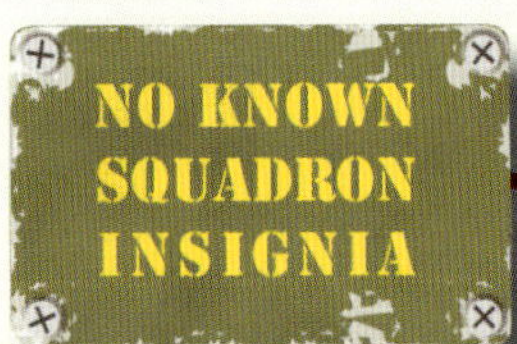

353d Bomb Sqdn (H)

Insignia; (unknown)

Constituted:
353d Bomb Sqdn (H)/28-Jan-42
Activated: 3-Feb-42
Redesignated:
353d Bomb Sqdn (VH)/5-Aug-45

419th Bomb Sqdn (H)

Insignia; (unknown)

Constituted:
29th Rcn Sqdn (H)/28-Jan-42
Activated: 3-Feb-42
Redesignated:
419th Bomb Sqdn (H)/22-Apr-42
419th Bomb Sqdn (VH)/5-Aug-45

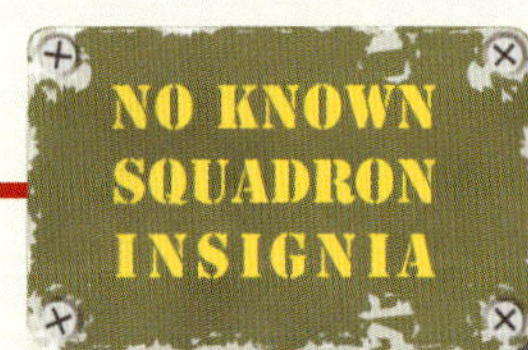

• Eighth USAAF • Twelfth USAAF • Fifteenth USAAF •

Boeing B-17 'Flying Fortress'
circa: Sep-42 thru V-E Day

Early Twelfth AAF Markings:

Like many other AAF units seeing early service in the Mediterranean Theater, the 301stBG began combat operations with no tactical markings other than national insignia and aircraft serial number. This changed in mid-1943 when the B-17 groups serving in the Twelfth AAF were assigned geometric symbols for identification purposes. These new devices were applied with white paint on the upper fin area with any number of different line weights. Each squadron within the 301stBG was assigned a numerical code and these were similarly applied directly below the serial number.

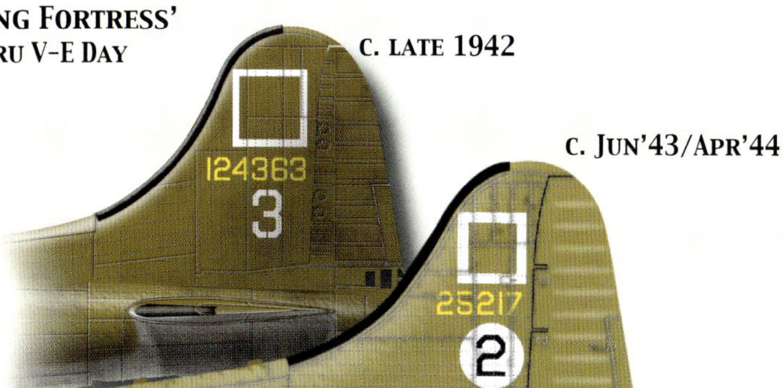

Early Fifteenth AAF Markings:

The 301stBG retained their original rectangular geometric symbol after transferring to the Fifteenth AAF, but two modifications quickly took effect in early 1944. All B-17's were directed to paint their respective group symbols a solid white upon which would be affixed, in black, the upper case 'Y' designator of the 5th Bomb Wing. The second change was the addition of a white disc below the serial number, onto which the respective squadron numerical designator was to be centered using black paint. Those ships without camouflage paint were directed to comply in like kind with their own applications. However, given the ever increasing arrival of NMF aircraft it soon became apparent that an enhanced method of applying tactical unit markings would have to be decided upon.

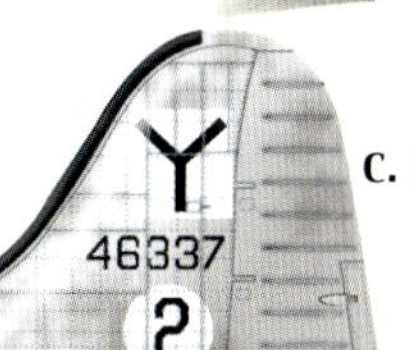

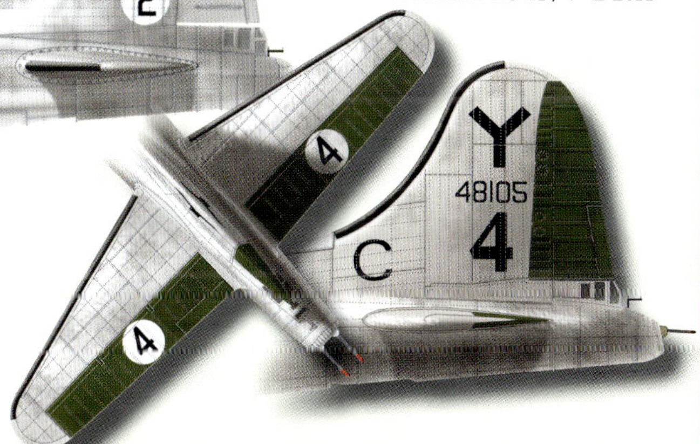

Late War NMF Markings:

Although by no means unilaterally applied within the unit, in the final months of the conflict the 301stBG adopted the practice of applying a Medium Green-42 paint (or equivalent) to tail rudders and elevator surfaces. The individual squadron numerical designators were replaced with a letter code ('A' thru 'D') and now located on the lower forward fin area. The white rectangle was dropped entirely and replaced with a much heaver weighted 'Y' configuration. A large numeral '4' (now representing the 301stBG) was positioned directly below the serial number where the squadron numbers had previously been located. This number '4' was also applied to both upper elevator surfaces, irregardless of green paint.

1.) Tafaraoui, Algeria c.26-Nov-42

2.) Maison Blanche, Algeria 5-Dec-42

3.) Biskra, Algeria c.16-Dec-42

4.) Ain M'lila, Algeria c.17-Jan-43

5.) Saint Donat, Algeria 6-Mar-43

6.) Oudna, Tunisia 6-Aug-43

7.) Cerignola, Italy c.7-Dec-43

8.) Lucera, Italy 1-Feb-44

• Assigned Twelfth AAF, Oct-1942 thru V-E Day •

57TH Bomb Wng 1944-1945

XII Ftr Cmnd 1944

47TH Bomb Wng 1942-1944

310TH Bombardment Group (M)

Insignia: (unofficial)

Constituted:
310TH Bomb Grp (M)/28-Jan-42

Activated: 15-Mar-42

Alternate 381stBS Motif:
Due to the complexity of the original design the outer border was generally reduced to a simple blue contour for most clothing and signage applications.

379TH Bomb Sqdn (M)

Insignia; Replaced/21-Jan-58

Constituted:
379TH Bomb Sqdn (M)/28-Jan-42
Activated: 15-Mar-42

NO SQUADRON CODES ISSUED

380TH Bomb Sqdn (M)

Insignia; Replaced/10-Jan-55

Constituted:
380TH Bomb Sqdn (M)/28-Jan-43
Activated: 15-Mar-42

NO SQUADRON CODES ISSUED

381ST Bomb Sqdn (M)

Insignia; Replaced/7-Mar-56

Constituted:
381ST Bomb Sqdn (M)/28-Jan-42
Activated: 15-Mar-42

NO SQUADRON CODES ISSUED

428TH Bomb Sqdn (M)

Insignia; Replaced/14-Jul-60

Constituted:
39TH Rcn Sqdn (M)/28-Jan-42
Activated: 15-Mar-42
Redesignated:
428th Bomb Sqdn (M)/22-Apr-42

NO SQUADRON CODES ISSUED

• Twelfth USAAF •

North American B-25 'Mitchell'

circa: Oct-42 thru V-E Day

First MTO Markings:
There is enough photographic evidence available today to suggest that early in 1943 the Group at least experimented with the use of individual aircraft call letters. These appear to have been affixed using non-standard stencils and white paint on the forward mid-nose area. The full extent to which these particular type of markings were used within the 310th is currently unknown.

Early Deployment:
Other than national insignia and serial number, the only other markings present on the original compliment of B-25's assigned to the 310thBG was an American flag located on the lower forward portion of each ships tail fin.

Squadron 'Nose Art':
Squadron insignia began to appear on forward fuselages of 310thBG aircraft shortly after the units deployment.

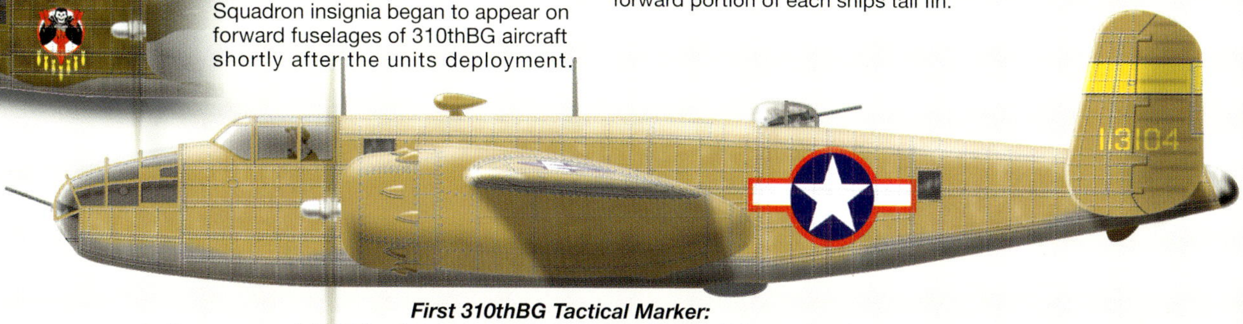

First 310thBG Tactical Marker:
In the summer of 1943 the first group marker was introduced. This consisted of a yellow horizontal band bordered top and bottom with thin black stripes. This marker was located on both inner and outer upper tail fin surfaces.

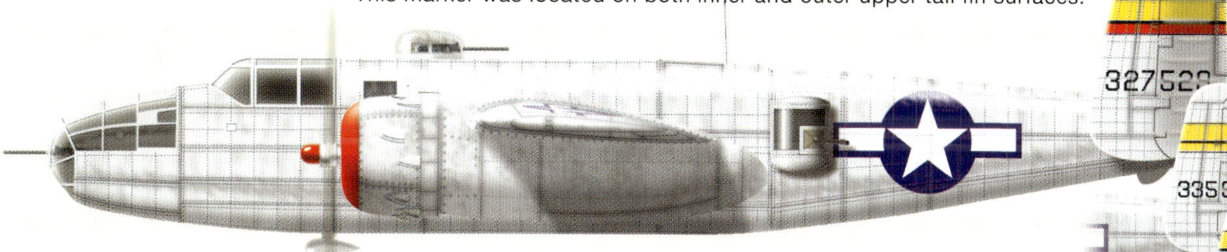

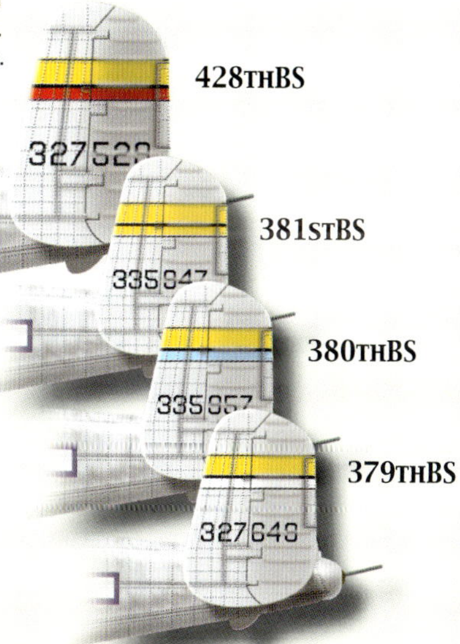

Modified Group Markings:
Early in 1944 the use of color as a means of squadron identification was introduced within the 310thBG. The lower third of the Group tail marker was repainted with the respective new squadron color, which was segregated from the upper yellow band by the use of a black stripe, approximately twice the thickness of the outer borders. In addition to these modifications, squadron colors were applied to engine cowling rings and propeller bosses.

• Assigned Twelfth AAF, Nov-1942 : Fifteenth AAF, Nov-1943 thru Jan-1944 : Twelfth AAF, Jan-1944 thru Jan-1945 : Seventh AAF, Apr-1945 thru V-J Day •

42d Bomb Wng
Aug/Nov-1943

47th Bomb Wng
August-1942

42d Bomb Wng
January-1944

319th Bombardment Group (M)

Insignia: (unofficial)
Sobriquet: 'Big Tail Birds'
aka; 'Col. Randy's Flying Circus'
Constituted:
319th Bomb Grp (M) / 19-Jun-42
Activated: 26-Jun-42
Redesignated:
319th Bomb Grp (L) / Feb-45

Design Variations:
The problem with unofficial insignia is apparent when researching units such as the 437thBS. Represented on this page are Four of several variations to this insignia that can be encountered when studying and analyzing war time photos of this particular squadron. The image at lower left is the design which shows up most frequently.

437th Bomb Sqdn (M)

Insignia: (unofficial)

Constituted:
437th Bomb Sqdn/19-Jun-42
Activated: 26-Jun-42
Redesignated:
437th Bomb Sqdn (L)/3-Feb-45

Aircraft Number-In-Squadron
01-24

438th Bomb Sqdn (M)

Insignia: (unofficial)

Constituted:
438th Bomb Sqdn/19-Jun-42
Activated: 26-Jun-42
Redesignated:
438th Bomb Sqdn (L)/3-Feb-45

Aircraft Number-In-Squadron
25-49

439th Bomb Sqdn (M)

Insignia: (unofficial)

Constituted:
439th Bomb Sqdn/19-Jun-42
Activated: 26-Jun-42
Redesignated:
439th Bomb Sqdn (L)/3-Feb-45

Aircraft Number-In-Squadron
50-74

440th Bomb Sqdn (M)

Insignia: (unofficial)

Constituted:
440th Bomb Sqdn/19-Jun-42
Activated: 26-Jun-42
Redesignated:
440th Bomb Sqdn (L)/3-Feb-45

Aircraft Number-In-Squadron
75-99

• Twelfth USAAF • Fifteenth USAAF •

Martin B-26 'Marauder'
circa: Nov-42 thru Nov-44

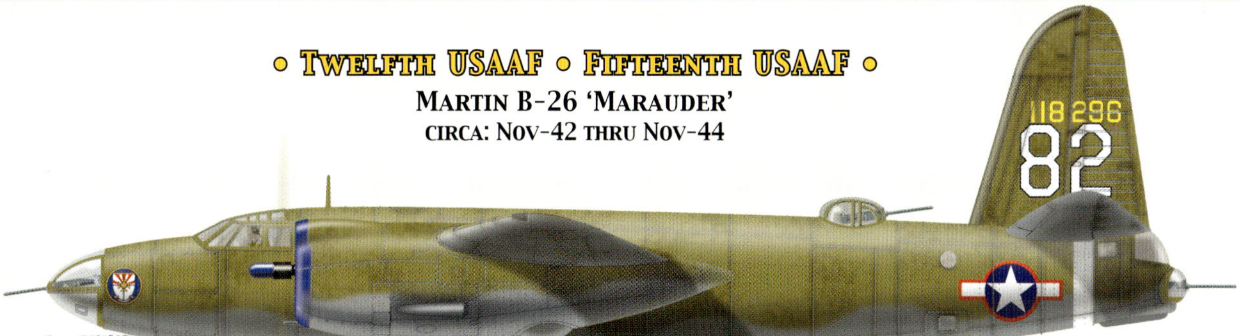

Group Markings:
The 319thBG displayed no distinctive tactical markings until the July of 1943 when the Group adopted Insignia White as the official unit color and began to display a vertical band of same on the rear fuselage, just forward the gunners station. Exact location and thickness of these devices varied considerably from one application to another. When natural metal finishes began to arrive at the Group, this device was outlined on either side with thin black stripes to enhance legibility. During this same time frame, the use of a 'number-in-squadron' system of aircraft identification was adopted. These numerical devices were also applied with white paint to the tail fin and rudder immediately below the serial number, being outlined in black on both camouflaged as well as metal finished surfaces. On short tailed Marauders the serial number was simply over painted. In the majority of these applications, condensed and often thinner weight numerals were utilized.

Insignia:
The 437thBS was known to have adorned a number of its Marauders with their squadron insignia. To what extent this practice may have been employed by the other three squadrons within the Group is uncertain.

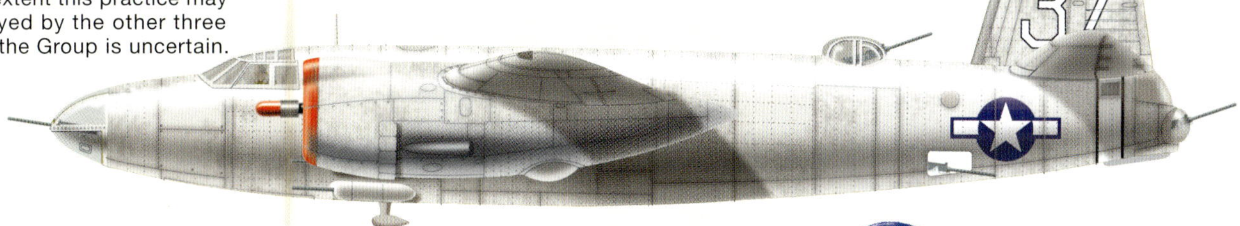

New Group Color:
Beginning in late 1944 the 319thBG began making a transition from the B-26 to the B-25 medium bomber. Cobalt blue was selected as the color to represent the Group, and the tail fins of their new aircraft were soon adorned with this hue. The 'number-in-squadron' system of individual aircraft recognition was retained and these designators were applied with white paint atop the serial number, the latter having been masked-out prior to applying the blue paint. Engine cowling rings and prop bosses similarly continued to be painted in respective squadron colors.

• Twelfth USAAF •

North American B-25 'Mitchell'
circa: Nov-44 thru Jan-45

• Assigned Twelfth AAF, Dec-1942 : Fifteenth AAF, Nov-1943 : Twelfth AAF, Jan-1944 : 1stTAF(P), Dec-1944 thru V-E Day •

42D Bomb Wng
August-1943

320th Bombardment Group (M)

Insignia/Approved: 3-Mar-43
Motto: 'Forever Battling'
Constituted:
320th Bomb Grp/19-Jun-42
Activated: 23-Jun-42

Early 441stBS
The image above was the original insignia of the 441stBS throughout the squadrons deployment in North Africa. Retained were the Lion Heart symbol and pilots wings in addition to the motto which roughly translates as...'the end depends upon the beginning'.

441st Bomb Sqdn (M)

Insignia/Replaced: 7-Apr-54

Constituted:
441st Bomb Sqdn (M)/19-Jun-42
Activated: 1-Jul-42

Aircraft
Number-In-Squadron
01-24

442d Bomb Sqdn (M)

Insignia/Replaced: 10-Aug-53

Constituted:
442d Bomb Sqdn (M)/19-Jun-42
Activated: 1-Jul-42

Aircraft
Number-In-Squadron
25-49

© Walt Disney

443d Bomb Sqdn (M)

Insignia/Replaced: 5-Mar-54

Constituted:
443d Bomb Sqdn (M)/19-Jun-42
Activated: 1-Jul-42

Aircraft
Number-In-Squadron
50-74

444th Bomb Sqdn (M)

Insignia/Replaced: 10-Aug-53

Constituted:
444th Bomb Sqdn (M)/19-Jun-42
Activated: 1-Jul-42

Aircraft
Number-In-Squadron
75-99

• Twelfth USAAF • Fifteenth AAF • First TAF(P) •

Martin B-26 'Marauder'
circa: Dec-42 thru V-E Day

Early Markings:
The 320thBG reportedly began combat operations using the last three digits of any given aircraft's serial number as a means of identification. To date no photographic evidence supporting this premise has yet surfaced. There are however, early deployment photos which do show the use of single call letters applied to the rear fuselage area in yellow paint.

Squadron Designators:
The application of individual unit insignia/markers was a common practice among all squadrons comprising the 320thBG. These devices were displayed on both sides of the forward fuselage area.

Permanent Tail Markings:
White, 48in. tall, two digit numbers began being applied to all 320thBG vertical stabilizers by the end of 1943. Identification Yellow began being used for these applications beginning in early 1944. In some cases the serial numbers were repainted white for contrast. Stencils used for the two digit identification applications were heaver in weight than those normally found on USAAF medium bombers serving in the Mediterranean.

© Walt Disney

Walt Disney's 'Thumper' was the 444thBS's first insignia and originally decorated the noses of many of the squadrons ships. In early 1943 a sharks mouth motif began to appear on some of the squadrons B-26's and the image caught on. The sharks mouth quickly became the unofficial nose art for the entire squadron and thereafter became a common symbol applied to a significant number of 444thBS Marauder noses. This same image was also included in the redesign of the squadron insignia (opposite page).

Group Color Marking:
In July 1943 the 42dBW issued a directive stating that all medium bomb groups within its command would henceforth display an 10in. vertical band of distinguishing unit color. In compliance with this directive the 320thBG began applying an Identification Yellow color strip 'in the neighborhood' of the rear gunners station. The location of these devices varied somewhat in actual applications.

Natural Metal Finishes:
The dual number yellow tail codes were retained after the introduction of NMF's, although the digits were now outlined in black for enhanced legibility. Similar black stripes were also added as borders to the either side of the vertical tail color recognition band.

Additional Color Markings:
In July of 1944 the 320thBG began painting the cowling rings and prop bosses of their assigned combat aircraft Insignia Red, even though Identification Yellow was the Groups designated color. Yellow cowling rings and prop bosses did appear occasionally on 320thBG aircraft, however red was the dominate color and the reason for this is as yet unanswered.

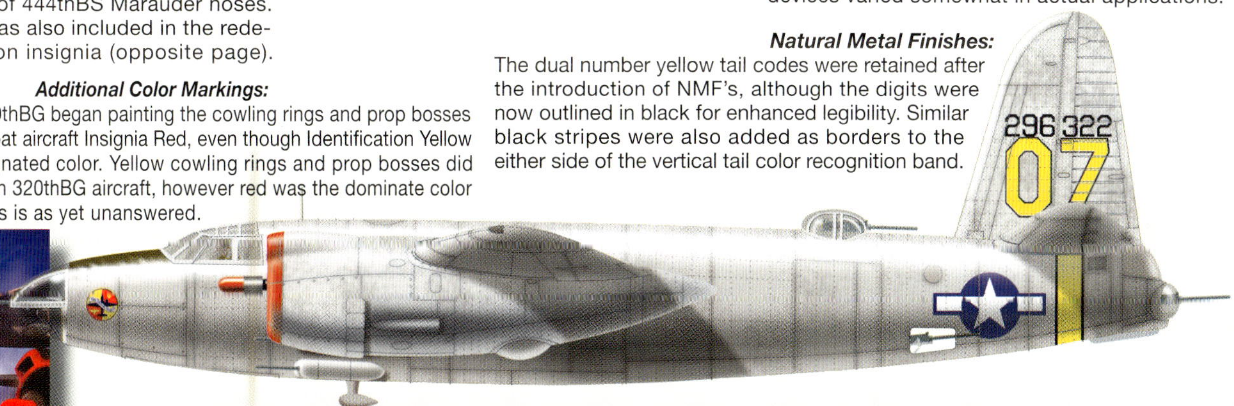

1.) La Senia, Algeria
c.2-Dec-42

2.) Tafaraoui, Algeria
28-Jan-43

3.) Montesquieu, Algeria
9-Apr-43

4.) Massicault, Tunisia
29-Jun-43

5.) El Bathan,Tunisia
28-Jul-43

6.) Decimomannue, Sardinia
c.1-Nov-43

7.) Alto, Corsica
c.18-Sep-44

8.) Y-7 Dijon/Longvic, France
11-Nov-44

9.) Y-9 Dole/Tavaux, France
1-Apr-45

• Assigned Twelfth AAF, Mar-1943 thru V-E Day •

57th Bomb Wng
January-1944

47th Bomb Wng
February-1943

321st Bombardment Group (M)

Insignia: Approved: 7-Nov-42
Motto:
'Perseverance, Vision And Duty'
Constituted:
321st Bomb Grp (M) / 19-Jun-42
Activated: 26-Jun-42

Alternate 321stBG Insignia:
Although the image depicted at left was the officially approved design for this group, the modified version above was commonly in evidence during the course of World War II.

445th Bomb Sqdn (M)

Insignia / Unapproved

Constituted:
445th Bomb Sqdn (M)/19-Jun-42
Activated: 26-Jun-42

I
Roman Numeral / 1943-1944
1-25
Number-In-Squadron-1945

446th Bomb Sqdn (M)

Insignia / Unapproved

Constituted:
446th Bomb Sqdn (M)/19-Jun-42
Activated: 26-Jun-42

II
Roman Numeral / 1943-1944
26-50
Number-In-Squadron-1945

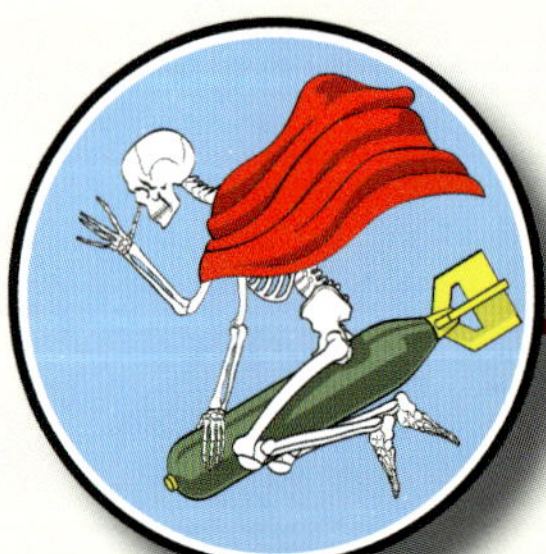

447th Bomb Sqdn (M)

Insignia / Unapproved

Constituted:
447th Bomb Sqdn (M)/19-Jun-42
Activated: 26-Jun-42

III
Roman Numeral / 1943-1944
51-75
Number-In-Squadron-1945

448th Bomb Sqdn (M)

Insignia / Unapproved

Constituted:
448th Bomb Sqdn (M)/19-Jun-42
Activated: 26-Jun-42

IV
Roman Numeral / 1943-1944
76-99
Number-In-Squadron-1945

• Twelfth USAAF •

North American B-25 'Mitchell'
circa: Mar-43 thru V-E Day

Tactical Tail Markings:
In the Summer of 1943 the 321stBG adopted the practice of identifying its aircraft by painting the entire tip of both tail fins. Although Insignia Red was definitely used for this purpose there are some indications that early on Identification Yellow was sometimes employed for the same purpose until late 1944. As of the publication deadline for this volume however, no authoritative documentation has surfaced to confirm this latter use of yellow as a unit designator. What is known for certain is that beginning in early 1944 the 321stBG began identifying its individual squadrons via the use of large Roman numerals painted on the upper surface area of both tail fins, white on camouflaged surfaces, black on NMF's.

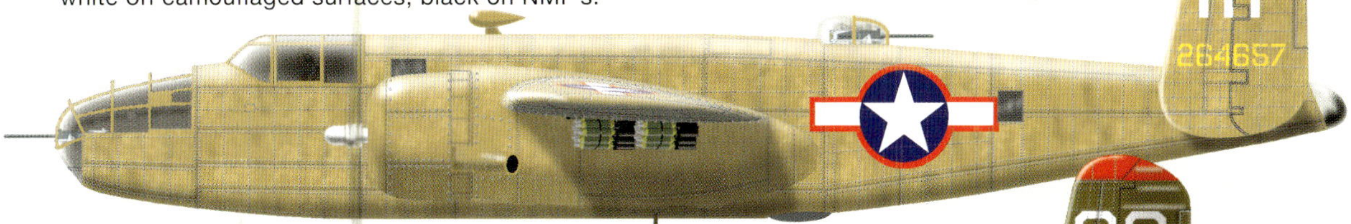

Change Of Tactical Markings:
In January 1945 the 319thBG(M), another unit operating B-25's and likewise assigned to the 57thBW, was rotated back to the U.S. in preparation for that units re-deployment to the Pacific Theater. The departure of the 319th made available its Arabic 'number-in-squadron' method of aircraft identification, which was quickly adopted by the 321st as a replacement for its existing system of Roman numerals. These new Arabic two-digit devices were applied as had been their predecessors, white on camouflaged aircraft and black for NMF's. The use of the Insignia Red fin tips on both surface types was continued until wars end.

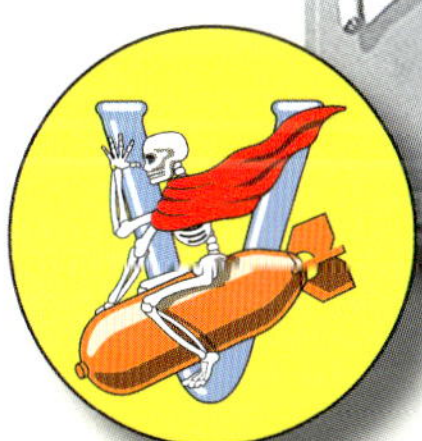

447thBG Variations:
By far the most common alteration to this insignia during the war years can be seen in the black & white inset at left. This Headquarters signage was typical of a simplified skeletal figure than that which was to be found in the original design. This simplification was carried over onto many A-2 jackets. The addition of the background 'V' for Victory symbol, while not part of the original configuration, was nevertheless popular with many crewmen.

More On The Color Quandary:
The question over use of tactical colors by the 321st is perhaps best illustrated by these two photos. The top image was taken sometime in 1944 while the bottom photo dates to 1945. There is a distinct contrasting variation in tonal value between the two fin tip applications. Whether simply a matter of light refraction or color differential is the issue currently under scrutiny.

• Assigned Ninth AAF, Mar-1943 : Twelfth AAF, Aug-1943 thru V-E Day •

57th Bomb Wng 1943-44/1944-45

XII Tac Air Comd 1943-1944

IX Bmr Comd 1943

340th Bombardment Group (M)

Insignia: Replaced / 12-Sep-55

Motto: (none)

Constituted: 340th Bmb Grp/10-Aug-42

Activated: 20-Aug-42

Common 486thBS Variation:
Whether due to un-refined artistic skills, indifference or other factors, the images above were the result of some field applications of this particular insignia.

486th Bomb Sqdn (M)

Insignia/Arrroved: 26-Aug-43

Constituted:
486th Bomb Sqdn (M)/10-Aug-42
Activated: 20-Aug-42

487th Bomb Sqdn (M)

Insignia/Readopted: 15-May-59

Sobriquet: 'The Dogface Squadron'

Constituted:
487th Bomb Sqdn (M)/10-Aug-42
Activated: 20-Aug-42

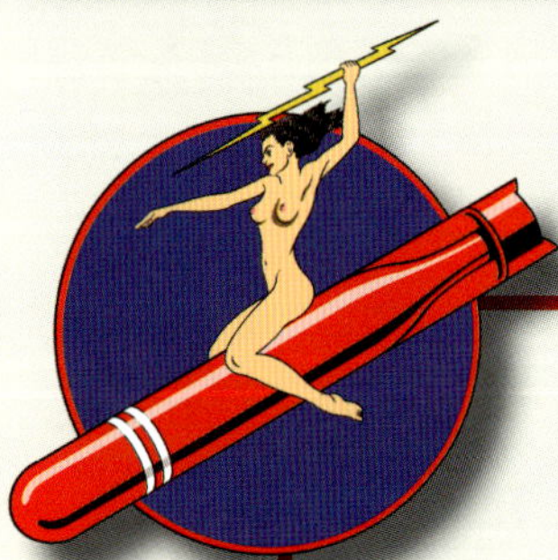

488th Bomb Sqdn (M)

Insignia/Replaced: 16-Sep-54

Constituted:
488th Bomb Sqdn (M)/10-Aug-42
Activated: 20-Aug-42

489th Bomb Sqdn (M)

Insignia/Replaced: 27-Oct-59

Organized:
77th Aero Sqdn/13-Aug-17
Redesignated:
489th Sero Sqdn/1-Feb-18
Consolidated/Constituted:
489th Bomb Sqdn (M)/10-Aug-42
Activated: 20-Aug-42

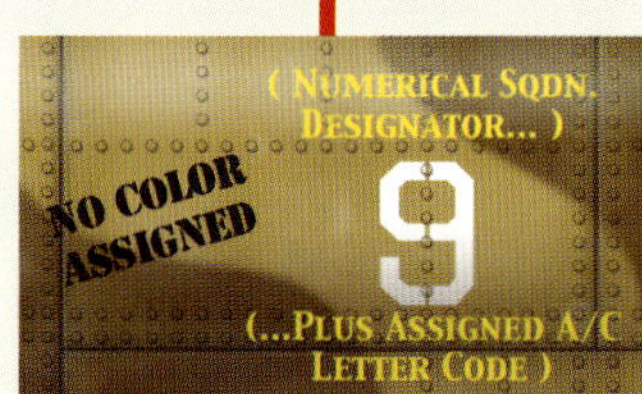

• Twelfth USAAF •

North American B-25 'Mitchell'

circa: Mar-43 thru V-E Day

Original Inventory: The 340thBG'sfirst consignment of Mitchell's arrived in Egypt painted an overall RAF Desert Pink. Allied Recognition Flashes were applied to both sides of each tail fin, the outward facing images affixed immediately above the a/c serial number. The squadron numerical designator and individually assigned aircraft letters were positioned near the upper tail fin outfacing surfaces and painted with Insignia White.

Second Phase: With subsequent re-postings to airfields along the Tunisian coastline, a new paint scheme was called for, one that was more compatible with the lusher surroundings. A standard tri-color camouflage pattern was thus adopted.

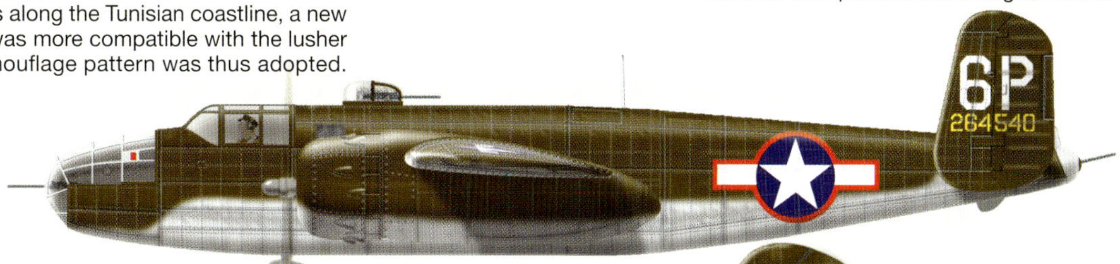

Tail Fin Codes: As with other B-25 groups of the 12thAAF, the 340thBG employed the use of a narrower character width for tail code applications than what would normally be found in use by other AAF units serving in the Mediterranean Theater during the course of the war.

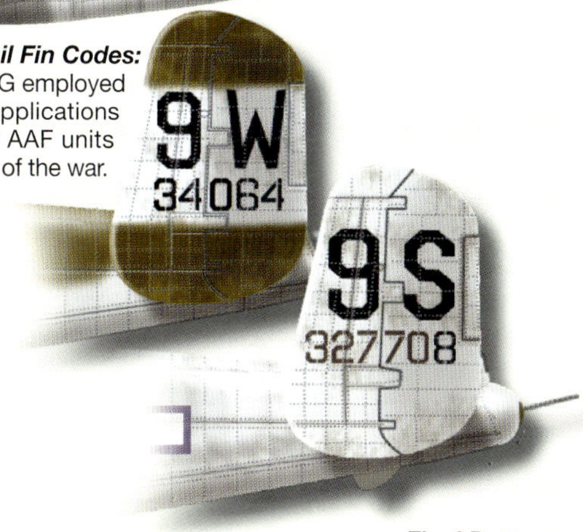

'The Dogface Squadron': Although outside the 'tactical marking' arena, the dominate nose art of the 487thBS is historically worthy of note here. While it might seem unusual for a bunch of fly boys to adopt Bill Mauldin's long suffering infantrymen, ***Willie & Joe***, as the squadrons overall nose art theme, this was nevertheless the case. So many 487thBS B-25's ended up with images of Mauldin's now famous ground pounders, that the squadron proudly earned its very un-Army Air Force like non-de-plume...'Dogface'.

Final Patterns: As the threat of attacks by the Luftwaffe began to diminish, so too did the complexity of paint schemes on 340thBG Mitchells'. The tri-color camouflage made way for a simple upper surface coat of Olive Drab until finally, by wars end, all replacement aircraft were assigned for combat operations with metal finishes. With the exception of dropping the Recognition Flash and the subsequent increase in size of the tail codes, the tactical tail markings of the 340thBG remained unchanged throughout the war.

• Assigned Ninth AAF, Oct-1942 : Twelfth AAF, Sep-1943 : Fifteenth AAF, Nov-1943 thru V-E Day •

47th Bomb Wng 1943

IX Bmr Comd 1942

376th Bombardment Group (H)

Insignia: Approved: 8-Nov-51
(from WWII design)
Motto: 'Liberandos'
Constituted:
387th Bmb Grp (H) / 19-Oct-42
Activated: 31-Oct-42

376thBG Insignia:
In spite of the post war approval application date, there are ample wartime photos depicting the use of this image to ensure that this design did in fact represent the 376th during the course of WWII.

512th Bomb Sqdn (H)

Insignia/Arroved: 6-Jan-44

Constituted:
512th Bomb Sqdn (H)/19-Oct-42
Activated: 31-Oct-42

No Color Assigned — Squadron Codes Unknown

513th Bomb Sqdn (H)

Insignia/Arroved: 6-Jan-44

Constituted:
513th Bomb Sqdn (H)/19-Oct-42
Activated: 31-Oct-42

No Color Assigned — Squadron Codes Unknown

514th Bomb Sqdn (H)

Insignia/Replaced: 26-Mar-57

Constituted:
514th Bomb Sqdn (H)/19-Oct-42
Activated: 31-Oct-42

No Color Assigned — Squadron Codes Unknown

515th Bomb Sqdn (H)

Insignia/Arroved: 6-Jan-44

Constituted:
515th Bomb Sqdn (H)/19-Oct-42
Activated: 31-Oct-42

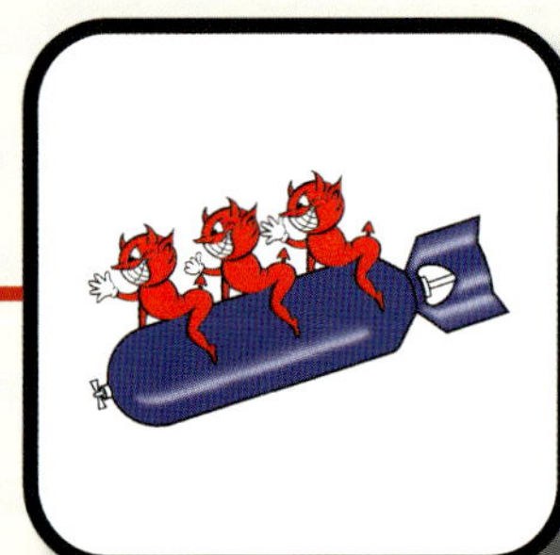

No Color Assigned — Squadron Codes Unknown

• Ninth USAAF, Twelfth USAAF, Fifteenth USAAF •

Consolidated B-24 'Liberator'

circa: Oct-42 thru V-E Day

Early 9th/12thAAF Tactical Markings:
Initial combat operations created little need for elaborate aircraft markings. What little there was consisted of a numerical or single call letter located on the outward facing surfaces of both tail fins accompanied by an Allied Recognition Flash. This latter devise was typically located on both outward and inward facing surfaces. A large number of assigned aircraft were repainted RAF Desert Pink soon after arrival in the T/O, and serial numbers were reapplied using either yellow, black and sometimes white paint.

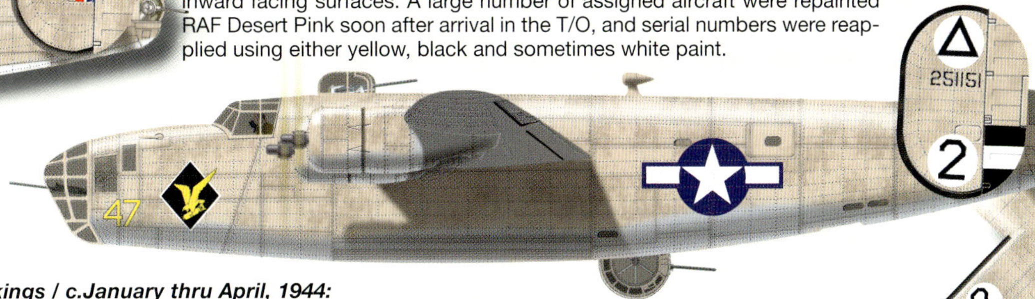

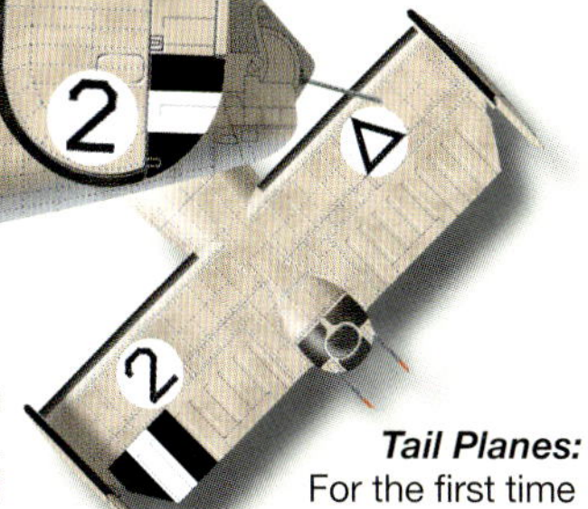

15thAAF Tactical Markings / c.January thru April, 1944:
As the strategic bombing offensive intensified, the larger Heavy Bomber formations gave rise to the need for an improved method of unit recognition. In the early part of 1944, the 476thBW adopted a heavy black outlined equilateral triangle mounted on a white disc as its tactical marker. Each bomb group assigned to the 47thBW was allocated a numerical designator (No.2 in the case of the 376thBG) which was likewise to be displayed on a similar white disc. This latter devise was directed to be affixed near the bottom of the tail fin, while the former would be located at the top. The use of the b&w panel tactical group marking is reputed to pre-date these circular devices, but precise dates regarding this are uncertain. Two (sometimes three) digit aircraft numbers, either in-line or stacked, were known to have been applied to the tail rudders in some instances, prior to the later more standardized useof two-digit nose numbers.

Tail Planes:
For the first time within the 376thBG tactical unit markings were also adopted for use on the upper tail surfaces. These were identical to those devices located on the fins.

15thAAF Tactical Markings / c.May 1944 thru V-E Day:
By this time the application of squadron insignia to individual aircraft was a wide spread practice throughout the 376thBG. So too was the use of individual two-digit aircraft codes these were generally located forward the respective squadron insignia with a large number applied using yellow paint with a solid black contour outline. In other instances solid black numerals were used. Although there appears to have been some distinct sequential allocation of these numbers to the respective squadrons (I.E., number-in-squadron) the specific lot assignments is unknown.
With the ever increasing number of NMF replacement aircarft an improved method of airborne visual identification was needed. In the case of the 376thBG, the entire tail surface was divided diagonally with the bottom half receiving a coat of solid black paint as the Groups new tactical tail marking. The former 376thBG 'Circle/2' designator was discarded while the 47thBW's 'Circle/Triangle' was retained on outward facing tail fin surfaces, straddling the upper fin and rudder intersection seam. Serial numbers were generally eliminated entirely with this application.
An even more dramatic change was in evidence on the upper tail plane surfaces. The earlier geometric symbols were completely replaced with an extensive application of black and yellow paint. The upper image at right depicts the new tactical marking as first proposed. The lower image represents the vast majority of actual field applications.

• ASSIGNED: FIFTEENTH AAF, JAN-1944 THRU V-E DAY •

47TH BOMB WNG
JANUARY-1944

449TH BOMBARDMENT GROUP (H)

INSIGNIA: (UNOFFICIAL)
SOBRIQUET: 'THE FLYING HORSEMEN'
CONSTITUTED:
449TH BMB GRP (H)/6-APR-43
ACTIVATED: 1-MAY-43
REDESIGNATED:
449TH BMB GRP (VH): 1-MAY-43

449thBG Marker

While at first glance this tactical marker may appear to resemble an airfield layout, it is in fact a Western livestock brand, the ***'Bar A'***. This device was developed in honor of the 449th's first combat C/O, Col. Darr H. Alkire, who's ship was lost to enemy flak on a bombing mission over Aviano A/F, Italy on 31-Jan-44.

716TH BOMB SQDN (H)

INSIGNIA: (UNOFFICIAL)
SOBRIQUET: '?'

CONSTITUTED:
716TH BMB SQDN (H)/6-APR-43
ACTIVATED: 1-MAY-43
REDESIGNATED:
716TH BMB SQDN (VH)/23-MAY-45

NO COLOR ASSIGNED
TWO-DIGIT TAIL RUDDER CODES

717TH BOMB SQDN (H)

INSIGNIA: APPROVED/10-JUL-44

CONSTITUTED:
717TH BMB SQDN (H)/6-APR-43
ACTIVATED: 1-MAY-43
REDESIGNATED:
717TH BMB SQDN (VH)/23-MAY-45

NO COLOR ASSIGNED
TWO-DIGIT TAIL RUDDER CODES

718TH BOMB SQDN (H)

INSIGNIA: APPROVED/21-MAR-57
(FROM WWII DESIGN)

CONSTITUTED:
718TH BMB SQDN (H)/6-APR-43
ACTIVATED: 1-MAY-43
REDESIGNATED:
718TH BMB SQDN (VH)/23-MAY-45

NO COLOR ASSIGNED
TWO-DIGIT TAIL RUDDER CODES

719TH BOMB SQDN (H)

INSIGNIA: (UNOFFICIAL)

CONSTITUTED:
719TH BMB SQDN (H)/6-APR-43
ACTIVATED: 1-MAY-43
REDESIGNATED:
719TH BMB SQDN (VH)/7-SEP-45

NO COLOR ASSIGNED
TWO-DIGIT TAIL RUDDER CODES

• Fifteenth USAAF •

Consolidated B-24 'Liberator'
circa: Jan-44 thru V-E Day

1st Pattern Markings:
The 449thBG was assigned as its tactical marking an Insignia Blue equilateral triangle and an Arabic number '3', both to be enclosed within white circular discs on both tail fins. These two tactical markings were duplicated on the upper tail plane surfaces where additionally, the ***Bar-A*** group symbol was located on the upper port side elevator surface. Use of this latter devise on Tail rudders appears to have been sporadic and eventually phased out entirely when individual two-digit aircraft identification numbers were adopted and subsequently applied to the rudders with white paint. The positioning of these numerical devices varied from mid to upper rudder surface area. Serial numbers were likewise handled in a wide assortment of ways ranging from re-application to complete removal from the tail fin altogether.

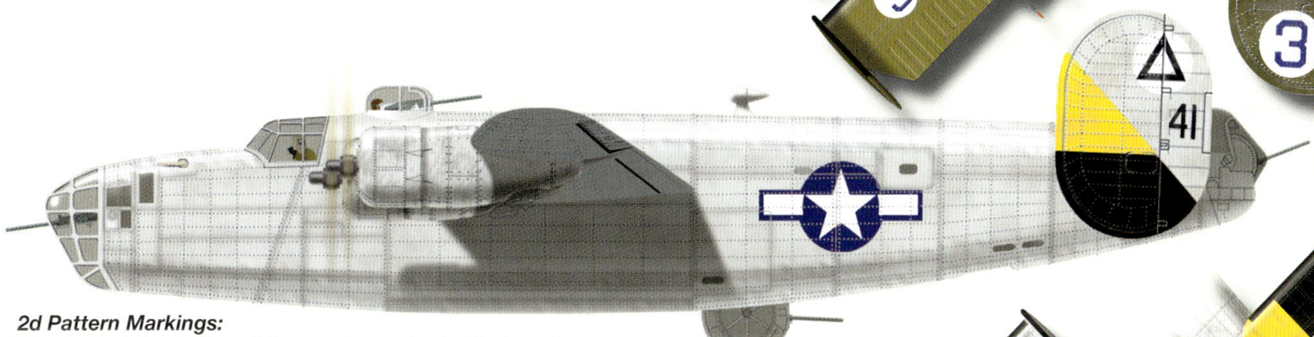

2d Pattern Markings:
Prior to the introduction of the new two-color tactical markings, numerous replacement aircraft had upper tail-planes adorned with only the 'Bar-A' Group designator, This linear configuration consisted of an intersecting series of 6 to 8in. wide stripes, Insignia Blue or Black in color. As with earlier applications these devices were located on the upper port side elevator surface ,but by late 1944 time had disappeared from the tail fins altogether. In early 1945 a new tactical tail marking was approved for the 449thBG, and this consisted of the tail fin being divided in half diagonally with the lower half being further divided in half horizontally. The upper half of this sub-division was painted yellow while the lower half was solid black.
Use of the Triangle/Circle was retained albeit repositioned straddling the intersection of fin and rudder. The two-digit numerical aircraft codes were, from this point on, pretty much consistently located in the mid rudder area. The use of color on upper tail-plane surfaces was similarly adopted.

• Assigned: Fifteenth AAF, Dec-1943 thru V-E Day •

47TH Bomb Wng
December-1943

450TH Bombardment Group (H)

Insignia: (unofficial)
Sobriquet: 'The Cottontails'
Constituted:
450TH Bmb Grp (H)/6-Apr-43
Activated: 1-May-43
Redesignated:
450TH Bmb Grp (VH)/May-45

Group Insignia Note:
Although no official documentation relating to this design has yet been located, the design at left represents the insignia reputedly displayed by the 450thBG during WWII. A slightly modified version (as depicted above) is the current official insignia of the 450thBG Association.

720TH Bomb Sqdn (H)

Insignia/Replaced: 11-Aug-54

Constituted:
720TH Bomb Sqdn (H)/6-Apr-43
Activated: 1-May-43
Redesignated:
720TH Bomb Sqdn (VH)/23-May-45

Two-Digit Tail Rudder Codes
No Color Assigned
1 thru 20

721ST Bomb Sqdn (H)

Insignia/Replaced: 22-Jun-55

Constituted:
721ST Bomb Sqdn (H)/6-Apr-43
Activated: 1-May-43
Redesignated:
721ST Bomb Sqdn (VH)/23-May-45

Two-Digit Tail Rudder Codes
No Color Assigned
21 thru 39

722[D] Bomb Sqdn (H)

Insignia/(unofficial)
Sobriquet: 'Holy Joes'

Constituted:
722[D] Bomb Sqdn (H)/6-Apr-43
Activated: 1-May-43
Redesignated:
722[D] Bomb Sqdn (VH)/23-May-45

Two-Digit Tail Rudder Codes
No Color Assigned
40 thru 59

723[D] Bomb Sqdn (H)

Insignia/Replaced: 22-Jun-55

Constituted:
723[D] Bomb Sqdn (H)/6-Apr-43
Activated: 1-May-43

Two-Digit Tail Rudder Codes
No Color Assigned
60 thru 99

• Fifteenth USAAF •

Consolidated B-24 'Liberator'

circa: Dec-43 thru V-E Day

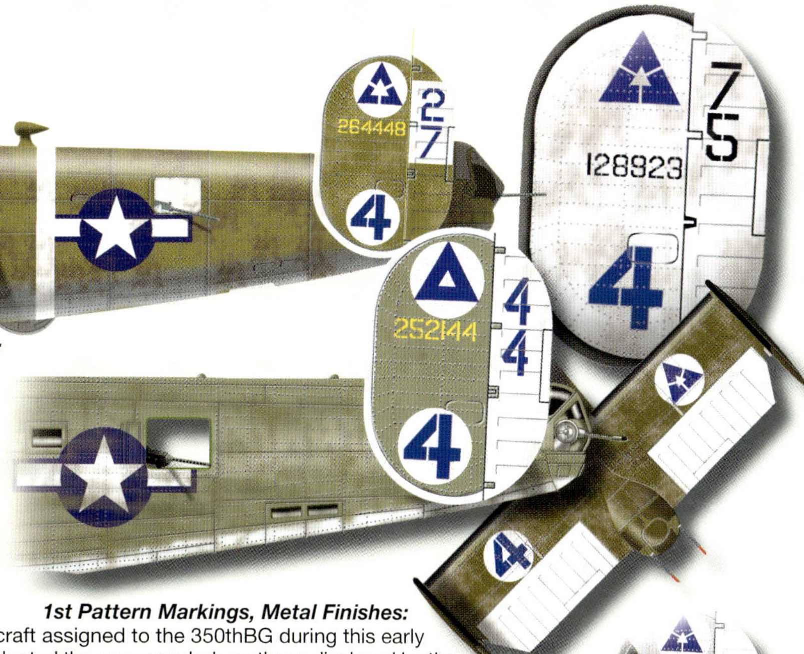

1st Pattern Markings, Painted Surfaces:
In the early part of 1944, all fundamental markings utilized by the 450thBG(H) were consistent with 47thBW directives. The 450thBG was assigned the Arabic numeral Four (4) as its unit designator which, along with the blue 47thBW equilateral triangle, was affixed to both the outer fin and upper tail plane surfaces as depicted. Two color camouflaged empennage had outer rudder and upper Elevator surfaces painted white. Individual aircraft 'number-in-squadron' two-digit designators were applied to the upper rudder surfaces using Insignia Blue paint. There were numerous variations among these applications as evidenced by the few examples shown.

1st Pattern Markings, Metal Finishes:
NMF aircraft assigned to the 350thBG during this early period adopted the same symbols as those displayed by the camouflaged ships, some with one notable difference. While many of the 450thBG's metal airframes carried the white discs, others in this category applied the 47thBW triangle and numerical designator directly onto the metal surface, sans the white circles. With or without the discs however, during this time period both the rudder and elevator surfaces were generally painted white.

Insignia:
Validation of unofficial unit insignia all to often hinges upon random photos such as these of the 450thBG(H).

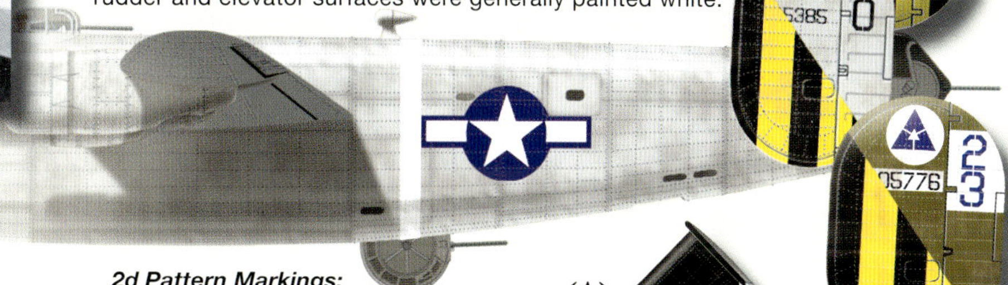

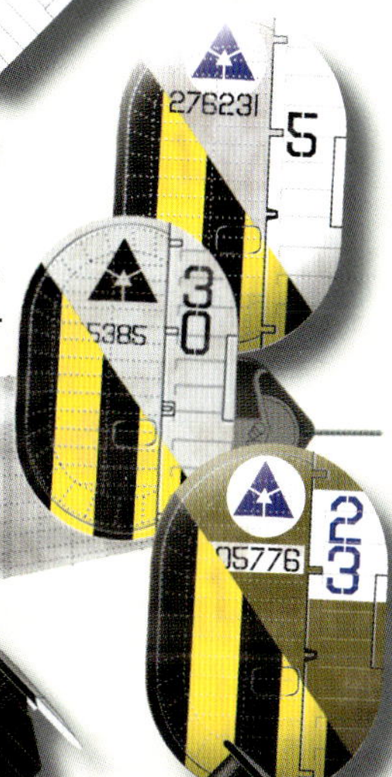

2d Pattern Markings:
The earlier 'Circle-4' Group designator began disappearing by mid-summer 1944, replaced with a series of five alternating black & yellow vertical stripes on the lower forward diagonal half of tail surfaces. The use of the 47thBW 'Circle-Triangle' on the upper tail fin area was retained, as was the use of the two-digit 'number-in-squadron' rudder markings. As with First Pattern tactical markings, there were numerous various in actual field applications. As with other 47thBW groups, the 450thBG adopted a new color pattern as a replacement to the original marking system employed on the upper tail plane surfaces. Original specifications (A) differed from the actual color pattern (B) which ultimately ended up on the operational combat aircraft of the 450thBG(H).

• Assigned: Fifteenth AAF, Jan-1944 thru V-E Day •

49TH Bomb Wng
January-1944

451ST Bombardment Group (H)

Insignia: (unofficial)

Sobriquet: 'The Fighting 451ST'

Constituted:
451ST Bmb Grp (H) / 6-Apr-43

Activated: 1-May-43

Runner-Up:
In early 1945 an inter-unit design contest was held to come up with an insignia for the 451stBG. The winning submission (at left) was from Sgt. McAvin of the 727thBS. The above design was a very close contender, and was the creation of Lt. C.L. March of the 724thBS.

*724TH Bomb Sqdn (H)

Insignia/(unofficial)

Constituted:
724TH Bomb Sqdn (H)/6-Apr-43
Activated: 1-May-43

* All attempts to date to establish the colors used in this insignia have proved unsuccessful, thus the b&w image.

01-24
Aircraft
'Number-In-Squadron'

725TH Bomb Sqdn (H)

Insignia/(unofficial)

Constituted:
725TH Bomb Sqdn (H)/6-Apr-43
Activated: 1-May-43

25-49
Aircraft
'Number-In-Squadron'

726TH Bomb Sqdn (H)

Insignia/Approved: 8-Jul-44

Constituted:
726TH Bomb Sqdn (H)/6-Apr-43
Activated: 1-May-43

50-74
Aircraft
'Number-In-Squadron'

727TH Bomb Sqdn (H)

Insignia/Approved: 29-Aug-44

Constituted:
727TH Bomb Sqdn (H)/6-Apr-43
Activated: 1-May-43

75-99
Aircraft
'Number-In-Squadron'

• Fifteenth USAAF •

Consolidated B-24 'Liberator'

circa: Dec-43 thru V-E Day

1st Pattern Markings:
Early markings were simple devices confined to the tail fins and entailed of a 49th Bomb Wing designator and the 451stBG symbol, an Arabic No. '1'. The 49thBW symbol consisted of a circle within a disc which was positioned on the upper fin surface, with the 451stBG designator near the bottom. Overall average height of both these devices was approximately 36in.

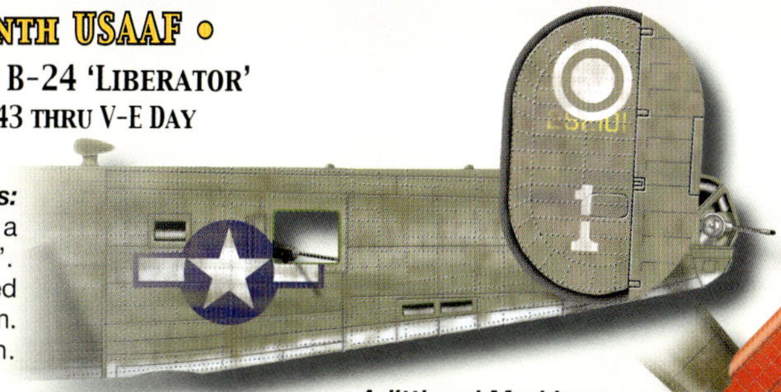

Adittional Markings:
In the early Spring (c.March) of 1944, a directive was issued instructing the squadrons to begin marking the upper tail plane surfaces (as depicted). From a maintenance point of view, this configuration presented a certain set of problems entailing elevator balancing, and it is thus uncertain just how extensively this marking pattern was actually employed.

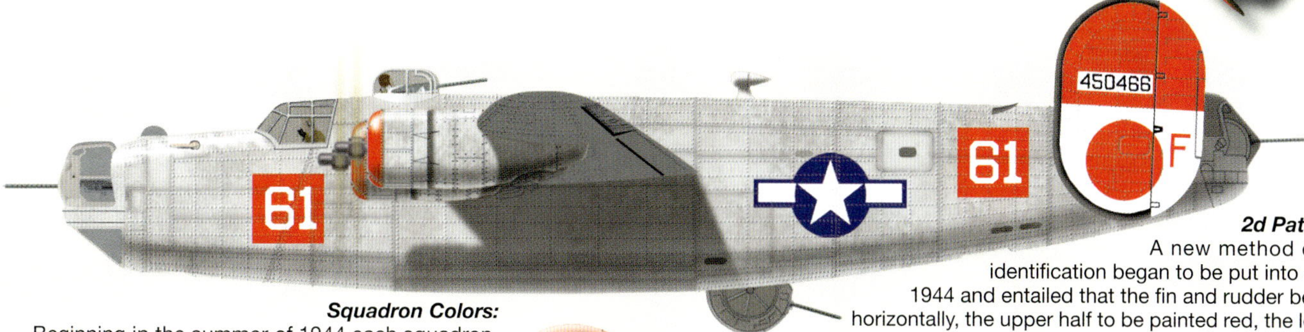

2d Pattern Markings:
A new method of aircraft unit identification began to be put into effect in May of 1944 and entailed that the fin and rudder be divided in half horizontally, the upper half to be painted red, the lower half white. A large (approx. 48in.) red circle was to be centered on the bottom white section, with an individual red call letter (approx. 28in.) located just aft, on the rudder surface. Aircraft serial numbers were generally masked out, thus eliminating the need of re-paint these devices following the application of the red paint. Ultimately the white paint was eliminated entirely, letting the metal finish stand alone as a contrast to the red. 'Number-in-squadron' numerical designators were often, but not always, affixed to both the forward and aft fuselage areas in a variety of methods. The images below depict the originally prescribed upper tail plane tactical markings **(A)** versus **(B)**, the actual pattern actually incorporated within the 451stBG.

Squadron Colors:
Beginning in the summer of 1944 each squadron within the 451stBG began a policy of painting the engine cowling rings in their respective colors.

(A)

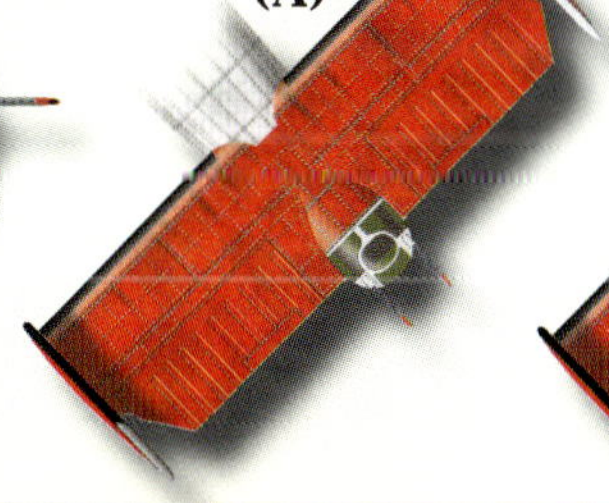

(B)

• ASSIGNED: FIFTEENTH AAF, DEC-1943 THRU V-E DAY •

304TH BOMB WNG
JANUARY-1944

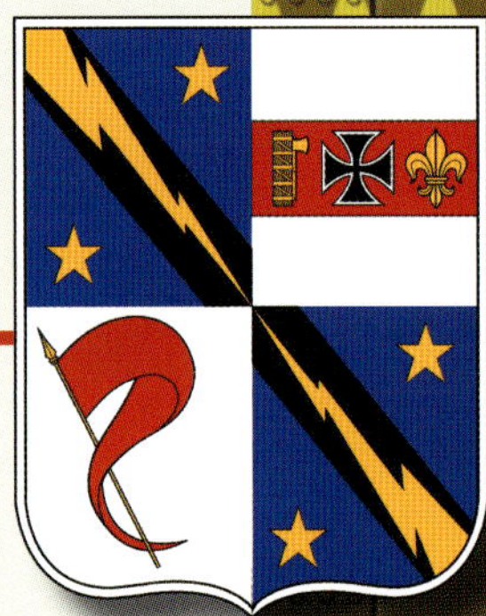

454TH BOMBARDMENT GROUP (H)

INSIGNIA: (UNOFFICIAL)
CONSTITUTED:
454TH BMB GRP (H)/14-MAY-43
ACTIVATED: 1-JUN-43
REDESIGNATED:
454TH BMB GRP (VH)/AUG-45

736TH BOMB SQDN (H)

NO KNOWN SQUADRON INSIGNIA

INSIGNIA/(UNKNOWN)

CONSTITUTED:
736TH BOMB SQDN (H)/14-MAY-43
ACTIVATED: 1-JUN-43
REDESIGNATED:
736TH BOMB SQDN (VH)/5-AUG-45

SQUADRON CODES (SEE TEXT)

737TH BOMB SQDN (H)

NO KNOWN SQUADRON INSIGNIA

INSIGNIA/(UNKNOWN)

CONSTITUTED:
737TH BOMB SQDN (H)/14-MAY-43
ACTIVATED: 1-JUN-43
REDESIGNATED:
737TH BOMB SQDN (VH)/5-AUG-45

SQUADRON CODES (SEE TEXT)

738TH BOMB SQDN (H)

NO KNOWN SQUADRON INSIGNIA

INSIGNIA/(UNKNOWN)

CONSTITUTED:
738TH BOMB SQDN (H)/14-MAY-43
ACTIVATED: 1-JUN-43
REDESIGNATED:
738TH BOMB SQDN (VH)/5-AUG-45

SQUADRON CODES (SEE TEXT)

739TH BOMB SQDN (H)

NO KNOWN SQUADRON INSIGNIA

INSIGNIA/(UNKNOWN)

CONSTITUTED:
739TH BOMB SQDN (H)/14-MAY-43
ACTIVATED: 1-JUN-43
REDESIGNATED:
739TH BOMB SQDN (VH)/5-AUG-45

SQUADRON CODES (SEE TEXT)

Consolidated B-24 'Liberator'

circa: Dec-43 thru V-E Day

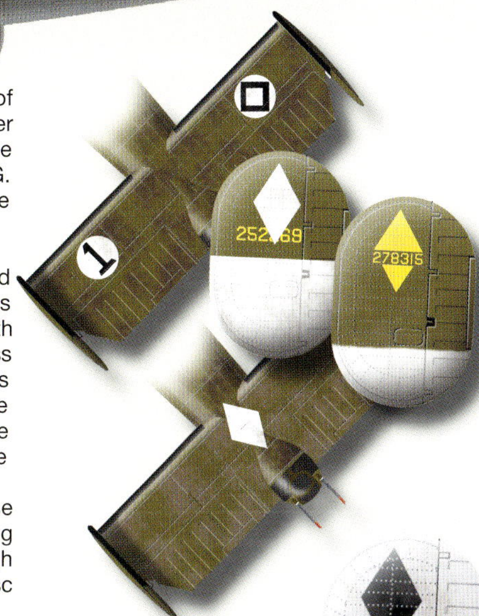

1st Pattern Markings:

When first deployed to the MTO, 454thBG tactical markings consisted of dual 36in. white discs positioned on the outer tail fin surfaces. The upper disc contained the 304thBW black geometric diamond shape while the lower contained the Arabic #1, the numerical designator for the 454thBG. Both of these marking devices were duplicated on the upper tail plane surfaces, the Group designator located on the port side.

2d Pattern Markings:

Officially adopted in late May of 1944, Identification White was assigned as the official color to represent the 454thBG. The lower fin disc was replaced with this newly assigned color which was generally outlined with a thin black border on NMF's. Use of this color was intended to encompass the entire lower half of the tail surface. In actual practice however, this 'equal division' often ended up being somewhat less than that, the result of which was that the surface area actually allocated for the white paint could end up being little more than 1/4 of the tail surface rather than the specified 50/50 split.

A single large diamond replaced the previous tactical device and these were applied using either yellow or white paint, sometimes over-painting the serial number or masked out to allow the numbers to show through after application of the new 304thBW designator. The upper tail-plane disc devices were similarly replaced with a single diamond shape.

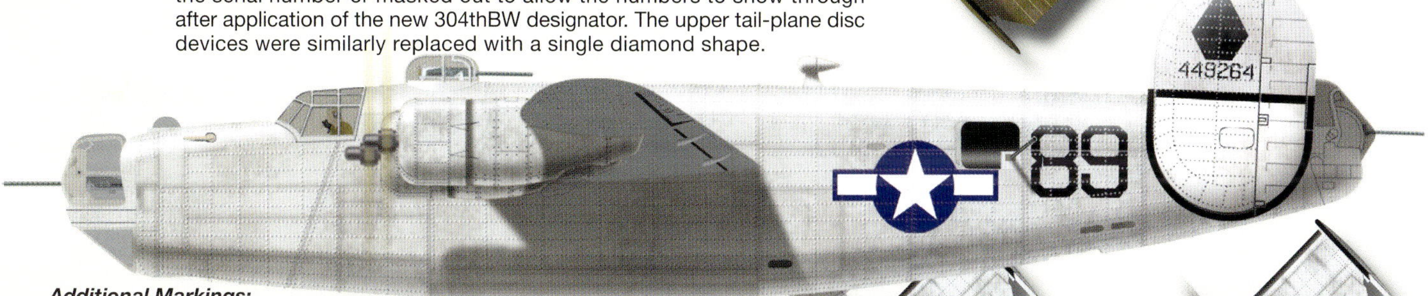

Additional Markings:

At some point in late 1944 the 454thBG adopted the use of what appears to be a 'number-in-squadron' method of aircraft identification. These devices were approximately 48in. tall standard USAAF block Arabic numerals, and were applied aft the waist gunners station using black paint on NMF, white or yellow on camouflaged surfaces. Although not confirmed at this time the numerical squadron assignment is believed to be as follows;

736thBombSqdn = 0-20 **737thBombSqdn = 21-39**
738thBombSqdn = 40-59 **739thBombSqdn = 60-99**

Tail-plane surface markings were modified as shown in the examples at right.

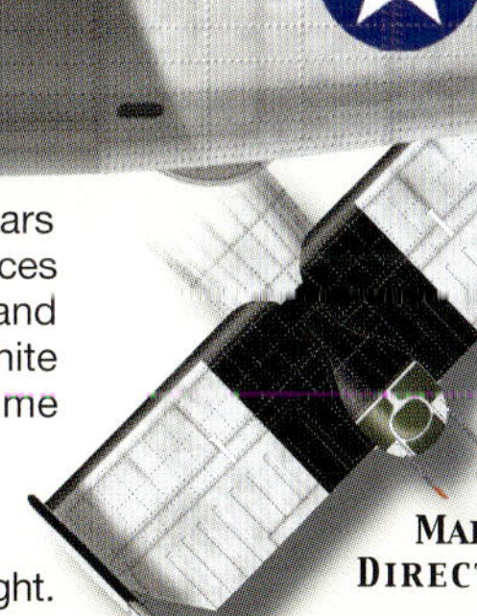

Tail-Plane Marking As Directed

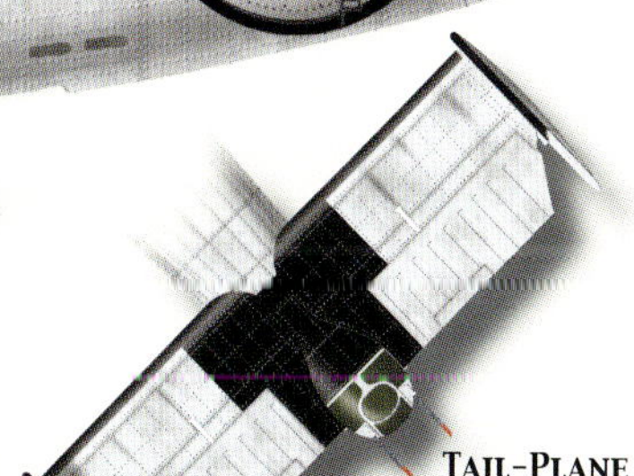

Tail-Plane Marking As Adopted

• Assigned: Fifteenth AAF, Jan-1944 thru V-E Day •

304th Bomb Wng
January-1944

455th Bombardment Group (H)

Insignia: (Unofficial)
Sobiquet:
The Vulgar Vultures'
Constituted:
455th Bmb Grp (H)/14-May-43
Activated: 1-Jun-43

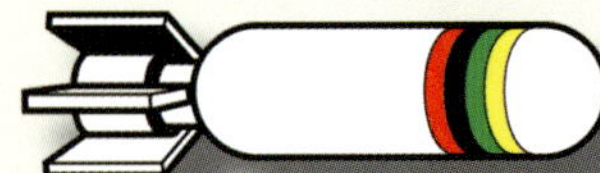

Color Notes:
With the exception of its use in differentiating squadron insignia, the 455thBG is not known to have employed the use of color as a tactical marking devise on their combat aircraft at any time during their overseas deployment in WWII.

740th Bomb Sqdn (H)

Insignia/(Unofficial)

Constituted:
740th Bomb Sqdn (H)/14-May-43
Activated: 1-Jun-43

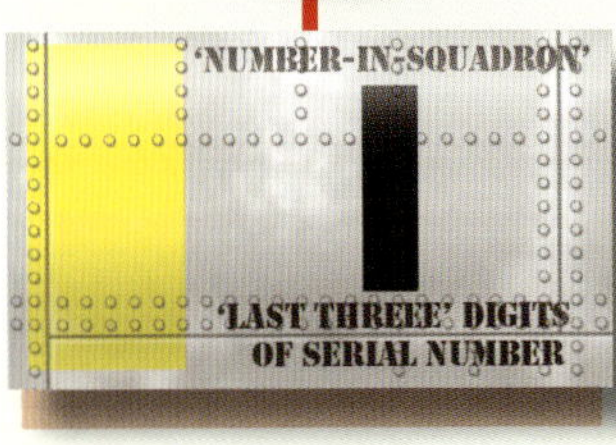

741st Bomb Sqdn (H)

Insignia/(Unofficial)

Constituted:
741st Bomb Sqdn (H)/14-May-43
Activated: 1-Jun-43

742d Bomb Sqdn (H)

Insignia/(Unofficial)

Constituted:
742d Bomb Sqdn (H)/14-May-43
Activated: 1-Jun-43

743d Bomb Sqdn (H)

Insignia/(Unofficial)

Constituted:
743dBomb Sqdn (H)/14-May-43
Activated: 1-Jun-43

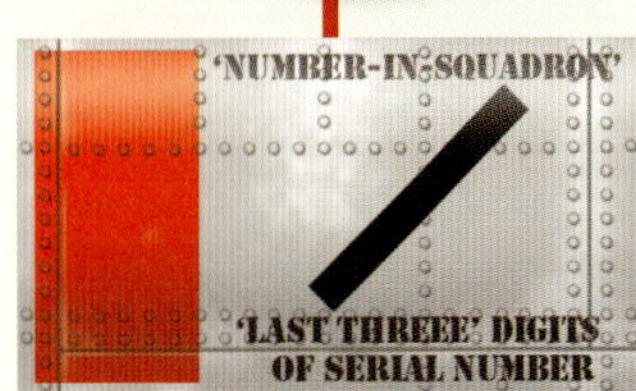

• Fifteenth USAAF •

Consolidated B-24 'Liberator'

circa: Jan-44 thru V-E Day

1st Pattern Markings:
These markings were consistent with those adopted for use within the 304thBW beginning in early 1944. An Arabic numeral '2' was chosen to stand for the 455thBG and was displayed as shown. Several symbols were adopted in this same time frame to represent the four squadrons (see opposite page).

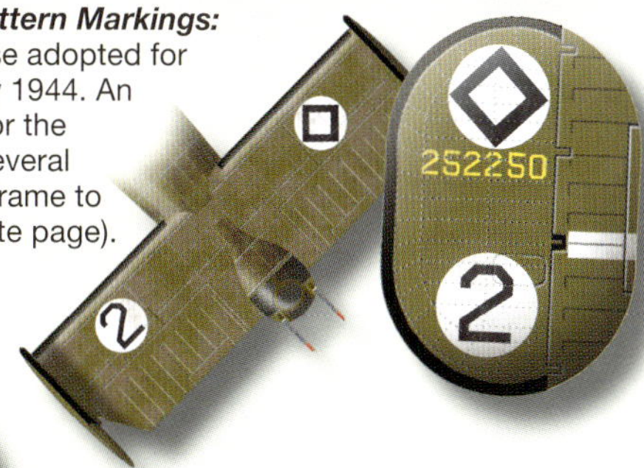

2d Pattern Markings:
A large diamond symbol (48-52 in.) and the color yellow replaced the original tactical fin markings beginning in May 1944. The squadron symbols were retained, white being employed on camouflaged surfaces, black on natural metal finishes. (note: there were some early variations to this theme, I.E. s/n 42-52257 below). Aircraft serial numbers were handled differently from one application to another. In some instances these numbers were simply over painted, obliterating most of the numerals. In other instances the s/n was re-applied, below the diamond configuration, while still others were masked over (some rather elaborately) prior to the application of the new 304thBW geometric devise.

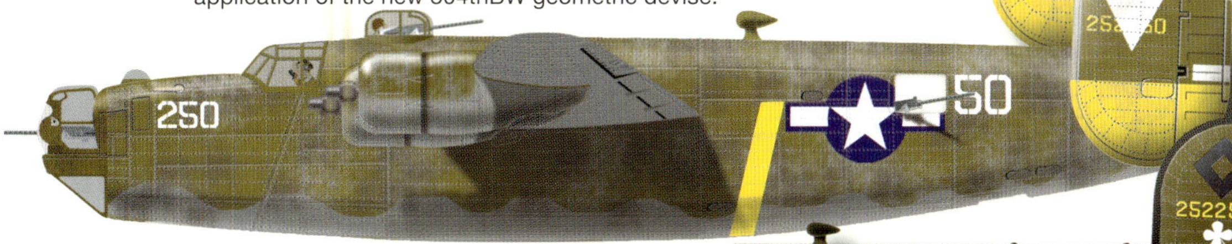

Special Note:
The 743dBS devise was approx. 6-8in. wide and was applied at an angle of 45°.

Additional Markings:
'Hash Marks'; these color stripes show up on several photos of the groups early deployment in the MTO. Although no official documentation has yet been discovered that explains the actual function of these devices, it is safe to say that they were, in all probability, 'Command' or 'Lead Ship' designators. The first **confirmed** use was by Group CO Col. Cool in April 1944 on his ship 'Bestwedu', and consisted of a vertical white stripe, approximately 10-12in. width, and located just aft the wing trailing edge (s/n #42-52257). The second confirmed use was on 'Virginia Princess aka Flak Alley Sally' belonging to 742dBS CO Lt.Col. Edwin Ambrosen. This similar stripe was applied with yellow paint and approximately of the same dimensions and mid-fuselage location as 'Bestwedu', but at an angle of 75° (s/n 42-52250). It only seems logical that the other squadrons also utilized similar markings, but no additional photographs depicting this have yet to surface.

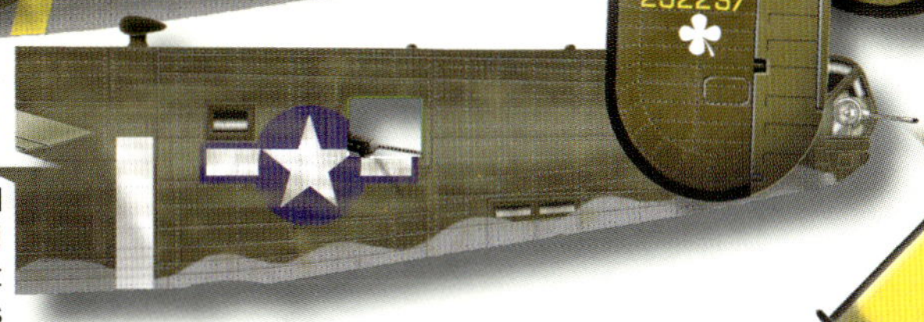

The 455thBG employed a dual method of battle numbers for their combat aircraft. A 'number-in-squadron' was assigned to each ship and affixed aft the waist gunners station while the 'last-three' digits of the serial number were applied (with a wide variety of sizes and locations) on the nose area.

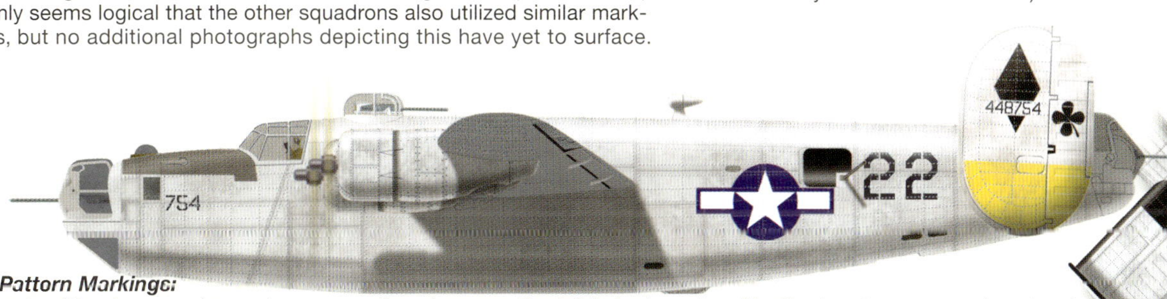

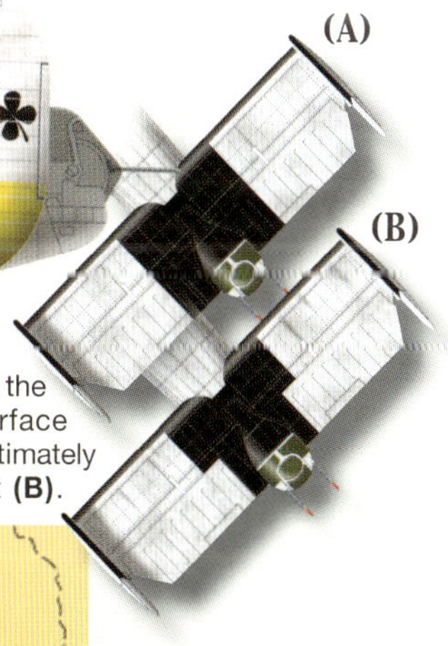

2d Pattern Markings:
The use of fuselage number codes was continued as were the tail fin/rudder markings and 455thBG color. Black paint replaced white for Wing and Squadron symbols on NMF's. The new standardized 304thBW upper tail-plane surface pattern replaced the earlier configuration.

As with other bomb groups assigned to the 304thBW, there was the tail-plane surface as proposed **(A)**, and that which was ultimately applied to 455thBG combat aircraft **(B)**.

• Assigned: Fifteenth AAF, Dec-1943 thru V-E Day •

304TH Bomb Wng
January-1944

456TH Bombardment Group (H)

Insignia: (unofficial)
Motto: 'Strength-Loyalty'
Sobriquet: 'Steed's Flying Colts'
Constituted:
456TH Bmb Grp (H)/14-May-43
Activated: 1-Jun-43
Redesignated:
456TH Bmb Grp (VH)/Aug-45

744TH Bomb Sqdn (H)

Insignia/(unofficial)
Sobriquet: 'The Deliverators'

Constituted:
744TH Bomb Sqdn (H)/14-May-43
Activated: 1-Jun-43
Redesignated:
744TH Bomb Sqdn (VH)/5-Aug-45

Individualy Assigned Aircraft Call Letters

745TH Bomb Sqdn (H)

Insignia/(unofficial)

Constituted:
745TH Bomb Sqdn (H)/14-May-43
Activated: 1-Jun-43
Redesignated:
745TH Bomb Sqdn (VH)/5-Aug-45

Individualy Assigned Aircraft Call Letters

746TH Bomb Sqdn (H)

Insignia/(unofficial)
Sobriquet: 'Lardassarus Rex'

Constituted:
746TH Bomb Sqdn (H)/14-May-43
Activated: 1-Jun-43
Redesignated:
746TH Bomb Sqdn (VH)/5-Aug-45

Individualy Assigned Aircraft Call Letters

747TH Bomb Sqdn (H)

Insignia/(unofficial)

Constituted:
747TH Bomb Sqdn (H)/14-May-43
Activated: 1-Jun-43
Redesignated:
747TH Bomb Sqdn (VH)/5-Aug-45

Individualy Assigned Aircraft Call Letters

• Fifteenth USAAF •

Consolidated B-24 'Liberator'
circa: Jan-44 thru V-E Day

1st Pattern Markings:
An Arabic numeral '1' was designated to represent the 460thBG and was applied as depicted along with the 55thBW's concentric square. Some time during the early stages of their combat deployment, the 460thBG began the practice of utilizing individual aircraft call letters. These devises were located aft the waist gunners station on both sides of the fuselage, and were generally in yellow paint with a thin white full contour outline,

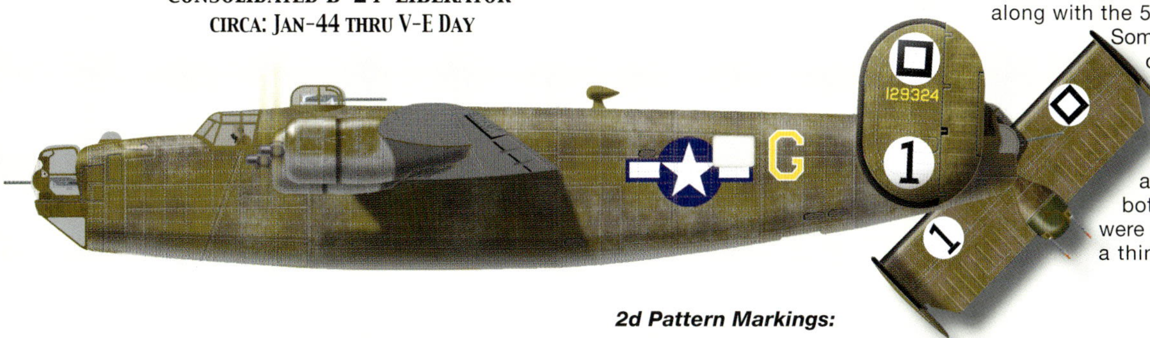

2d Pattern Markings:
Equally divided yellow and black outer vertical tail surfaces were adopted in May of 1944. Two geometric symbols were additionally selected to represent the 460thBG; a square and a concentric circle. As seen in the accompanying illustrations, each of these new symbols were utilized on both the outward horizontal and upper vertical tail surfaces.

The use of call letters was carried over, however these devices were somewhat larger than those originally used. White letters featuring a yellow contour outline began to be applied to both camouflaged and NMF surfaces. By wars end the call letters were being located closer to the vertical tail and the application of group insignia to the nose area were less common.

Unit Insignia:
Although no squadron insignia have surfaced to date, combat aircraft with the 460thBG did make use of the group insignia. Numerous ships displayed this image on the forward fuselage nose area, albeit in a rectangular rather than circular format.

Rear Horizontal Stablizer Tactical Markings:
The upper tail surfaces of combat aircraft serving with the 460thBG underwent numerous modifications to their tactical tail markings.

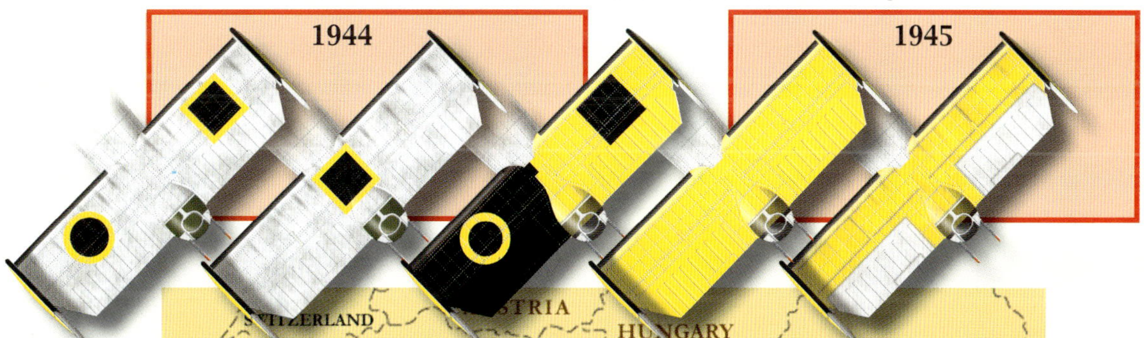

• Assigned Fifteenth AAF, Feb-1944 thru V-E Day •

49TH BOMB WNG
FEBRUARY-1944

461ST BOMBARDMENT GROUP (H)

INSIGNIA: (UNOFFICIAL)
MOTTO: 'TO THE ATTACK'
CONSTITUTED:
461ST BOMB GRP (H) /19-MAY-43
ACTIVATED: 1-JUL-43
INACTIVATED: 28-AUG-45

461st BG Variation:
This slightly modified version of the group insignia was a frequent replacement for the original design. Of the latter image it should be noted here that the motto scroll was sometimes omitted, even when used for official purposes.

764TH BOMB SQDN (H)

INSIGNIA: APPROVED/24-NOV-44

CONSTITUTED:
764TH BOMB SQDN (H): 19-MAY-43
ACTIVATED: 1-JUL-43
INACTIVATED: 28-AUG-45

AIRCRAFT NUMBER-IN-SQUADRON
1-19

765TH BOMB SQDN (H)

INSIGNIA: REPLACED/27-AUG-54

CONSTITUTED:
764TH BOMB SQDN (H): 19-MAY-43
ACTIVATED: 1-JUL-43
INACTIVATED: 28-AUG-45

AIRCRAFT NUMBER-IN-SQUADRON
20-39

766TH BOMB SQDN (H)

INSIGNIA: APPROVED/30-MAY-44

CONSTITUTED:
764TH BOMB SQDN (H): 19-MAY-43
ACTIVATED: 1-JUL-43
INACTIVATED: 28-AUG-45

AIRCRAFT NUMBER-IN-SQUADRON
40-59

767TH BOMB SQDN (H)

INSIGNIA: APPROVED/8-AUG-44

CONSTITUTED:
764TH BOMB SQDN (H): 19-MAY-43
ACTIVATED: 1-JUL-43
INACTIVATED: 28-AUG-45

AIRCRAFT NUMBER-IN-SQUADRON
60-79

• Fifteenth USAAF •

Consolidated B-24 'Liberator'

circa: Feb-44 thru V-E Day

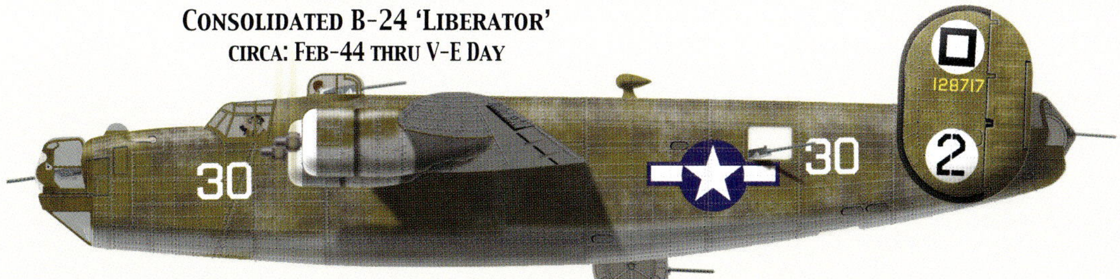

1st Pattern Markings:
The 461stBG drew an Arabic numeral '2' as its unit designator which was used in conjunction with the 49thBW tactical marking system. This included the application of the standard 'dual disc' pattern to both outward facing vertical and upper rear horizontal stabilizer surface areas, as depicted. Research indicates that the 461st BG adopted early the use of both squadron colors (engine cowling rings) as well as individual aircraft battle numbers. These latter devises were considerably smaller than what the group would eventually use after May, 1944.

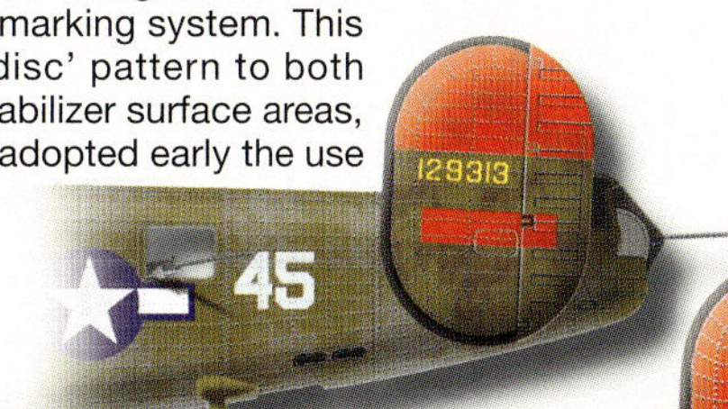

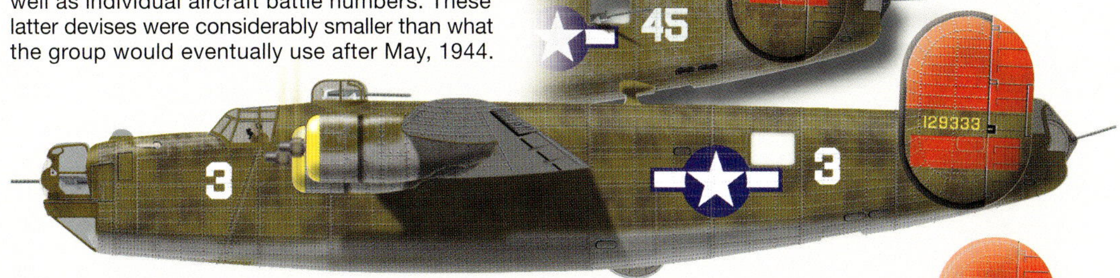

More On The Aircraft Codes:
Early fuselage codes were applied to both sides of the fuselage using either Insignia White or RAF/Sky paint, positioned aft the waist gunners station and on the forward nose area. Later applications included white numerals on both red and white rectangles, and were later simple applied using black paint on NMF's. Late in the war it was not uncommon to see aircraft displaying these devises on either the fuselage or nose, one or the other, but not both.

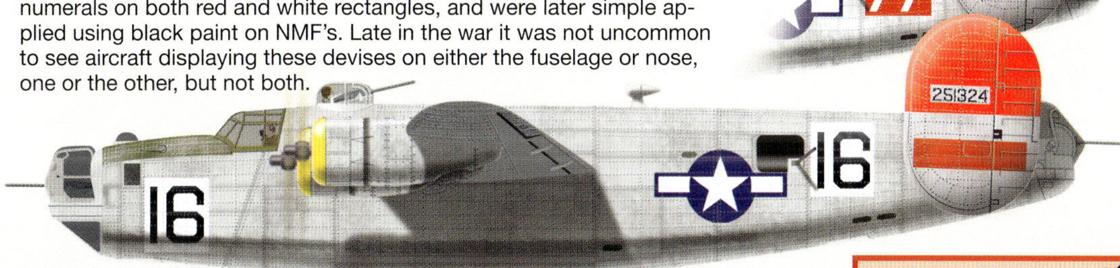

2d Pattern Markings:
The new replacement markings called for the outer vertical tail surface to be divided in half chord wise, the upper half to be painted red while the lower section was to receive a wide horizontal bar, also in red. The aircraft serial numbers were either retained via masking or reinstated after the paint application. There were numerous modifications to the marking schemes located on the rear horizontal stabilizer upper surfaces, as evidenced by the illustrations. The image at the bottom of this stack is the one finally adopted by wars end all units serving with the 49thBW.

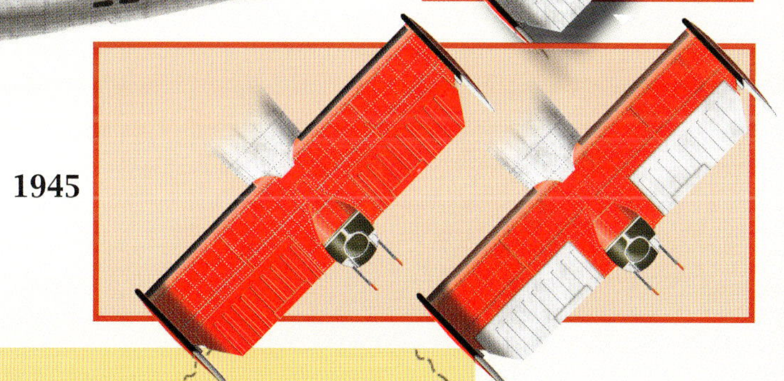

• Assigned Fifteenth AAF, Feb-1944 thru V-E Day •

5th Bomb Wng
February-1944

463d Bombardment Group (H)

Insignia: Replaced/30-Aug-54
Motto:
'Fortress In The Clouds'
Sobriquet: 'The Swoose Group"
Constituted:
463d Bomb Grp (H) /19-May-43
Activated: 1-Aug-43

The Other Group Insignia: The story behind this image is, unfortunately, too lengthy for this format. The above design was nevertheless a popular alternative to the more traditional 463dBG insignia and appeared frequently on A-2 and B-3 uniform jackets.

772d Bomb Sqdn (H)

Insignia: Approved/16-Feb-44

Constituted:
772d Bomb Sqdn (H): 19-May-43
Activated: 1-Aug-43

Squadron Codes Unknown

773d Bomb Sqdn (H)

Insignia: Replaced/23-Dec-57

Constituted:
773d Bomb Sqdn (H): 19-May-43
Activated: 1-Aug-43

Squadron Codes Unknown

774th Bomb Sqdn (H)

Insignia: Replaced/15-Sep-53

Constituted:
774th Bomb Sqdn (H): 19-May-43
Activated: 1-Aug-43

Squadron Codes Unknown

775th Bomb Sqdn (H)

Insignia: Approved/3-May-45
Sobriquet:
'Allyn's Irish Orphans'

Constituted:
775th Bomb Sqdn (H): 19-May-43
Activated: 1-Aug-43

Squadron Codes Unknown

• FIFTEENTH USAAF •

BOEING B-17 'FLYING FORTRESS'

circa: Feb-44 thru V-E Day

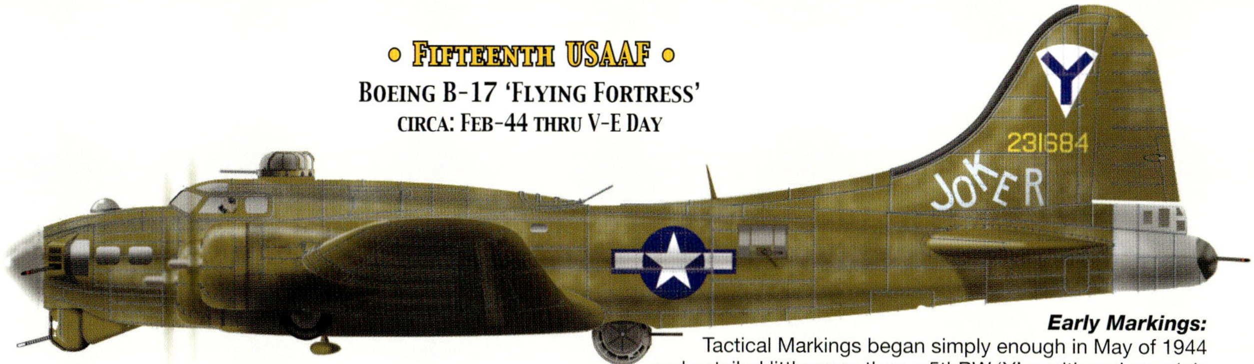

Early Markings:
Tactical Markings began simply enough in May of 1944 and entailed little more than a 5thBW 'Y' positioned on a 'pie slice' which was simply an inverted triangle featuring a 60° arc between the top two corner edges. This devise was applied using either black or Insignia Blue on a white base (camouflaged surfaces) or white over black on later natural metal finished aircraft. In the latter case, the 'Y' was sometimes simply masked out prior to the application to the black paint, letting the metal surface show through the geometric 'pie' configuration.

Early 775thBS Insignia:
Although the design depicted on the facing page is the final, and offical insignia representing this squadron, this was the original patch worn on many an A-2 and B-3 Bomber jacket.

Alternate 'Swoose' Insignia:
This image represents a popular patch variation of the 'official / unofficial' 463dBG design featured on the facing page.

2d Stage Markings:
During the summer of 1944 the 463dBG adopted Identification Yellow as its group color and this was applied to the rudder surfaces in addition to both upper elevator surfaces. The Group/Wing marker was also added to the elevator top surfaces in the same manner used on the vertical fin. There is some photographic evidence to indicate that the wing tips similarly received a coat of yellow paint, however the extent and duration of this additional application of group color is uncertain at this juncture.

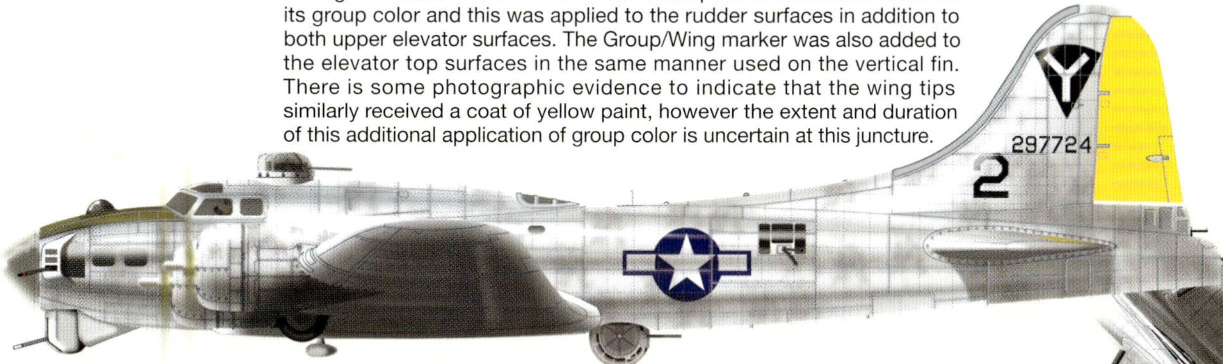

Another short lived tactical marking was the use of the 'last-digit' of each squadrons numerical designation as a means of aircraft assignment, I.E.;
'2' = **772dBS • '3'** = **773dBS • '7'** = **774thBS • '5'** = **775thBS**
These numbers were applied towards the lower leading edge of the vertical fin, and were approximately 36in. tall. By all accounts it would appear that this marking system was all but totally discarded by late summer '44. By wars end the 463dBG had dispensed with virtually all unit markings.

• Assigned Fifteenth AAF, Feb-1944 thru V-E Day •

55th Bomb Wng
February-1944

464th Bombardment Group (H)

No known group insignia

Insignia: (unknown)
Constituted:
464th Bomb Grp (H) /19-May-43
Activated: 1-Aug-43
Inactivated: 31-Jul-45

Although never submitted for approval, this design was used on the masthead of the 464thBG's newsletter during 1944. The art work for this periodical was so poor however as to be almost unrecognizable from the original.

776th Bomb Sqdn (H)

No known squadron insignia

Insignia: (unknown)

Constituted:
776th Bomb Sqdn (H): 19-May-43
Activated: 1-Aug-43
Inactivated: 31-Jul-45

Individual 'aircraft-in-squadron' call letters assigned

777th Bomb Sqdn (H)

No known squadron insignia

Insignia: (unknown)

Constituted:
777th Bomb Sqdn (H): 19-May-43
Activated: 1-Aug-43
Inactivated: 31-Jul-45

Individual 'aircraft-in-squadron' call letters assigned

778th Bomb Sqdn (H)

Insignia: (unofficial)

Constituted:
778th Bomb Sqdn (H): 19-May-43
Activated: 1-Aug-43
Inactivated: 31-Jul-45

Individual 'aircraft-in-squadron' call letters assigned

779th Bomb Sqdn (H)

Insignia: (unofficial)
Sobriquet: 'Li'l Stinky"

Constituted:
759th Bomb Sqdn (H): 19-May-43
Activated: 1-Aug-43
Inactivated: 31-Jul-45

Individual 'aircraft-in-squadron' call letters assigned

• Fifteenth USAAF •

Consolidated B-24 'Liberator'

circa: Feb-44 thru V-E Day

Vertical Stabilizer/Rudder:
The 464thBG utilized essentially the same vertical stabilizer marking configuration throughout their entire combat tour. Originally applied using O.D. and Identification Yellow, the former was eventually replaced with Black-44 almost exclusively by wars end. The single vertical yellow bar on the lower half of the tail surface denoted 464thBG while the rectangle in the upper half identified aircraft as 55thBW. Early applications retained serial numbers.

Squadron Colors:
Assigned squadron colors were applied to aircraft engine cowling rings, albeit sporadically throughout the entire group. Analysis of photographic evidence points to an apparent steady decline of this marking practice until its use had virtually been entirely discarded by the end of hostilities.

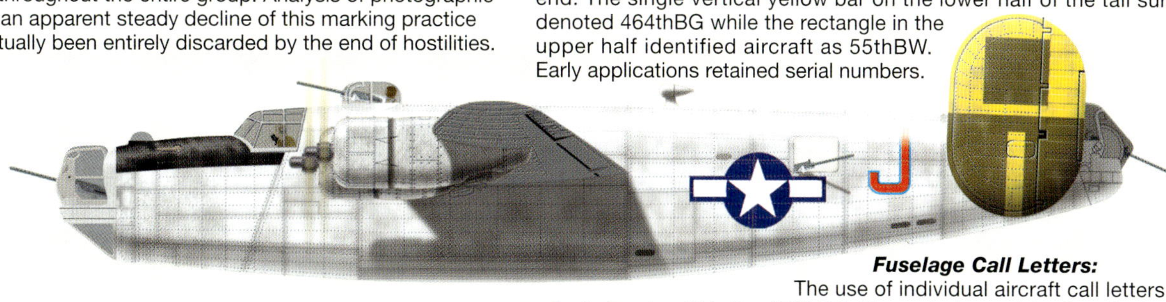

Fuselage Call Letters:
The use of individual aircraft call letters was adopted early within the 464thBG. These devices originally called for the letter to be positioned on a black rectangle between the waist gunners station and the vertical fin. Actual applications of these devices varied considerably throughout the war. Many aircraft within the 464thBG displayed these letters, sans rectangle, applied using the respective squadron color, generally featuring a contrasting contour color outline. Solid black call letters were also used but with much less frequency.

Horizontal Stabilizer/Elevator:
Unlike its vertical counterpart, the upper rear tail-plane surface underwent numerous changes from May of 1944 through V-E Day. By wars end there were numerous aircraft within the 464thBG that carried no markings at all on this surface whatsoever. As depicted below the colors used for this purpose evolved throughout the war beginning with O.D./Yellow to Black/Yellow and finally, a solid IdentificationYellow tactical marking.

By late 1945, replacement 464thBG a/c vertical stabilizers were monochromatic, receiving a coat of black paint over a natural metal finish.

1.) Pantanella A/F, Italy c.Mar-44

2.) Gioia del Colle A/F, Italy 21-Apr-44

3.) Pantanella A/F, Italy 1-Jun-44 thru V-E Day

• Assigned Fifteenth AAF, Feb-1944 thru V-E Day •

55TH Bomb Wng
February-1944

No Known Group Insignia

465TH Bombardment Group (H)

Insignia: (unknown)
Constituted:
465TH Bomb Grp (H) / 19-May-43
Activated: 1-Aug-43
Inactivated: 31-Jul-45

781th BS Variation:
The prevailing differences in the wartime use of this design was in the use of color. The presence or absence of color within the bomb configuration in particular varied greatly from one use to another throughout the course of the war.

780TH Bomb Sqdn (H)

Insignia: (unofficial)

Constituted:
780TH Bomb Sqdn (H): 19-May-43
Activated: 1-Aug-43
Inactivated: 31-Jul-45

Individual 'Aircraft-in-Squadron' Call Letters Assigned

781ST Bomb Sqdn (H)

Insignia: (unofficial)

Constituted:
781ST Bomb Sqdn (H): 19-May-43
Activated: 1-Aug-43
Inactivated: 31-Jul-45

Individual 'Aircraft-in-Squadron' Call Letters Assigned

782D Bomb Sqdn (H)

Insignia: (unofficial)

Constituted:
782D Bomb Sqdn (H): 19-May-43
Activated: 1-Aug-43
Inactivated: 31-Jul-45

Individual 'Aircraft-in-Squadron' Call Letters Assigned

783D Bomb Sqdn (H)

Insignia: (unofficial)

Constituted:
783D Bomb Sqdn (H): 19-May-43
Activated: 1-Aug-43
Inactivated: 31-Jul-45

Individual 'Aircraft-in-Squadron' Call Letters Assigned

• Fifteenth USAAF •

Consolidated B-24 'Liberator'

CIRCA: FEB-44 THRU V-E DAY

Tail Markings:
A horizontal yellow bar dividing the lower half of the Olive Drab vertical stabilizer was the designated tactical marking of the 465thBG. In many later applications, the use of yellow was eliminated and black replaced O.D., which in turn was applied directly to metal finished tail surfaces.

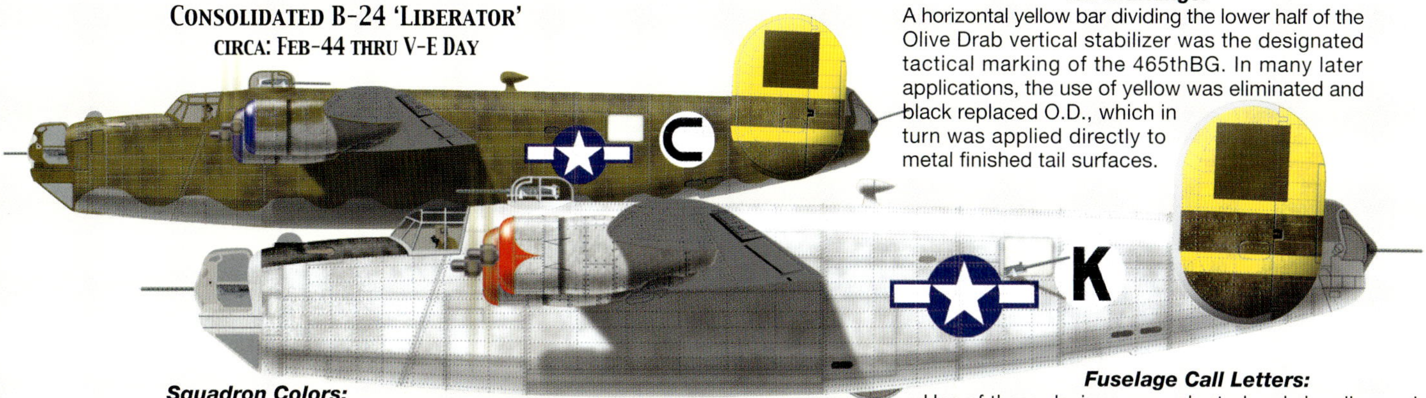

Squadron Colors:
The application of designated colors to the engine cowling rings was another identification method put into use early within all squadrons of this group. This policy use of color as a tactical marking appears to have been employed fairly consistently throughout the 465thBG's combat tour of duty.

Fuselage Call Letters:
Use of these devices was adopted early by all squadrons and initially entailed a black individually assigned RCL (approximately 36in.) centered on a white circular disc which was positioned aft the waist gunners station.

Additional Markings:
Some, but by no means all, aircraft within the 465thBG carried an additional three-digit numerical code located on the nose area. These designators were not tied to the typical 'last-three' in the serial numbers and their use appears to have been sporadic.

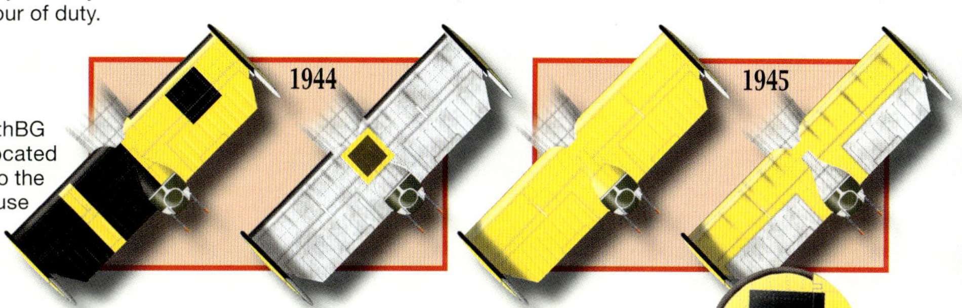

Late War Call Letters:
By the end of 1944 the circular white disc had disappeared from the fuselages of the 465thBG. The use of a single letter was retained and these were generally applied in two colors, white, with the squadron color serving as either the fill or contour outline.

• Assigned Fifteenth AAF, Feb-1944 thru V-E Day •

5th Bomb Wng
March-1944

483d Bombardment Group (H)

Insignia: (unofficial)
Motto:
'From The Skies We Conquer'
Constituted:
483d Bomb Grp (H) /14-Sep-43
Activated: 20-Sep-43

840th BS (unofficial): When the 818thBS(H) was redesignated as the 840thBS(H) many within the unit felt a new squadron insignia was in order. The above design was the result which, for obvious reasons, was never officially sanctioned.

815th Bomb Sqdn (H)

Insignia: (unofficial)

Constituted:
815th Bomb Sqdn (H): 14-Sep-43
Activated: 20-Sep-43

No color assigned — Squadron codes unknown

816th Bomb Sqdn (H)

Insignia: Appproved/22-Mar-44

Constituted:
816th Bomb Sqdn (H): 14-Sep-43
Activated: 20-Sep-43

No color assigned — Squadron codes unknown

817th Bomb Sqdn (H)

Insignia: (unofficial)

Constituted:
817th Bomb Sqdn (H): 14-Sep-43
Activated: 20-Sep-43

No color assigned — Squadron codes unknown

818th Bomb Sqdn (H)

Insignia: Approved/12-Jan-44

Constituted:
840th Bomb Sqdn (H)/ 14-Sep-43
Activated:
1-Oct-43
Redesignated:
818th Bomb Sqdn (H)/ 15-Feb-44

No color assigned — Squadron codes unknown

• Fifteenth USAAF •

Boeing B-17 'Flying Fortress'

circa: Feb-44 thru V-E Day

Tactical Markings:

The 483dBG began combat operations using the standard white 5thBW 'Y' coupled with the newly adopted white star as the group designator. Both of these devices were displayed on either side of the vertical tail fin in addition to the upper surfaces of the horizontal tail-planes as depicted.

In the summer of 1942 the 483dBG adopted the practice of applying Insignia Red to their B-17's rudders in addition to both upper and lower elevator surfaces. The tactical markings remained unchanged with the exception that the groups 'star' was sometimes masked-out prior to the application of the red paint, letting the silver doped surface beneath show through. The 483dBG did not incorporate any type of individual aircraft fuselage call letters or numbers during its entire overseas combat tour. Neither did they apparently see a need for the use of squadron color for recognition purposes.

• Assigned Fifteenth AAF, Mar-1944 thru V-E Day •

49th Bomb Wng March-1944

484th Bombardment Group (H)

Insignia: (unofficial)
Motto: 'Always Ascending'
Constituted:
484th Bomb Grp (H) /14-Sep-43
Activated: 20-Sep-43
Redesignated:
484th Bomb Group (Pathfiner): May-44
484th Bomb Group (H): 11-Nov-44
Inactivated: 25-Jul-45

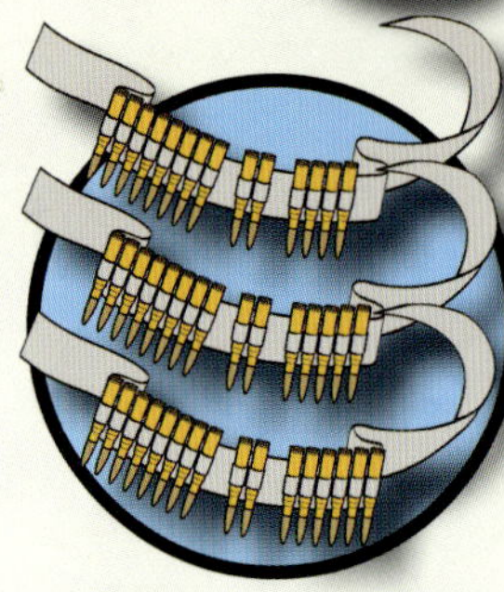

Squadron Designators:
At first glance, three of the groups squadron insignia appear identical. The key differentiation is the bullet count: ***8-2-4***, ***8-2-5*** and ***8-2-6***. The 827th opted to retain their original officially sanctioned design.

824th Bomb Sqdn (H)

Insignia: (unofficial)

Constituted:
824th Bomb Sqdn (H): 14-Sep-43
Activated: 20-Sep-43
Redesignated:
824th Bomb Sqdn (Pathfinder): 14-Feb-44
824th Bomb Sqdn (H): 11-Nov-44
Inactivated: 25-Jul-45

Aircraft Number-In-Squadron
01-19

825th Bomb Sqdn (H)

Insignia: (unofficial)

Constituted:
825th Bomb Sqdn (H): 14-Sep-43
Activated: 20-Sep-43
Redesignated:
825th Bomb Sqdn (Pathfinder): 14-Feb-44
825th Bomb Sqdn (H): 11-Nov-44
Inactivated: 25-Jul-45

Aircraft Number-In-Squadron
20-39

826th Bomb Sqdn (H)

Insignia: (unofficial)

Constituted:
826th Bomb Sqdn (H): 14-Sep-43
Activated: 20-Sep-43
Redesignated:
826th Bomb Sqdn (Pathfinder): 14-Feb-44
826th Bomb Sqdn (H): 11-Nov-44
Inactivated: 25-Jul-45

Aircraft Number-In-Squadron
40-59

827th Bomb Sqdn (H)

Insignia: Approved/11-Jul-42

Constituted:
41st Bomb Sqdn (M): 20-Nov-40
Activated: 15-Jan-41
Redesignated:
5th Antisub Sqdn (H): 29-NOv-42
827th Bomb Sqdn (H): 1-Oct-43
Inactivated: 25-Jul-45

Aircraft Number-In-Squadron
60-79

• Fifteenth USAAF •

Consolidated B-24 'Liberator'

circa: Dec-43 thru V-E Day

Group Marking:

The symbol selected to designate the 484thBG was a chord-wise Insignia Red complex quadrangle or polygon, more commonly referred to as an hour-glass or bow tie. These devices were originally applied directly to Olive Drab paint surfaces but this policy was quickly replaced with an outlined version for improved legibility. The outlines were applied using white on camouflage, black on metal surfaces. In all cases the upper portion of the vertical stabilizer surfaces were painted a solid Insignia Red in compliance with the standard 49thBW directive.

Unlike the other two groups comprising the 49thBW, which pretty much divided their vertical tail surfaces 50/50 top to bottom, 484thBG tail surfaces were divided less equally than this. There does not appear to have been any fixed rule concerning the geometric properties of the groups quadrangle application, as evidenced by a review of available wartime photos of this unit.

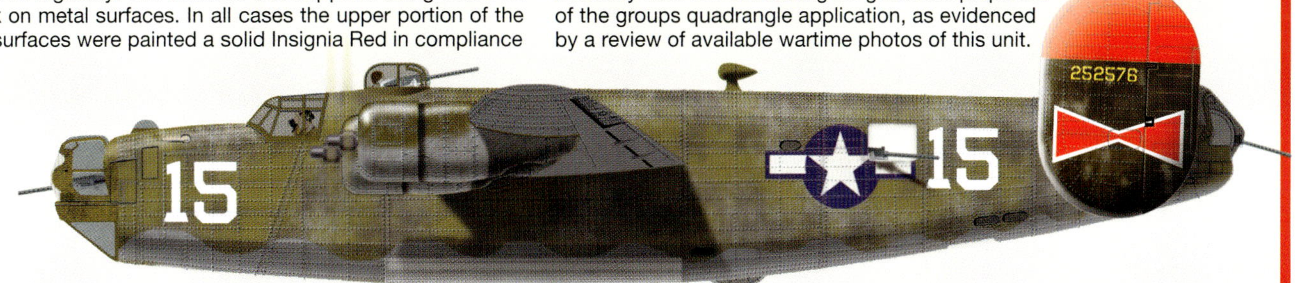

Radio Call Numbers:

Whereas the other two groups comprising the 49thBW incorporated a rectangular shape with their RCN's, the 484thBG opted instead to affix their numerals without the addition of these geometric devices. Individually assigned call numbers were approximately 36in.- 48in. overall height and generally applied in two locations, aft the waist gunners station and slightly forward the cockpit windscreen. Originally applied with either a solid black or white (depending upon surface type) a color contour outline was later added to many of these devices from late 1944 until wars end.

Squadron Colors:

While it is known that the 484thBG adopted and used color as a means of squadron identification, researchers have to date been unable to determine precisely which colors were assigned to each squadron comprising the 484thBG. Within the structure of the 49thBW, the colors authorized for use by squadrons within its three groups were as follows; Yellow / White / Green / Red.

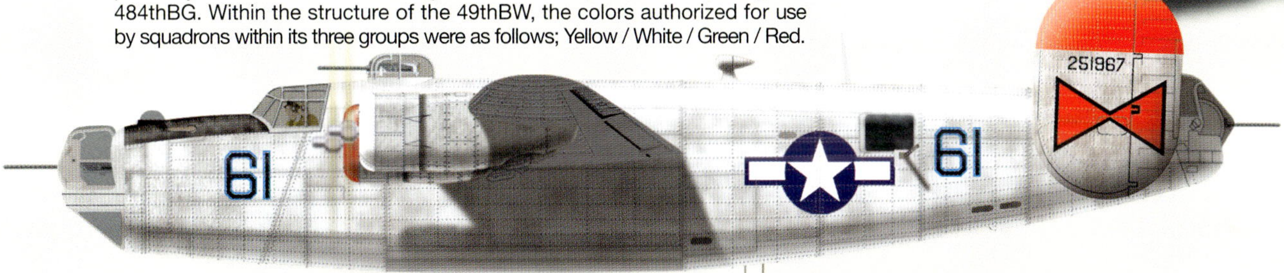

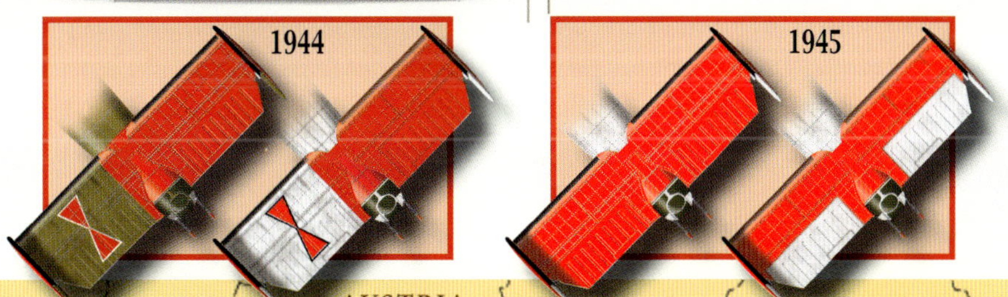

• Assigned Fifteenth AAF, Feb-1944 thru V-E Day •

55TH Bomb Wng
March-1944

485TH Bombardment Group (H)

Insignia: (unofficial)
Constituted:
485TH Bomb Grp (H) /14-Sep-43
Activated: 20-Sep-43
Redesignated:
485TH Bomb Group (VH) /Aug-45

Alternate 485thBG(H) Insignia: This device was simply a derivative of the early General Jimmy Doolittle design for what was at the time the fledgling Fifteenth USAAF. While this design was frequently applied to airmen's jackets, it is uncertain today whether it was used officially.

828TH Bomb Sqdn (H)

Insignia: (unofficial)

Constituted:
828TH Bomb Sqdn (H): 14-Sep-43
Activated: 20-Sep-43
Redesignated:
828TH Bomb Sqdn (VH): 5-Aug-45

Individual 'Aircraft-in-Squadron' Call Letters Assigned

829TH Bomb Sqdn (H)

Insignia: (unofficial)

Constituted:
829TH Bomb Sqdn (H): 14-Sep-43
Activated: 20-Sep-43
Redesignated:
829TH Bomb Sqdn (VH): 5-Aug-45

Individual 'Aircraft-in-Squadron' Call Letters Assigned

830TH Bomb Sqdn (H)

Insignia: (unofficial)

Constituted:
830TH Bomb Sqdn (H): 14-Sep-43
Activated: 20-Sep-43
Redesignated:
830TH Bomb Sqdn (VH): 5-Aug-45

Individual 'Aircraft-in-Squadron' Call Letters Assigned

831ST Bomb Sqdn (H)

Insignia: Approved/9-Feb-43

Constituted:
516TH Bomb Sqdn (H): 13-Oct-42
Activated: 18-Oct-42
Redesignated:
11TH Antisub Sqdn (H): 29-Nov-42
11TH Antisub Sqdn (M): 3-Mar-43
11TH Antisub Sqdn (H): 20-Apr-43
831ST Bomb Sqdn (H): 1-Oct-43
Inactiated: 20-Aug-45

Individual 'Aircraft-in-Squadron' Call Letters Assigned

• Fifteenth USAAF •

Consolidated B-24 'Liberator'

circa: Mar-44 thru V-E Day

Radio Call Letters:

The use of single letter call signs was adopted when the 485thBG was first deployed to the MTO. These devices were approximately 48in. overall height and applied using either white or yellow paint, aft the waist gunners station. On later applications these markings were applied in squadron colors and often featured a contour outline.

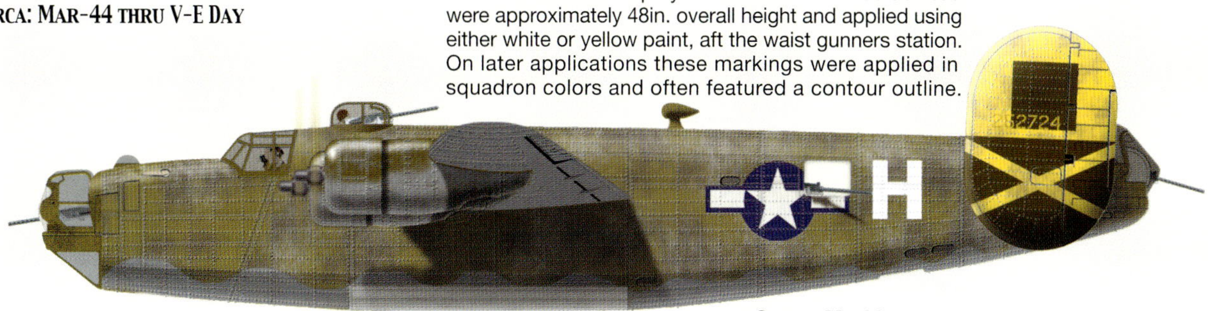

Group Marking:

The 484thBG adopted a large 'X' as its unit designator and this device was applied to the lower portion of the vertical stabilizers. This 'X' symbol was additionally located on the upper port horizontal stabilizer surface (as depicted) but its use was eventually dispensed with in favor of a simplier 55thBW marking device. By wars end use of these markings had all but ended.

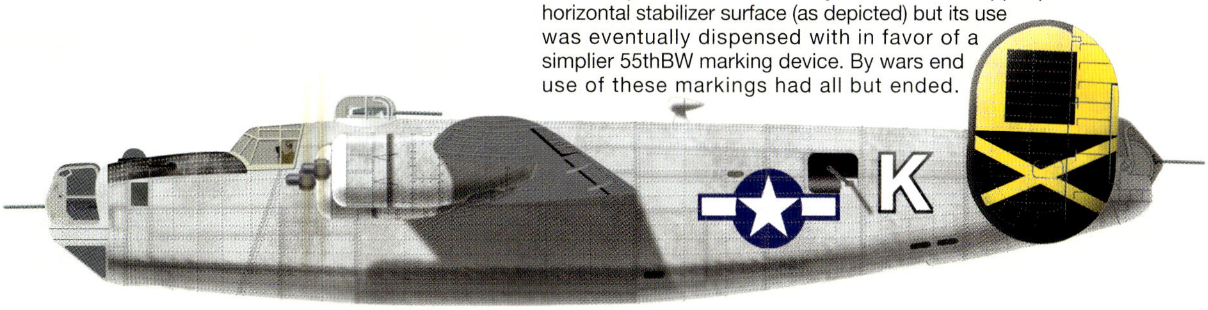

Squadron Colors:

Although approved for use on engine cowling rings as tactical squadron marking devices, actual applications for this purpose were, by all accounts, sporadic at best.

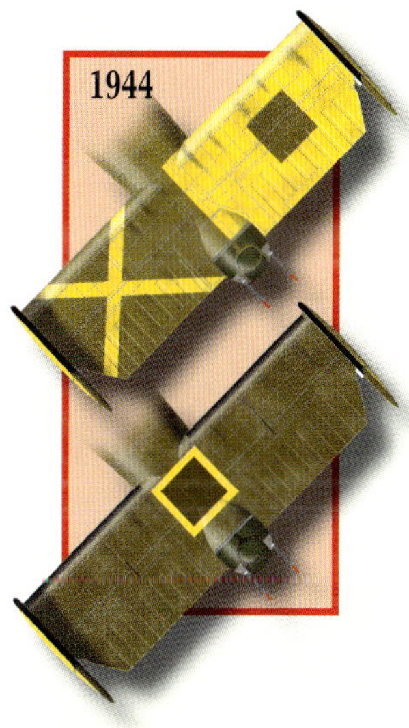

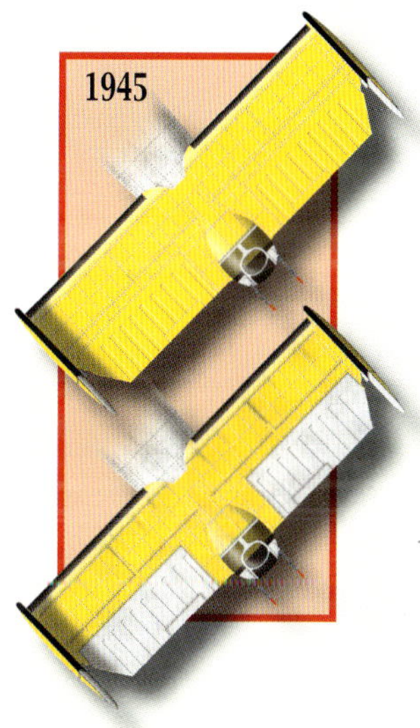

©

The 'Other' Squadron Insignia:

Although the approved design depicted on the facing page was the authorized insignia for the 516thBS, it still appears in many official historical documents as representing the 831stBG. The fact is however, that the design depicted at left is the actual Disney design developed for, and adopted by, the men of 831stBS squadron in World War II.

U.S.A.A.F. RECON/SPEC OPS UNITS

MEDITERRANEAN THEATER OF OPERATIONS

Because of the transitory conditions under which the reconnaissance and other special duty squadrons operated, few specific details regarding their tactical markings exist today. It should also be acknowledged that due to the very nature of reconnaissance and other special operations missions, high visibility airframe markings were both unnecessary as well as a detriment. Those few tactical markings that were employed by the various recon, antisubmarine and other special units deployed to the MTO are as follows;

3d Photographic Group (Reconnaissance)

• At one time or another all four elements assigned to the 3dPG(R), the 5th, 12th, 15th and 23d Photographic Reconnaissance Squadrons, operated with Lockheed F-4 and later F-5 and L-5 aircraft. The early F-4's began operations utilizing a standard two color Olive Drab / Neutral Gray paint scheme, the latter being quickly replaced with RAF Sky or other similar shade of blue. In January 1943 Lockheed introduced Synthetic Haze Paint and many photo recon Lightnings soon displayed this new color.

Supply of this shade was limited however and numerous F-4 and F-5's received an overall coat of RAF PRU Blue and although not as effective as the Lockheed paint, it was readily available. Most of the recon Lightnings in all three groups employed the policy of applying 'last-three' serial number digits to both sides of the nacelle nose in either white or yellow paint.

The 15thPRS additionally operated with standard two color camouflaged B-17;s from November 1942 until January 1944.

5th Photographic Reconnaissance Group

• This unit operated primarily with F-5 Lightnings augmented with a few F-4 Models which all followed along the same marking pattern as those employed by the 3dPRG.

68th Tactical Reconnaissance Group

• This outfit operated with just about everything with wings in the AAF inventory; A-20, A-36, B-17, B-24, L-5, P-38, P-39, P-40, and P-51. All served at one time or another with the 60th-TRG conducting operations ranging from photographic to visual reconnaissance which even included antisubmarine patrols in the Mediterranean Sea. While some photographic evidence does exist clearly showing various aircraft displaying some type of tactical marking at one time or another, there is no concise documentation currently known that defines just what was used on what type of aircraft and when. The only thing known for certain concerns the 111th Reconnaissance Squadron which utilized a two-digit code on the fuselage of their P-51's. Located just aft the national insignia on both sides, these codes were applied as standard AAF block letters with white paint and were approximately 24" tall. With receipt of natural metal finished airframes, use of these same codes was retained and were than applied using black paint.

An earlier unusual method of aircraft identification adopted by the 111thRS was the use of the 'first-four' digits of the aircraft serial number. These were applied in a similar location, aft the national insignia on both sides of the rear fuselage, using yellow numerals approximately 18" tall.

1st Photo Recon Sqdn / 2d AntiSub Sqdn / 15th BmbSqdn (L) 19th PhotoChrtngSqdn / 859th BmbSqdn (H)

Of the squadrons on detached service from other parent units, little is known in regards to specific tactical markings. It can only be speculated that these outfits continued to display whatever markings, if any, they may have carried on their aircraft at the time of posting. What provisions were made for marking replacement aircraft while TDY is currently unknown.

3d Photo Group (Rcn)

Insignia: Approved: 29-Oct-42
Motto: 'Shoot Well'
Constituted: 3d Photo Grp/ 9-Jun-42
Activated: 20-Jun-42
Redesignated:
3d Photo Rcn & Mpng Grp/ May-1943
3d Photo Grp (Rcn)/ Nov-1943
3d Rcn Grp/ May-1945

5th Photo Rcn Sqdn

Insignia/(unofficial)
Constituted:
5th Photo Sqdn/ 19-Jun-42
Activated: 1-Feb-42
Redesignated:
5th Photo Rcn Sqdn/ 9-Jun-42
5th Photo Sqdn (L)/ 6-Feb-43
5th Cmbt Mpng Sqdn/ 21-Jan-44
5th Photo Rcn Sqdn/ 31-Aug-44

NO KNOWN SQUADRON INSIGNIA

12th Photo Rcn Sqdn

Insignia/ (unknown)
Constituted:
11th Photo Sqdn/ 7-May-42
Activated: 14-May-42
Redesignated:
12th Photo Sqdn/ 9-Jun-42
12th Photo Sqdn (L)/ 6-Feb-43
12th Photo Rcn Sqdn/ 13-Nov-43

15th Photo Rcn Sqdn

Insignia/Arroved: 21-Feb-45
Constituted:
15th Photo Mpng Sqdn/9-Jun-42
Activated: 20-Jun-42
Redesignated:
15th Photo Sqdn (H)/ 6-Feb-43
15th Cmbt Mpng Sqdn/ 21-Jan-44
15th Photo Rcn Sqdn/ 31-Aug-44

23d Photo Rcn Sqdn

Insignia/ (unofficial)
Constituted:
23d Photo Rcn Sqdn/ 14-Jul-42
Activated: 2-Sep-42
Redesignated:
23td Photo Sqdn (L)/ 6-Feb-43
23d Photo Rcn Sqdn/ 13-Nov-43

5th Photo Rcn Group

Insignia: Approved: 25-Jan-43
Motto: 'Beware, We Snap'
Constituted: 5th Photo Grp/ 14-Jul-42
Activated: 23-Jul-42
Redesignated:
5th Photo Rcn & Mpng Grp/ Aug-1943
5th Photo Rcn Grp/ Aug-1943
5th Rcn Grp/ May-1945

15th Photo Rcn Sqdn

Insignia/Arroved: 21-Feb-45
Constituted:
15th Photo Mpng Sqdn/9-Jun-42
Activated: 20-Jun-42
Redesignated:
15th Photo Sqdn (H)/ 6-Feb-43
15th Cmbt Mpng Sqdn/ 21-Jan-44
15th Photo Rcn Sqdn/ 31-Aug-44

32d Photo Rcn Sqdn

Insignia/unofficial
Constituted:
45th Rcn Sqdn (Ftr)/ 25-Jun-43
Activated: 1-Jul-43
Redesignated:
32d Photo Rcn Sqdn/ 11-Aug-43

37th Photo Rcn Sqdn

Insignia/Replaced: 26-Oct-59
Designated:
152d Obs Sqdn/21-Aug-39
Activated: 13-Oct-39
Redesignated:
152d Obs Sqdn (M)/ 13-Jan-42
(additional designations omitted)
37th Photo Rcn Sqdn/ 29-Mar-44

68th Tac Rcn Group

Insignia: Approved: 17-Sep-42
Motto: 'Victory Through Observation'
Constituted: 68th Obs Grp/ 21-Aug-41
Activated: 1-Sep-41
Redesignated:
68th Rcn Grp/ May-1943
68th Tac Rcn Grp/ Nov-1943

16th Rcn Sqdn(H,S)

Insignia: Approved/ 1-Apr-24
Organized:
3d Avn Sch Sqdn/ 9-May-17
Redesignated:
16th Aero Sqdn/ 31-Aug-17
Reconstituted:
16th Sqdn/ 30-Aug-21
Redesignated:
16th Obs Sqdn / 25-Jan-23
16th Obs Sqdn (M)/ 13-Jan-42
16th Obs Sqdn/ 4-Jul-42
16th Rcn Sqdn (Bmr)/ 31-May-43
16th Rcn Sqdn (H,S)/ 12-May-44

111th Tac Rcn Sqdn

Insignia: Approved/ 6-Jun-33
Organized:
111th Aero Sqdn/ 4-Aug-17
Redesignated:
632d Aero Sqdn/ 1-Feb-18
Reconstituted:
111th Obs Sqdn/ 29-Jun-23
Redesignated:
111th Obs Sqdn (M)/ 13-Jan-42
111th Obs Sqdn/ 4-Jul-42
111th Rcn Sqdn (Ftr)/ 31-May-43
111th Tac Rcn Sqdn/ 13-Nov-43

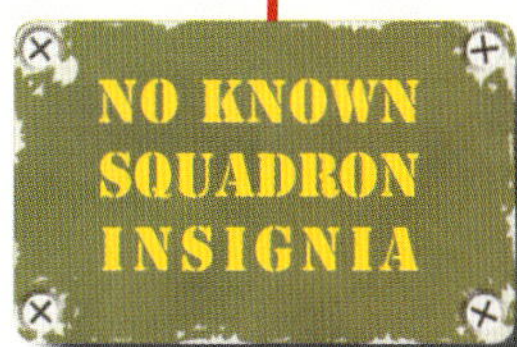

122d Obs Sqdn

Insignia/(unknown)
Designated:
122d Obs Sqdn/30-Jul-40
Activated: 2-Mar-41
Redesignated:
122d Obs Sqdn (L)/ 13-Jan-42
122d Obs Sqdn (M)/ 12-Mar-42
122d Obs Sqdn/ 4-Jul-42
122d Ln Sqdn/ 31-May-43
885th Bmb Sqdn (H)/ 12-May-44

154th Wea Rcn Sqdn (M)

Insignia: Reinstated/ 29-Apr-54
Organized:
154th Aero Sqdn/ 8-Dec-17
Reconstituted:
154th Obs Sqdn/ 24-Oct-25
Redesignated:
154th Obs Sqdn (M)/ 13-Jan-42
154th Obs Sqdn/ 4-Jul-42
154th Rcn Sqdn (Ftr)/ 31-May-43
154th Tac Rcn Sqdn/ 13-Nov-43
154th Wea Rcn Sqdn (M)/ 12-May-44

•Temporary Duty Units•

1st Photo Rcn Sqdn

Insignia: Approved/ 3-Oct-41

2d Antisub Sqdn

Insignia: (unofficial)

15th Bmb Sqdn (L)

Insignia: Approved/ 27-May-40

19th Photo Chrtng Sqdn

Insignia: Approved/ 23-Nov-43

859th Bomb Sqdn (H)(S)

Insignia: (unofficial)

•Insignia Variations, Reconnaissance•

5th PhotoRcnSqdn

Insignia/(unofficial, variation)

111th TacRcnSqdn

Insignia/(unofficial)

5th Photographic Reconnaissance Group:
Shortly after transferring to the Fifteenth AAF the 5thPRG an adopted aircraft marking system that they would retain until wars end. Propeller spinners were uniformly painted red and a dual set of horizontal bars soon adorned the upper vertical tails, red for the 15thPRS, yellow for the 32dPRS and blue for the 37thPRS. Each bar was approximately 6"-8" wide and spaced apart at roughly the same, or slightly greater measure than the overall bar width.

154th Weather Reconnaissance Squadron:
All aircraft within the 154thWRS were consistently marked with a single horizontal bar, approximately 10" wide on the upper vertical stabilizer surfaces. A numerical designation ranging from 01-20 was assigned each aircraft and affixed in two locations, the forward nacelle nose and the radiator housings. Sizes were approximately 10" and 18" respectively and were applied with white paint on camouflaged airframes and with black paint on later natural metal surfaces.

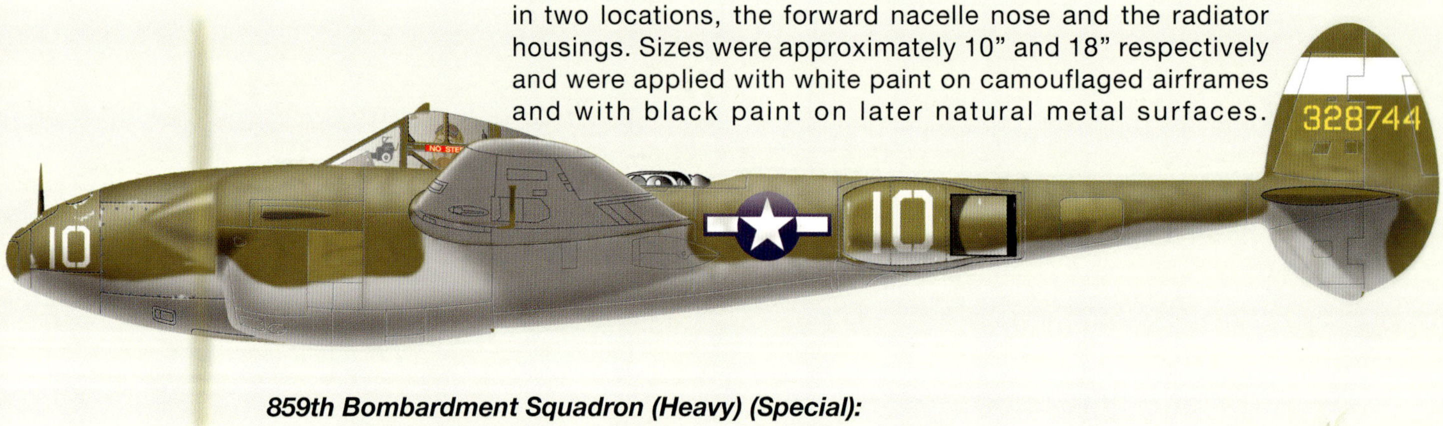

859th Bombardment Squadron (Heavy) (Special):
Formerly the 122d Observation/Liaison Squadron, this unit conducted mostly nighttime missions for the Fifteenth AAF beginning in Mid-June 1944, most of which were in conjunction with top secret OSS operations. Operating primarily with B-24's, the majority of these were painted overall ANA Jet (black) No.622, in keeping with their mission type. There were no special unit tactical markings, and most displayed red aircraft serial numbers on the vertical tail fins, and subdued national insignia on both the fuselage and both upper and lower wing surfaces. No additional markings of any kind were used.

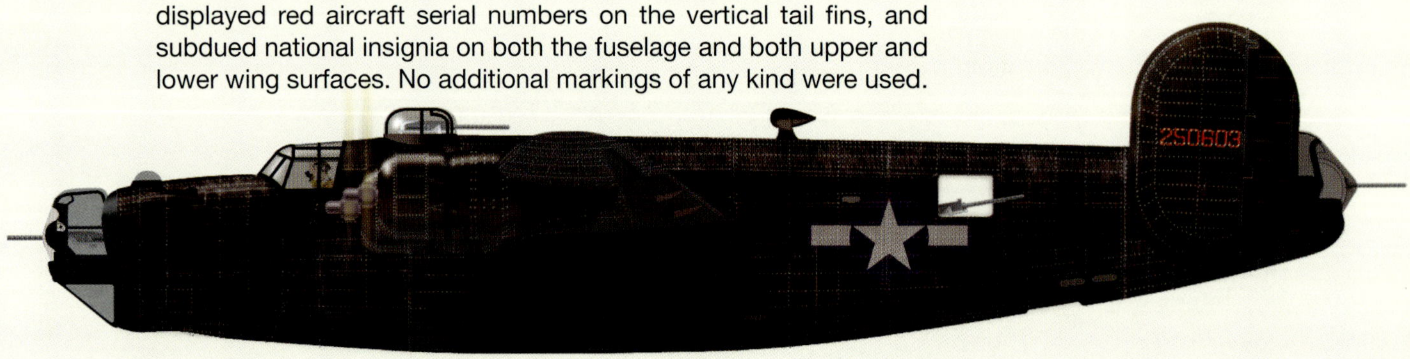

To set the game above renown,
To love the game above the prize,
To honor, while you strike him down,
The foe that comes with fearless eyes;
To count the life of battle good
And dear the land that gave you birth,
And dearer yet the brotherhood
That binds the brave of all the earth.

Sir Henry Newbolt

• Appendix-I •

USAAF Abbreviations

AAA .... Anti-Aircraft Artillery
AAF .... Army Air Force
AB .... Air Base
AAB .... Army Air Base
A/C .... Aircraft
ALG .... Advanced Landing Ground
AD .... Air Division
Air.Div .... Air Division
A/D .... Air Depot
AEF .... American Expeditionary Force
AF .... Air Force
A/F .... Airfield
ANA .... Army-Navy Aeronautical
AS / Antisub .... Anti-Submarine
A/S .... Airstrip
ATO .... American Theater of Operations
Avn. .... Aviation
BD .... Bombardment (later Air) Division
BG .... Bombardment (Bomb) Group
- BG(H) .... Bomb Group (Heavy)
- BG(M) .... Bomb Group (Medium)
- BG(L) .... Bomb Group (Light)
- BG(VH) .... Bomb Group (Very Heavy)

Bmr. .... Bomber
Bomb .... Bombardment
BS .... Bombardment (Bomb) Squadron
BW .... Bombardment (Bomb) Wing
c. .... circa (approximate time period)
Carr. .... Carrier
CBI .... China-Burma-India (Theater of Operations)
Chrtng .... Charting
Cmbt. .... Combat
Cmd. .... Command
Cmdo. .... Commando
CO .... Commanding Officer
Cmpst. .... Composite
Crgo. .... Cargo
CW .... Combat Wing
DB .... Dive Bomber
Det. .... Detachment
EAME .... European-African-Middle Eastern (Theater of Operations. See also MTO)
ERS .... Emergency Rescue Squadron
ETO .... European Theater of Operations
F/B .... Fighter-Bomber
FG / FtrGrp .... Fighter Group
FLAK .... Anti-Aircraft Fire
Fld. .... Field
Flt. .... Flight
Ftr. .... Fighter
FS / FtrSqdn .... Fighter Squadron
FW / FtrWng .... Fighter Wing
GB .... Great Britain
GHQ .... General Headquarters
GP / Grp. .... Group
HQ .... Headquarters
Incpt. .... Interceptor
L/G .... Landing Ground
LN .... Liaison
MTO .... Mediterranean Theater of Operations
Mpng. .... Mapping
NLS .... Night Leaflet Squadron
NMF .... Natural Metal Finish
PS .... Photographic Squadron
OBS .... Observation
OPS .... Operations
QIM .... Quick Identification Markings (Allied)
OSS .... Office Of Strategic Services (US)
(P) / Prov. .... Provisional
PG .... Photographic Group
Photo .... Photographic
POM .... Preparation for Overseas Movement
POW .... Prisoner Of War
PR .... Photographic Reconnaissance
PRG .... Photographic Reconnaissance Group
PS .... Photographic Squadron
PTO .... Pacific Theater of Operations
Pur. .... Pursuit
RAF .... Royal Air Force (British)
RCM .... Radio Counter Measures
Rcn. .... Reconnaissance
RG .... Reconnaissance Group
RS .... Reconnaissance Squadron
SF .... Scouting Force
SHAEF .... Supreme Headquarters Allied Expeditionary Force
SOE .... Special Operations Executive (British)
Spt. .... Support
Sq. / Sqdn. .... Squadron
Srch. .... Search
Stn. .... Station
Tac. .... Tactical
TDY .... Temporary Duty
Trng. .... Training
Tr. .... Troop
Trnsp. .... Transport
T/O .... Theater Of Operations
TRG .... Tactical Reconnaissance Group
TRS .... Tactical Reconnaissance Squadron
Triple-A .... Anti-Aircraft Artillery
USA .... United States Army
UK .... United Kingdom
USN .... United States Navy
US .... United States
USAAF .... United States Army Air Force
USSAFE .... United States Strategic Air Forces, Europe
WR .... Weather Reconnaissance
Wthr. .... Weather
Wng. .... Wing

• Appendix-II •

Biliography

Aircraft Insignia-Spirit Of Youth:
National Geographic, June 1943 / Gerard Hubbard
Air Force Units Of World War II:
Dr. M. Maurer
USAF Historical Research Center
C-47 / R4d Units Of The ETO & MTO:
David Isby
Combat Insignia Stamps Of The United States Army & Navy:
Hearst Publications
Combat Squadrons Of The Air Force, World War II:
Dr. M. Maurer
Command And Employment Of Air Power:
War Department Field Manual / FM 100-20
Camouflage & Markings Of The USAAF In WWII:
ModelArt Publication No.713
Consolidated B-24 Liberator
Krzysztof Janowicz
Fifteenth Ait Force Combat Markings, 1943-1945
E.A. Munday
Insignia & Decorations Of The US Armed Forces:
National Geographic, 1944
Jagdwaffe / Holding The West, 1941-1943:
David Wadman / Martin Pegg
Jagdwaffe / Defending The Reich, 1943-1944:
Robert Forsyth / Eddie J. Creek
Jagdwaffe / Defending The Reich, 1944-1945:
Robert Forsyth
L-Birds/American Combat Liaison Aircraft Of World War II:
Terry M. Love
Martin B-26 Marauder:
Fredrick A. Johnsen
P-38 Lightning:
Bert Kinzey
Republic P-47 Thunderbolt In USAAF, RAF & Foreign Service
Argo-Aircam Aviation Series, No.2
The Army Air Forces In World War II;
Combat Chronology / 1941-1945
Kit C. Carter / Robert Mueller
The Luftwaffe / Strategy For Defeat:
Williamson Murray
The Ninth Air Force in World War II:
Ken C. Rust
The Official Guide To The Army Forces:
Army Air Forces Aid Society
The Organization And Lineage Of The United States Air Force:
Charles A. Ravenstein
USAAF Aircraft Markings & Camouflage;1942-1947
Robert D.Archer / VictorG.Archer
USAAF Heavy Bomb Group Markings & Camouflage
a) Boeing B-17 Flying Fortress
b) Consoludater B-24 Liberator
Aircam Aviation Series

Acknowledgemtnts

Grateful appreciation is extended to the following institutions for providing much of the invaluable historical data and photo images used in the creation of this work:
American Battle Monuments Commission
National Air and Space Museum
P-38 National Association
Planes of Fame / Air Museum
United States Air Force Museum / Wright-Patterson AFB
United States National Archives and Records
9th Air Force Association

A special thanks to ***Scott Burris*** for hosting what is perhaps the finest on-line research web site pretaining to the USAAF.
I enthusiastically encourage anyone researching any aspect of the Army Air Force during WWII to visit this web site;

www.armyairforces.com

I would additionally like to extend my appreciation to the following *ArmyAirForces.com Forum* members who went 'above and beyond' in assisting me with the research for this volume;
Lynn Cotterman, 'Jerry', Nick King, Viliam Kladnik, Mark LaScotte, Jan Lindquist, Bernie Shearon, Tom Walsh.

S/Sgt. Dean Ottaway & Crew
782dBS, 465thBG
Fifteenth USAAF
Giulia Air Field, Italy-1944

Johnny 'Siggy' Signor
-Insignia Reproductions-
714 Atlantis Road S.E.
Palm Bay FL 32909-4811

• Visual Index: Fighter Groups: 'A' •

1st FtrGrp: Pg.14

14th FtrGrp: Pg.16

27th FtrGrp: Pg.18

31st FtrGrp: Pg.20

33d FtrGrp: Pg.22

52d FtrGrp: Pg.24

57th FtrGrp: Pg.26

• Visual Index: Fighter Groups: 'B' •

79th FtrGrp: Pg.30

81st FtrGrp: Pg.32

82d FtrGrp: Pg.34

86th FtrGrp: Pg.36

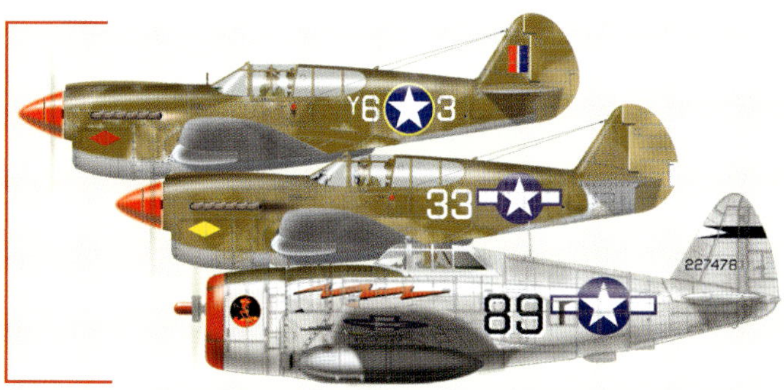

324th FtrGrp: Pg.38

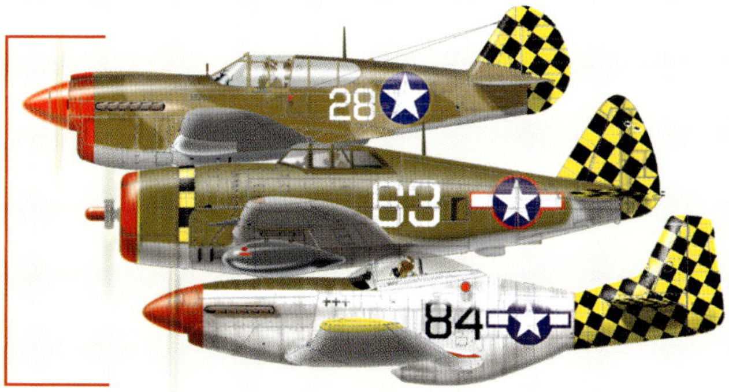

325th FtrGrp: Pg.40

• Visual Index: Fighter Groups: 'C' •

332D FtrGrp: Pg.42

350TH FtrGrp: Pg.44

• Visual Index: Bomb Groups: 'A' •

2D BmbGrp: Pg.64

2D BmbGrp: Pg.64

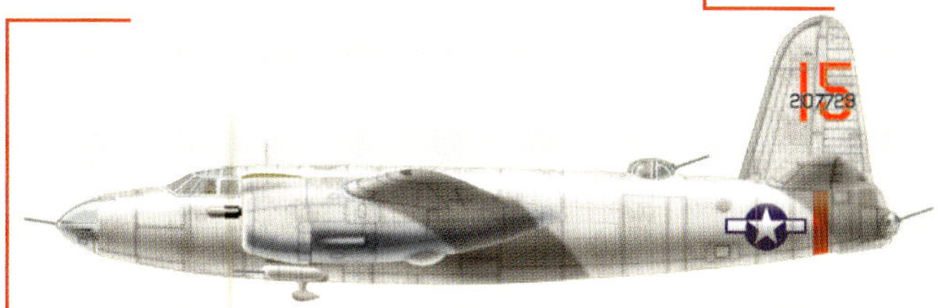

17D BmbGrp: Pg.68

47TH BmbGrp: Pg.70

97TH BmbGrp: Pg.72

98TH BmbGrp: Pg.74

• Visual Index: Bomb Groups: 'B' •

99th BmbGrp: Pg.76

301st BmbGrp: Pg.78

310th BmbGrp: Pg.80

319th BmbGrp: Pg.82

320th BmbGrp: Pg.84

321st BmbGrp: Pg.86

• Visual Index: Bomb Groups: 'C' •

340th BmbGrp: Pg.88

376th BmbGrp: Pg.90

449th BmbGrp: Pg.92

450th BmbGrp: Pg.94

451st BmbGrp: Pg.96

454st BmbGrp: Pg.98

• Visual Index: Bomb Groups: 'D' •

455th BmbGrp: Pg.100

456th BmbGrp: Pg.102

459th BmbGrp: Pg.104

460th BmbGrp: Pg.106

461st BmbGrp: Pg.108

• Visual Index: Bomb Groups: 'E' •

463D BmbGrp: Pg.110

464TH BmbGrp: Pg.112

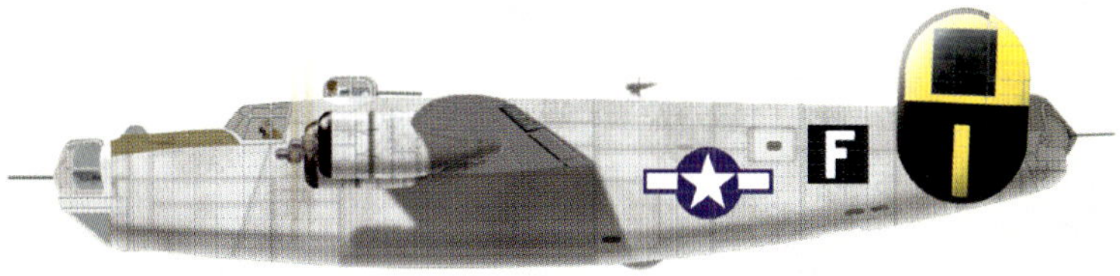

465TH BmbGrp: Pg.114

483D BmbGrp: Pg.116

484TH BmbGrp: Pg.118

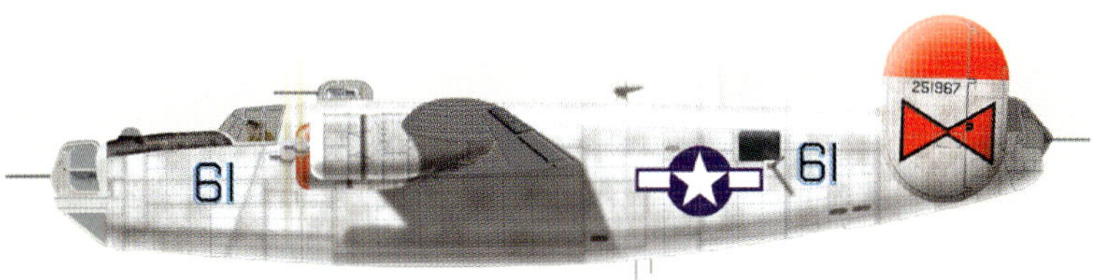

485TH BmbGrp: Pg.120

INDEX

GROUP/SQUADRON CODES

Fighters .... page

Troop Carrier.

Bombers .... page